AN OFFICIAL TRAINING GUIDE FROM MYTRAININGCENTER.COM

My CHECKLISTS

OVER 70 ESSENTIAL BUSINESS CHECKLISTS
SAVE TIME / SAVE MONEY / MAKE MONEY

FOR WEBSITE DESIGN, AFFILIATE MARKETING, INTERVIEWS, PRODUCT CREATION / LAUNCHES, INSTALLING WORDPRESS, MARKETING & MAKING $$$

BART SMITH

TheMarketingMan.com & MyTrainingCenter.com Founder

COPYRIGHT / LEGAL NOTICES

COPYRIGHT NOTICE

DISCLAIMER NOTICE

MY CHECKLISTS "MESSAGE"

A MESSAGE FROM THE AUTHOR:
BART SMITH
YOUR CHECKLIST COACH

I don't know about you, but I wouldn't be where I am today without my checklists. They help keep me organized, on track, even motivated, and help pull me through to the finish line each and every time no matter what project I'm working on. That goes for building small/large websites, writing/publishing books, conducting workshops/webinars/tele-seminars, launching new products, setting up affiliate programs, sending out eMail messages, setting up a shopping cart, adding products to the cart, ... the list (no pun) goes on!

Seriously, if there's something I want to do, I just whip up a quick list of "what to do" steps in my head. Then, I'll type it out in the computer, or for you "write here" in this book. I'll even get very detailed with my lists so I don't make any mistakes. This way, I can add to 'em, review 'em, rearrange a list item or two, and as I progress through my checklist, I'll mark "D→" next to those items that are "DONE!" That's what I do. That helps me stay motivated when I see all those D's in a column.

Because I use my own checklists so extensively, I don't even worry about what comes next. I just refer to my checklist. I have checklists for almost everything I do. Honestly, there's no way I could write all the books I have, or build the websites I have without checklists. I have to restate that one more time for the record. Checklists save me!

Knowing how important checklists are to my life, and the success of my businesses, making money, and getting things done FAST, I thought I would put this book together for you. If my checklists can help me, perhaps they can help you too!

May I suggest a few things, when it comes to using this book? (#1) Of course, pick out any checklist(s) that interests you, and read it. (#2) REALLY READ IT! Line by line. (#3) Don't worry about understanding it, or committing it to memory, or questioning why I put the items in the order I did, per se. Just read it for what it is. Then, (#4) read it one more time if you like. Let it really sink into your subconscious. (#5) Go after what it was you wanted to do, but now with the added confidence having read a checklist on that very topic you wish to tackle. You see, as you work on a certain project, having read my checklist, you have a greater understanding of what might come next. Even if a few steps might be reordered for your situation, that's okay. Every project is a little different. My checklists are merely guides. They guide me, and they can guide you. I, myself, might interject an item or two, or rearrange something to accommodate a new step. That's alright. That's reality. So, may my checklists bring to you the kind of success they've brought to me.

To your success,

Bart Smith

Bart Smith, TheMarketingMan.com
AND FOUNDER OF
MyTrainingCenter.com
BartsCookies.com

TABLE OF CONTENTS

HERE ARE "MY CHECKLISTS" TO HELP YOU SUCCEED!

MY CHECKLISTS

MY CHECKLISTS

CHECKLIST CONTENTS

BART'S BOOKS, WEBSITES & CONSULTING SERVICES

❏ *Link To My Checklist on MyTrainingCenter.com*

❏ *Bart's Other Books*

❏ *Bart's Other Websites*

❏ *Coach With Bart*

❏ *Train With Bart*

ADVERTISING CHECKLIST

Running ads, both online and offline, takes a fair amount of planning, precision and testing. Check out my advertising checklist below. Carefully review before designing or running any advertising campaign. What you'll learn will cover a wide variety of advertising strategies and how-to tips to ensure your advertising campaigns are successful!

1. ❑ **Determine your target market first.** WHO do you want to reach with your ad? Make sure you're not wasting time or money advertising to a market that has no interest in what you're selling. Identify your target and what you expect to get in return by advertising to that niche. Know your advertising objectives and then document them!

2. ❑ **WHERE does your market hang out?** Research the publications, websites, newspapers, magazines where your target market might be found. Are there any advertising statistics available such as demographics? For example, "Our magazine reaches 100,000 accountants, whose average income is between $X-Y."

3. ❑ **Collect information on pricing rates, ad terms, specials for extended ad runs, etc.** Compare advertising rates based on circulation rates before you buy space. Where can you spend the least amount of money and get the most exposure? Talk to other advertisers in publications you are interested in. You might ask, "Are you satisfied with your advertising efforts in XYZ magazine/newspaper/journal, etc. Are you getting the response you expected? Will you continue your advertising campaign?"

4. ❑ **Create an advertising budget.** Take an average of all media costs to assess what you can afford to spend. Know the costs for advertising in different publications, venues, websites, etc., you might test your ad in a smaller publication or one with a less expensive advertising medium before spending big bucks. When you find out what ad lines pull the most response, you can expand your advertising campaign by going national or spending more for greater exposure on pay-per click engines, for example. Budget for different time blocks and observe their performance to mark any significant differences.

5. ❑ **Is the time right for your ad?** Do you want

to control the times your ads run? Is holiday advertising good for your product/service? Are there events occurring out of your control (in the world, your town or country) that might negatively impact advertising? What trends are you seeing? What feedback are you getting from your prospects and customers?

6. ☐ **Are you prepared for the kind of response you expect?** Are you ready for the windfall of attention that your ads are generating such as sales and an increase number of inquiries? If you're ads are not resonating with your audience, rework the ad to ensure it gets results. Be sure that the information is clear, specific, focuses on benefits, solves a problem, has eye appeal, and has a strong headline. PREPARATION is the key to overall success for any ad campaign. Make it personal so people identify with you and believe that your product/service will meet their needs.

7. ☐ **What is the lead time for the ad you wish to place?** Some offline newspapers require advance notice (1-2 weeks) to run your ad while some magazines require a 2-3 month lead time due to production and printing schedules. Some print publications take much longer. Knowing the lead times for different publications will help you plan your advertising effectively. If you're promoting your product/service online, think Google, Yahoo, Bing, Yelp, Manta, Foursquare, DexKnows, Angie's List, Hotfrog, Kudzu. Most are FREE advertising venues with no wait period.

8. ☐ **Design the ad you want to see advertised.** What do you want to communicate to your potential prospect/customer. Remember, stress the benefits of what you're advertising in large headlines and sub-headlines. Don't be wordy; get to the point. Use fewer words to make the most impact. OR, if you have LOTS of room in your ad, and you can "tell a story", then write A LOT (using small print) and give a lot of detail. BUT, use large, powerful headlines to capture the reader's attention. People skim ads, they don't read them. The only thing they see, remember, are the headlines that grab them.

In addition to writing your own ad, it's a good idea to look at other ads in the same publication you'd like to advertise in and other publications to get ideas on how to design your ad. Get ideas for yours. Design, layout, wording, reverse text, bold, underline. Study, observe and learn what attracts YOU to a certain ad. Borrow what you like from their design, and learn what you don't like about certain ad designs too. Study your competition's advertisements and those who don't complete with you. What do their ads look like? How long have you seen them run their ads in the publication you'd like to advertise in? Is there another, similar venue/publication you could advertise in that doesn't have so much competition for space and eyeball/reader attention? Why aren't people advertising there? Hmm! Maybe advertising in a publication right next to your competition will be fine due to the high volume of readership and eyeballs scanning the ads.

Do you want to advertise up front in the publication, in the back or in the middle? How about a 1/2 page ad, 1/4 page add or full page ad? Ask the sales representative at the publication you'd like to advertise in to give you some feedback on ad placement, size, etc. It's in their best interest to help you succeed with your ad. When you do - you might advertise again!

Does you ad require a response? Make it clear. Use "call-to-action" verbs and words in your copy to elicit a response from your prospect / future client. "Call Now!" "Act Fast!" "Go to: www."

Can you design the ad yourself, or must you hire a professional to lay your ad out in a professional design program to be submitted to the publication where you'd like to advertise in. If you can simply give the advertiser your text and they convert it to an ad, great! On the other hand, if you have to submit a full-color (or black and white) ad with photographs, borders, special fonts, etc., you might have to hire a professional design artist to create that work for you.

If you have to hire someone to create the ad for you, first (you) design the ad yourself on a plain piece of paper, the way you see it, so you can give it to your design specialist. Or, create it in a program you're familiar with and send that design to them. Once your design artist has created the ad in the design program needed for the advertiser, follow these next few steps.

9. ❑ **Proof the ad and let 2-3 others review it prior to publication.** Don't trust your own eyes! Whether you created the ad or a professional designed it, you should proof it for misspellings, telephone numbers, brand names, trade names, website addresses, etc. before you agree to or sign off on it before it's forever in print and then, it's too late! Even when making minor changes, proof it again.

10. ❑ **Check the as soon as the ad is scheduled to display.** Advertising should capture prospective buyer attention and entice them to buy from you so on the day your ad displays, recheck it for errors. In certain cases, you can ask for credit, an extended re-run or a refund if there are mistakes in the ad that you had no control over.

11. ❑ **Test your ad! How is it working?** If you have a phone number in your ad and the phone isn't ringing, retest it. Running several ads, use different numbers or coupon codes in each ad. If a website listed, can you track click-through rates for the URL? Try some of the FREE ad-tracker programs such as ClixTrac.com or LinkTrack.info.

Using an ad-tracker can tell you how successful your ad campaign is. Depending on results such as knowing where traffic is coming from, you can refine or enhance your advertising. This is a "must have" for online advertising online. You'll want to track the click-through rates from your ad to your website. Other benefits are increase in sales, profitability, keywords working, identify changes in traffic and performance, etc. This tool will gives you useful information plus the ability to continuously monitor metrics as long as the ad runs.

If the response to your ad is low, revisit the header and content and modify it as needed. To entice a better response, offer an incentive (discounts or FREE gift). Remember, people are more inclined to trust information versus marketing; something to think about it.

12. ❑ **Keep a record of all the ads you run.** By maintaining copies of your ads and noting the ones that worked, you can copy any ad and revise it to meet your current needs. Here's a good way to track all of your ads:

Ad Campaign Name: _____

Publication/Site Advertised In: _____

Product/Service Advertised: _____

Target Market/Audience: _____

Advertising Sample: (ATTACH SAMPLE)

MY CHECKLISTS

Duration of Advertisement: _____

Cost Of Advertisement: _____

Tracking Method Used:

☐ Unique Telephone Number

☐ Mention Coupon Code in Ad

☐ URL Ad-Tracker

☐ Unique Domain Name: _____

☐ Other _____

Results (Good/Bad/Other): _____

Miscellaneous Comments: _____

Run The Ad Again? ☐ Yes ☐ No

How Long: _____

Any Changes: _____

Another way to organize your ads is to create a file folder for printouts or cutouts with a list of the publications you advertised in. Over time, these records will assist you when looking for new ideas for what and where to run your next ad.

Don't overlook the quality of the responses you are getting. You may receive a high number of responses, but are getting the reaction you expected? Are responders viable prospects? Did your ad reach the target audience you anticipated?

13. ☐ **Calculate the return on your advertising investment (ROI).** Did you get a good response? Did you make any sales? Did you increase the number of opt-ins into your list? What was the result of your advertising? Did the ad pay for itself, according to your own terms? If you are satisfied with your campaign efforts, work on new advertising strategies by knowing your cost per leads

and cost per sales. Like anything, sometimes, you have to spend money to make money. If your advertising is done right, you don't need to spend a lot of money and since you know what works by now, buying more ad space could increase your visibility with your ideal customers. Successful advertising might bring more customers to you, but delivering the goods and meeting their expectations will determine how your investment really pays off. Be sure that you honor all the terms of your ad and then surprise them by over-delivering, which can be done in many ways, so you can claim that retention that every business needs.

CHECKLIST

Track Sales → Earn Commissions

Join Affiliate Program

Affiliate Marketing

Promote Product

When it comes to promoting and selling products, services, coaching/consulting packages, webinars, seminars or tele-seminars online, get others to help you promote your event such as affiliates. What is an affiliate program? It's performance-based marketing in which a business rewards one or more "affiliates" for each paying customer brought by the affiliate's own marketing efforts. To create, launch and market your own Affiliate Program, here's my quick checklist to ensure your affiliate program is a complete success:

CHECKLIST

1. ❏ **Do you have a product or service you need help promoting?** Whatever you are offering, enlist affiliates to place promotions on their websites or communicate via their blogs and other venues. It's seemingly effortless for affiliates to "sell" your business since they don't have the responsibilities or concerns for traditional sales and the rewards can be very lucrative.

2. ❏ **Determine if you have enough money to attract/pay affiliates.** Is your product and/or service priced high enough to afford paying commissions? What's the profit margin? Digital products have high profit margins, whereas tangible products and even services that have a cost to produce and deliver them frequently have lower profit margins.

3. ❏ **Determine how much you will pay your affiliates.** (1) Will you pay your affiliates a % or a specific $ amount for each sale they make for you. (2) When you decide what you can pay, set those rates up in your own shopping cart. Typically, product/service that are delivered digitally and don't require handling or shipping, can generate a commission between 15% and 50%. Some affiliate commissions for digital products run as high as 100% for

the sole purpose of generating leads only. These types of leads will often upsell to something of more value.

For tangible goods like books, CDs and other products that require manufacturing and shipping, commissions can range between 10% to 40%. Overall, it's up to you to determine what you can afford vs. what will motivate affiliates to take action and promote your business. Their motivation will be how much money they can earn for little effort so be fair and make it worth their while. One sale is better than no sales.

4. ❑ **Determine the software that you'll use to track affiliate sales.** Depending on the shopping cart you use, will determine the affiliate program you use. Many carts either have an affiliate tracking system built in or, for an additional cost, you can install a plugin that works with your shopping cart.

If your shopping cart doesn't come with built-in affiliate tracking software, you can choose to use one of these affiliate software programs that might integrate with your shopping cart:

❑ iDevAffiliate.com (Multiple Integrations)

❑ AffiliateWP.com (WordPress Plugin)

❑ AffiliateRoyale.com (WordPress Plugin)

Perhaps you have a digital product for sale. Use one of the more popular affiliate networks such as:

❑ JVZoo.com	❑ Clickbank.com
❑ PayDotCom.com	❑ ShareASale.com
❑ CJ.com	❑ E-Junkie.com
❑ Payloadz.com	

5. ❑ **Set up your affiliate program inside your shopping cart system.** Once you've decided on an affiliate tracking software, set up and customize your affiliate program settings to manage it.

6. ❑ **How will you pay your affiliates?** By check, PayPal's "Mass Pay" service or a combination of both? Do you want to avoid stamps, envelopes and printing checks that might get lost in the mail? Pay your affiliates exclusively with PayPal's "Mass Pay" service.

7. ❑ **Create marketing materials for your affiliates.** Create at least 5-10 different sized banner ads, a variety of 5-10 eMail ads, and 10-20 various subject lines that will grab a prospect's attention that your affiliates can access from your web site and use to help them promote your products, services, seminars, tele-seminars, etc.

8. ❑ **Offer FREE training and tutorials for affiliates.** The more your affiliates know about your products or services and how passionate you are about your story, they'll be inspired to promote their lists and encourage sales. This is a win/win situation. You're excited about the program you offer and your affiliates are highly enthused to be part of your sales team.

8.1 ❑ **Create a web page dedicated to highlighting all the marketing tools.** Who is your ideal target market? Provide sample eMail letters, banners, and much more. The more informed they are, the better results for both of you.

8.2 ❑ **Create an Affiliate Terms & Conditions page.** Detail how you pay your affiliates, your rights to terminate an affiliate's account if needed and more.

8.3 ❏ Create a 5-10 day autoresponder series. Train your affiliates when you have promotions. All you have to do is create a sequence one time about how to sell for you can make money for years to come. Train them on how to use autoresponders to their advantage.

8.4 ❏ Create a number of video tutorials. Show new affiliates how to log in to their accounts once their affiliate links are assigned. They can check stats and earnings, even update their contact information. Imagine providing them with video tutorials about your products, specifically pointing out features and other details they can use in their own sales literature and letters to their lists.

8.5 ❏ Hold weekly, bi-weekly or monthly affiliate training calls by phone or webinar. Share with them what works, what doesn't. Recognize top affiliates and ask them to share their experiences as affiliates to motivate others to become top performers!

9. ❏ **Create incentives, prizes and contests for affiliates.** This will help drive sales. You could offer a cash prize, product prizes, bonuses for reaching a threshold, or a first sale bonus for the new affiliate. Get creative; shop for ideas on the web.

10. ❏ **Submit your affiliate program on the various affiliate directories.** Affiliate directories can help spread the word about your affiliate program and find affiliates to join you in your marketing efforts. In many cases, you only have to do this once per directory.

By doing this, you expose your affiliate program "opportunity" to both part-time and full-time affiliates who are consistently looking to promote to their list! Don't be surprised when seasoned affiliates approach because they like what you sell and your program meets their needs.

Here's a quick list of affiliate directories you can submit your program to:

- ❏ AffiliatesDirectory.com
- ❏ AffiliateSeeking.com
- ❏ AssociatePrograms.com
- ❏ AffiliateAnnouncement.com
- ❏ 5StarAffiliatePrograms.com
- ❏ WarriorPlus.com
- ❏ eCommerce-Guide.com
- ❏ BecomeAnAffiliate.com
- ❏ AffiliateFirst.com
- ❏ AffiliateGuide.com

If your goal is to increase the number of affiliates you have, you need to register affiliate directories. If affiliates are looking for more affiliate income, you need to be registered because they'll be looking for you there. Create a title for your program, a brief description, commission rates, etc. and link to a web page that provides more detail ... but not your home page.

You can also look into selling your (digital) products through affiliate networks, where that handle the selling transaction, collect monies, manage your affiliates and pay them. This is idea for digital products only. There may be a setup fee but compare programs for rules and setup instructions.

11.0 ☐ **Become familiar with running affiliate reports to pay your affiliates.** Learn how to run commission reports whether you manually issue checks or use PayPal so affiliates always have a record of what's paid and what's due. You'll need this too.

12.0 ☐ **Pay your affiliates on time and never miss a payment.** Review the procedures for paying your affiliates several times before you actually issue payments. If you let an affiliate network pay your affiliates, this is one task you won't have to worry about. They're generally reliable and trustworthy.

AFFILIATE/AD BANNERS
CHECKLIST

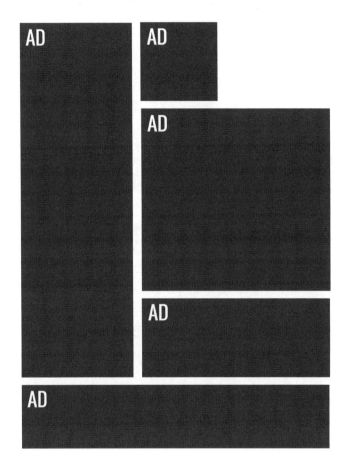

If you have an affiliate program, plan to implement one, or if you plan to do any kind of advertising that might involve the use of graphics, images, banners, and/or buttons, I recommend that you learn the basics for creating banners/buttons of different sizes and formats.

BANNERS & BUTTON ADS CAN BE DESIGNED & USED TO ADVERTISE

1. ❑ Your products/services ...
2. ❑ Others people's products/services ...
3. ❑ Events, workshops and seminars ...
4. ❑ Books, eBooks, eReports, etc. ...
5. ❑ Other: _____ ...

ONLINE BANNER & BUTTONS COME IN DIFFERENT SHAPES AND SIZES:

1. ❑ Letterboard (728 x 90)
2. ❑ Standard Banner (468 x 60)
3. ❑ Half Page (300 x 600)
4. ❑ Small Rectangle (300 x 100)
5. ❑ Medium Rectangle (300 x 200)
6. ❑ Vertical Rectangle (240 x 400)
7. ❑ Full Banner (468 x 60)
8. ❑ Skyscraper (120 x 600)
9. ❑ Wide Skyscraper (160 x 600)
10. ❑ Vertical Banner (120 x 240)
11. ❑ Button (120 x 60) or (120 x 90)
12. ❑ Square Button (125 x 125)

BANNERS & BUTTONS CAN BE DISPLAYED IN & ON

1. ❑ Front/Middle/Back of Books & eBooks
2. ❑ Header/Footer/Sidebar of Websites
3. ❑ Login/Logout Pages
4. ❑ Magazines (Both Online & Offline)
5. ❑ Member Home Pages

MY CHECKLISTS

6. ❑ Top/Middle/Bottom of Web Pages

7. ❑ Top/Middle/Bottom of eZines/Newsletters

AFFILIATE MARKETING TOOLS USING BANNERS, BUTTONS, ETC.

If you have an affiliate program, your affiliates will need marketing tools such as banners and buttons to enable them to better promote your products/services. Consider some of these examples below.

Plan to provide general banners and possibly holiday-specific banners. Have a creative, diverse collection and be open to creating custom banners/buttons for your affiliate clientele. If creating this type of promotional material is not your specialty, outsource it for a small fee. It will be worth investing in a professional to design what you need. At a minimum, plan to produce the following:

1. ❑ 7 different sized banners/buttons.

2. ❑ 3 different variations on those banners.

LEADERBOARD
728 x 90

3:1 RECTANGLE
300 x 100

MEDIUM RECTANGLE 300 x 200

VERTICAL RECTANGLE 240 x 400

WIDE SKYSCRAPER 160 x 600

FULL BANNER 468 x 60

SQUARE BUTTON 125 x 125

Make 3 or more banners of the same size with 3 varying content so you can test which ad pulls best response. Supplying several customized banners, your affiliates can choose not only the size banner they fits their sites, but also customize the message they send to their list/audience.

ASK CAMPAIGN
CHECKLIST

1.0 ❑ **What tools do you need? Have an autoresponder program that allows you to create a web form on your website.** Here's a good example of one. It's short, gets right to the point, and it's easy to use

> **WHAT'S YOUR BIGGEST QUESTION ABOUT:**
> **SETTING UP A WORDPRESS WEBSITE?**
>
> NAME:
>
> EMAIL:
>
> QUESTION:

An ASK CAMPAIGN is a laser sharp marketing strategy used to find out what your clients really want to know and how you can provide it. You, simply, allow them to ask a question about a topic you have expertise in. After you collect 20-100 questions from your clients, you then proceed to answer the top 10-20 questions at a tele-seminar call while your audience can hear your responses to the top questions you chose to answer.

"Asking" is a powerful tool. Imagine getting first hand information! While some ask campaigns can be performed independently, it's ideal to have another person narrate the questions while you respond with the answers, otherwise, you can do it all yourself.

Autoresponders are used to create individual lists for any campaign you run. You can use any number of autoresponder/eMail service provider companies out there today such as, **Aweber.com, GetResponse.com, MailChimp.com, etc.** to help create your "Ask (Your Name) ..." campaigns.

1.1 ❑ **Go to FreeConferenceCalling.com to sign up for a FREE account if you plan to conduct ask campaigns using tele-seminars.**

1.2 ❑ When using webinars to conduct your ask campaigns, choose a webinar software service such as WebinarJam.com or EasyWebinar.com. See other suggestions at MyTrainingCenter.com.

1.3 ❑ Choose an audio recording software program. Sony's SoundForge audio studio or Audacity can edit your ask campaign recorded tele-calls.

1.4 ❑ How about audio? Consider using MixPad or Audacity to mix in any intro/outro music to your ask campaign tele-calls.

2. ❑ **Setup and create the main components for your ask campaign.** Learn how to set up and execute your campaign to influence your audience to value the information they get.

2.1 ❑ What topics do you want people to ask you about? You could share your expertise or engage a guest expert to respond to some questions.

2.2 ❑ Decide date/time for your tele-seminar or webinar. Include the information, along with call-in details, in the autoresponder you created for this specific event.

2.3 ❑ Create an Ask Campaign web page on your site for people to register. This will help get attention, encourage participation, and ideally generate lots of good questions.

2.4 ❑ Create a "thank you" response on a web page. This should direct registrants to it once they've filled out the form.

2.5 ❑ Create the autoresponder for every ask campaign you solicit. Then create a custom field called "Ask Your Question" per the autoresponder service you're using such as Aweber.com.

2.7 ❑ Create a custom web form with a custom field that will be placed on your ask campaign web page. This will ask for names, eMail addresses and their questions.

2.8 ❑ Copy/paste the web form HTML code into the ask campaign web page **and TEST IT.** Do your name, eMail address and question display correctly?

3. ❑ **BEFORE** your Ask Campaign, eMail your list and invite them to join you for a Q&A. Direct them to your Ask Campaign web page well in advance of the date/time.

3.1 ❑ Prior to conducting your campaign, export the questions compiled in the autoresponder to an Excel spreadsheet. Begin compiling the questions every couple of days until the day of the event and giving you time to prepare your answers.

3.2 ❑ Sort the Excel spreadsheet data alphabetically by question. This helps you read faster and spot possible duplicates. Compile the top 15-20 questions.

3.3 ❑ Enter questions and answers into a WORD document and rehearse LIVE prior to responding to them.

4. ❑ **Conduct your Ask Campaign call or webinar** and record it so you can offer a playback for those who couldn't listen or view. Articulate the questions and answers slowly. If you run out of time, you can answer questions via eMail to those who registered.

5. ❑ **AFTER Your Ask Campaign Tele-Seminar or Webinar, download the MP3 file or recorded video embed code.** This will help you when editing as needed.

5.1 ❑ Post the audio or video on a web page so people can download it, listen or view.

5.2 ❑ Are you selling something? Include a buy button in your recording to collect sales. Include a countdown timer, too, so buyers understand that this is a one-time only deal for 48-72 hours (for example).

5.3 ❑ Create a product out of the questions and answers you have accumulated such as a brochure or guidelines.

5.4 ❑ Gear up to conduct your NEXT ask campaign soon after to stimulate enthusiasm and build relationships with customers/ prospects!

CHECKLIST

Audio-Technica AT2020 USB Condenser Microphone

(AVG. PRICE $110 ON AMAZON.COM)

When it comes to recording audio for your website, in product form, or for any other purpose, there's a lot you should know. For starters, this checklist will help you get on the right track.

1. ❑ **WHAT to record:**

1.1 ❑ Welcome message on your website's home page ...

1.2 ❑ Individual messages on various pages on your website (i.e., About Us, Contact Us, Product pages, etc.) ...

1.3 ❑ Audio products you can sell from your website, which are delivered digitally online (via downloadable MP3) to customers after they pay for them.

1.4 ❑ Audio libraries of recorded audio, such as your book or a recorded seminar, that people pay to have access to, then listen to it from your website by flicking different play buttons to hear different segments of the seminar or chapters of your book. With this option, there's nothing to download. Customers just listen online.

1.5 ❑ Telephone coaching, consulting or training calls you have with clients or large groups via tele-seminars.

2. ❑ **Decide the best way to record the audio you want within your budget and recording skill level.** Whether you decide to record it yourself, or higher someone to record your audio for you, consider this:

2.1 ❑ Use a USB microphone headset that plugs right into your computer for WEB-BASED audio! (Avg. cost $19-$29 on Amazon.com.)

2.2 ❑ Use a high quality condenser microphone that plugs into your computer via USB, such as the *Audio-Technica AT2020*. (Avg. cost $110 on Amazon.com.)

2.4 ❑ A portable MP3 digital recording device, such as the Zoom H4N Handy Portable Digital Recorder ($199 avg.) or the Zoom H4N Handy Portable Digital Recorder ($99 avg.). These can be used to record your presentations. Just hook up an *Audio-Technica ATR-3350 Lavalier Omnidirectional Condenser Microphone* ($29 avg.) and start recording. When you're done, transfer the recorded audio to your file for editing, mixing and publishing.

3. ❑ **Determine the audio recording software you'll use to record audio.** My favorite, when it comes to recording and editing a lot of audio, is *Sony's Sound Forge Audio Studio.* Some folks like to use Audacity, because it's free. I don't. I'll use Audacity for mixing, but not for recording. What's the difference? For me, it's the interface. I just like editing (and recording) my audio using Sound Forge. Audacity is free, whereas Sound Forge costs around $69. For me, it was worth it.

4. ❑ **Determine the audio mixing software you'll use to record audio, and learn how to use it.** When it comes to mixing sound effects and music into your spoken audio recordings, you can either use Audacity (which I've used before) or a program called MixPad. These two programs provide what you need, which is a multi-track interface (i.e., more than one track) for laying down layers of music, audio recordings, sound effects, and more, on top of one the other. Then, when you're done, you can export all those mixings into one single audio file that sounds great!

5. ❑ **Learn how to search for, download and even buy music loops and sound effects for commercial use in your audio recordings.** Check out more resources online at MyTrainingCenter.com.

6. ❑ **Start recording all the audio AFTER you read my special report on *Recording Tips & Techniques* available online at MyTrainingCenter.com.**

7. ❑ **Learn how to save and organize audio which you record on your computer so you know where they are and much more.** This is a critical step to learn if you plan on recording your own audio files. Learning where and how to record and save your audio files on your computer is important to you staying organized with so many audio files you might potentially record.

8. ❑ **Determine how you will duplicate the audio you record so you can sell in large quantities.** DO NOT even think about duplicating your own audio on CD (for example) at your home/office. Forget that idea. It's a waste of time, and money and the quality won't be as good as you paying a penny per disc at a professional CD replication company. IF you plan to offer your audio products for sale via CD format, consider using a company like TrepStar.com.

9. ❑ **Learn how to sell your audio products from your website.** After you record your audio product(s), how will you sell them? From your website? Learn what's involved in selling your audio products from your website. It's pretty simple, when you get to know the steps involved with that.

10. ❑ **Learn how to create your own audio library which you can sell from your website for pure profit.** If you have a lot of audio to sell, you might benefit from creating one or more audio libraries within your website to sell.

11. ❑ **Learn how to create your own audio books you can sell from your site for profits in your sleep.** If you have a book or eBook, have you recorded it yet? If not, then you're missing out on additional profits. If you have recorded it, good for you. Most authors don't record their books, why, who knows. If you can't record it yourself, search online for someone who will.

12. ❑ **Determine all the other places you can sell your audio products for big profits.** Make a list of all the places you can sell your audio at. Of course you can sell it online, but you can also sell it at seminars, workshops, expos, trade shows, networking events, etc. Bring order forms and your audio product with you to sell to folks on the spot.

AUTORESPONDER
CHECKLIST

WHAT IS AN AUTORESPONDER?

Autoresponders are eMails that automatically send information you create to others on your behalf without you having to touch a key. While you do have to set them up, you can program them to send anytime and any day for any length of time.

HOW CAN YOU USE AUTORESPONDERS

1. ❑ **Affiliate Support/Training** – Autoresponders make it easy to train your affiliates with automatic eMails that include support and training material. An affiliate who receives ongoing training and support is empowered to help you make more sales.

2. ❑ **Build Rapport** – What better way to build trust and relationships with prospects than to send out regular on-going eMails with content about how you can help them. Autoresponders can do this.

3. ❑ **Deliver Paid eCourse** – Autoresponders are great for communicating training information to those who pay to learn from you. Just set up an autoresponder series with your lessons and let it run automatically.

4. ❑ **Explain What You Do** – Maybe you have a story to tell about your business or service. Use an autoresponder so people can opt-in to learn more, but let your autoresponder do all the talking for you.

5. ❑ **Free Mini-eCourse** – Autoresponders can also deliver FREE training and course materials for you.

6. ❑ **Give Away Tips** – A great way to get people on your list is to offer FREE tips. Let autoresponders deliver the information seamlessly with no effort on your part.

7. ❑ **Customer Order Autoresponders** – A great use for autoresponders is to deliver contact information information to your customers should they reach out for support or have questions.

8. ❑ **Product Autoresponders** - Some products require instructions. So, why not put that information in an autoresponder. Once the customer buys a certain product from you, assign an autoresponder to it so paid customers receive information pertaining to

the item they purchased ASAP. People who don't buy, won't receive the information.

9. ❑ **Promote Something** - Autoresponders are a great way to promote a product/service/special/sale or even an old product you'd like to resell.

10. ❑ **Send Coupons & Discounts** - Imagine collecting an eMail list at your place of business or even online and then, imagine making an offer to "SIGN-UP for our list to regularly receive discount and coupon announcements!"

11. ❑ **Send Notifications** - A great way to notify alert people about anything is via autoresponder. For example, you might have a membership website with autorespodners that tell members that their memberships are expiring in one month, two weeks, one week, three days, etc. This lets them know so they should take action to renew or cancel. Informing customers about cancellation can work in your favor. You avoid emails and phone calls from customers asking for refunds because they were never notified of a charge to their credit card. Autoresponders are a certainty. Customers can also UPDATE their payment information when their cards will expire.

12. ❑ **Send Updates** - Another great use for autorespodners is to send your customers updates on what's new in your business or on your website. Now, you can easily send eMail blasts to your autoresponder subscription list.

13. ❑ **Share Archived Posts** - You can use autorespodners to send links to older, archived articles or posts you previously authored. This works great for old newsletter issues you published weeks, months or even years ago. If the information is still relevant, why not send special links where they can be located.

14. ❑ **Stay In Touch** - Out of sight out of mind, right? Maintain regular contact with autoresponders by programming your eMails to go out months following an event or special you ran. Those eMails could revive interest if what you're working on benefits them.

15. ❑ **Upselling** - Autoresponders are great at upselling subscribers to any FREE offer. Win them over with FREE material, earn their trust, and then offer something of more value reasonably priced for a specific promotion and then continue upselling.

WHERE DO YOU GET AUTORESPONDER SERVICES?

There are several companies today that provide autoresponder services. Most charge a monthly fee (or you can pay annually) based on the size of your list. You can use a company like www.MailerLite.com. To learn more about them, check out their website. Once you sign up with them, you can create your first autoresponder and get started using it immediately for any purpose I previously listed.

Now, let's review the steps for setting up your first autoresponder.

SETTING UP AUTORESPONDER + OPT-IN FORM

Log into the autoresponder service company you signed up for, and ...

1. ❑ **What's the purpose for creating your autoresponder.** Remember, you can create several different ones for different purposes.

2. ❑ **Give the autoresponder a descriptive title.** Depending on your purpose, the name

should have keywords that tell you why the autoresponder is needed. To organize your autoresponders (assuming you have more than one), sort them alphabetically. See the example below:

My Website Home Page / eZine Opt-in

- Free eCourse: (Enter Title #1)
- Free eCourse: (Enter Title #2)
- Paid eCourse: (Enter Title #1)
- Paid eCourse: (Enter Title #2)
- Landing Page Opt-In List For Website1.com
- Landing Page Opt-In List For Website2.com
- Landing Page Opt-In List For Website3.com
- Seminar Registration (Enter Title #1) 00/00/00
- Seminar Registration (Enter Title #2) 00/00/00
- Seminar Registration (Enter Title #3) 00/00/00
- Tele-Seminar (Title1) Registration 00/00/00
- Tele-Seminar (Title2) Registration 00/00/00

- Tele-Seminar (Title3) Registration 00/00/00
- Webinar (Title1) Registration 00/00/00
- Webinar (Title2) Registration 00/00/00
- Webinar (Title3) Registration 00/00/00

From the list, you know which ones are assigned to your home page, eZine/ newsletter opt-in list, registration forms, etc. Naming your autoresponders in this way helps to readily find them.

3. ☐ **Write the message for your autoresponder.** Some don't require messages, for example, if you're sending it only to collect names and eMails. You might just want to accumulate eMails for a special list that you manually broadcast an eMail for. There are some autoresponders that do require you to set up a sequence of pre-written eMail messages.

MailerLite

Below, you can see how I named these lists (autoresponders). You can see they are named in such a way that they alphabetize nicely so you can find them quickly.

| Home | Messages ⌄ | Subscribers ⌄ | Sign Up Forms | Reports ⌄ | List Options ⌄ |

Manage Your Lists (a.k.a. Autoresponders)
Create new lists, back up & deactivate lists.

Create A List

Email Marketing & Analytics

Back Up & Export All Active Lists

!My Website Home Page / eZine Opt-in This autoresponder is for my MAIN LIST + opt-in form on home page.	Active	3,751 Subscribers	51 Unsubscribers	Deactivate
Free eCourse : How To Design A Book Cover This is free eCourse has 7 lessons on how to design a book cover.	Active	375 Subscribers	25 Unsubscribers	Deactivate
Free eCourse : How To Make Affiliate Banners This is free eCourse has 10 lessons on how to make affiliate banners.	Active	291 Subscribers	15 Unsubscribers	Deactivate
Tele-Seminar : How To Conduct A Book Launch Party Date/Time: 07/8/15 3:00PM/EST (1Hr)	Active	503 Subscribers	17 Unsubscribers	Deactivate
Webinar : How To Use Adobe Fireworks To Design Book Covers Date/Time: 07/15/15 3:00PM/EST (1Hr)	Active	71 Subscribers	3 Unsubscribers	Deactivate
Webinar : WordPress Plugin Checklist Date/Time: 07/22/15 3:00PM/EST (1Hr)	Active	25 Subscribers	1 Unsubscribers	Deactivate

MESSAGE / SUBJECT:	GO OUT:
Message #1 - Welcome ...	Day 0 (IMMEDIATELY)
Message #2 - 1st Lesson	Day 1
Message #3 - 2nd Lesson	Day 2
Message #4 - 3rd Lesson	Day 3
Message #5 - 4th Lesson	Day 4
Message #6 - 5th Lesson	Day 5

As you can see from the message list above, that's how you would set up your sequential messages. You can choose what day, time and frequency. You have control over the schedule.

4. ❏ **Create an opt-in web form for your newly created autoresponder** so you can place it on your website. This is easily done.

5. ❏ **Install the opt-in form on your website** so people can sign up with their names and eMail addresses to join your list and/or subscribe to a specific autoresponder you set up.

6. ❏ **Test the opt-in form.** Enter YOUR own name and eMail address in the form and see what happens. Did you receive the message you created for this autoresponder? Were you added to the subscriber list as expected? Did you receive a "thank you" reply? Be satisfied that you get the results you anticipated, BEFORE you send it to others and then continue testing it to avoid any issues.

7. ❏ If everything's working related to your autoresponder, then it's **time to promote this autoresponder.**

These are the basic steps for creating an autoresponder, sequential messages, the opt-in web form, and posting it on your website or landing page. Once your autoresponder is in action, you can track your open rate, click-through rate, and any other statistics to find ways to improve its performance.

BOOK COVER DESIGN
CHECKLIST

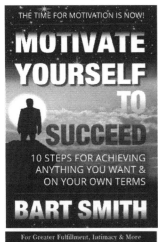

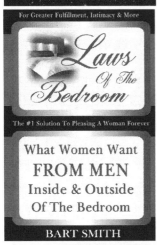

It's been said that one should be able to visualize a book cover from across the room. Frequently, a book cover will sell a book despite its contents. If you have a well-designed book cover, it should reach out to your intended audience of readers.

Allow me to share some valuable tips on what constitutes a great book cover design based on my own experiences:

FRONT COVER DESIGN LAYOUT FORMULA

What's the secret to designing world-class book covers? Whenever I am designing a book cover for my own books or for a client, this is how I approach the FRONT cover:

1. ❑ Every book cover should have an elegant BACKGROUND. Whether you make use gradients, shades or patterns, your book should be so appealing that it catches the reader's eyes and they feel compelled to examine it and buy it. It should be unique among all other books of similar genre.

2. ❑ The TITLE should not only captivate the reader's attention but it should relate, directly or indirectly, to what the book is about. It should fulfill a need, create intrigue, inform, etc.

3a. ❑ I also like to use unique fonts and colors (in the title) that bode well with the theme of the book. Titles should be about 5 words or less to make it memorable.

3b. ❑ I recommend choosing a GRAPHIC that helps

depict the story for your book. I've seen books with a photo of the author on the front cover. Spice it up. The title can make you or break you.

4. ❑ Using more than one GRAPHIC can also work if it supports what your book is about.

5. ❑ If your title is longer than 5 words, consider using a title and a SUBTITLE. The use of a subtitle can add value, but keep it concise and to-the-point.

6. ❑ What's a book cover without the AUTHOR'S NAME? If you co-author a book, put both names on the front cover. Ladies, first!

7. ❑ Adding a WEBSITE ADDRESS to the front book cover can be useful for prospective buyers or anyone whose interested in knowing more about the author. According to the expert book publishers, if you don't have a website or blog, particularly if you are a self-publisher, it's one of the biggest mistakes a writer can make.

① ② ③ ④ ⑤ ⑥ ⑦

Rich Coach Broke Coach

101+ Coaching Tactics To Start, Run & Explode Your Coaching Business & Your Income As A *"Rich Coach!"*

Bart Smith, TheMarketingMan.com

and Founder of MyTrainingCenter.com & BreakThroughBS.com

www.RichCoachBrokeCoach.com

BACK COVER DESIGN LAYOUT FORMULA

While I have my own FRONT cover design formula, I also have a 14-POINT CHECKLIST for designing the BACK cover of any book as well.

If the purpose of the FRONT cover, let's say, is to <u>ENTICE</u> a customer to <u>PICK UP</u> your book and check it out, then what's the purpose of the BACK cover? To <u>CONVINCE</u> the potential customer to <u>BUY</u> your book!

The back cover needs a design with interesting or inspiring information to make your reader open the book and look inside.

If you're interested in learning my BACK BOOK COVER CHECKLIST for designing the back covers of books, then head on over to **MyTrainingCenter.com**.

BOOK LAUNCH PARTY
CHECKLIST

WHAT IS A BOOK LAUNCH PARTY?

For starters, it's a "party" to celebrate the birth of a new book and to celebrate the author for recognizing an achievement that so few have accomplished! A book launch party (not to be confused with book signings) can be highly creative, carried out in a variety of venues and not necessarily a bookstore. Depending on your topics, book launch parties have occurred at open markets, wine stores, delis, niche retail stores, and more. Go where your readers hang out! You've worked hard writing it, getting it through the publishing and printing stages, etc. and now, you deserve a book launch party to signify the completion of an arduous, personal journey and share your ambitions to market and sell your book.

HOW DO YOU SET UP A BOOK LAUNCH PARTY?

Book launch parties can be a lot of fun (and profitable) when they're well-planned and promoted to family, friends, associates and others. Here are a few tips for orchestrating a successful book launch party:

1. ❑ **LOCATION**

   Depending on your budget, the number of people you invite and the environment will determine the venue for your party. If you have a small budget ($200-$500), you might have the party at your home if space is available or outdoors around a picnic theme. If you have a larger budget ($500-$2,500), consider having your party at a restaurant (in a private serving room) or in a hotel conference room.

2. ❑ **PARTY SUPPLIES & SETUP**

   A) Prepare a guest list for an intimate party, unless you invite a boatload of people and they invite their friends and partners.

B) Name tags are a good idea especially if it's a large group. First name basis creates more intimacy and encourages people to mingle and talk about your book.

C) Have 50-100 books available for purchase and/or distribution depending on the size crowd you anticipate. If you're selling your book at the party, designate a sales table and someone to manage it unless your books are unsigned and then you should be present, but have help to handle sales transactions. Your job it to meet, greet and autograph. If you expect a really large books, I suggest you pre-sign books.

D) Make it easy for guests can sign in or buy your book as soon as they walk in the door. When people are walking around with your book in hand, they can share your enthusiasm and encourage others to buy if they don't already have their copies.

3. ❑ GUEST LIST

Who should you invite to your book launch party? When selling books at your party, ask each person to bring guests and be prepared to serve a small beverage at a minimum such as bottled water.

Your goal should be to sell a lot of books so invite your clients, vendors, the local media (print/radio/TV), and special interest groups if appropriate, etc. Have a photographer on hand to capture special moments that you can share with the media.

If sending out invitations, ask invitees to RSVP so you know how to plan for the group you

expect. Many people have never attended a book launch party, so make your party is meaningful and memorable. This is your chance to shine and promote your celebrity/author status! Have fun!

4. ❑ CATERING

Depending on the size of your party, feed them! It's a party! Consider catering finger foods, veggies and dips (maybe), small sandwiches (food that doesn't require dishes or utensils), bottled water, beer/wine (optional), champagne (always a nice touch). Some local restaurants have catering services otherwise get referrals, check your local directories, and compare prices to get the best deal for your budget.

5. ❑ BOOKS FOR SALE

Most people who attend book launches will purchase a book so you need to be prepared to SELL. You can offer a special deal for people who attend your event (such as buy one, get the second one for half-price or buy two and get the third one FREE) versus paying full price for your book online! Set up a table that's easily accessed to all the traffic and have about $200 in change to cover any transaction. You can also manually enter credit cards on most mobile devices.

6. ❑ SPEECH PREPARATION

Be prepared to give speak about your book ... why you wrote it, how you wrote it, what you hope to accomplish with it. Now that you're a published author, maybe you can offer consulting services, conduct seminars, etc. Plan what you are going to say so you aren't winging it. Limit your speech to 10-15 minutes to ensure you have everyone's attention. Most people will be looking forward to a brief one on one with you so be ready for that. Work your book launch party the way a politician works a room.

7. ❑ DOOR PRIZES

Why not? You might offer a number of giveaway prizes at your party in keeping with the theme of your book or to add a little variety to the event. FREE autographed copies of your book would be a bonus! Timing is everything. Draw names to announce the winners when most of the group has gathered. This is a great opportunity for recognition and publicity, so get photos.

8. ❑ PUBLICITY

Consider contacting your local media networks (newspapers, magazines, radio and TV stations) to let them know that a local author is launching a new book! In most cases, a representative will ask to interview you, take a few pictures, etc. You can add these connections to your publicity campaign and your online press room. You do have a website, right?

9. ❑ PHOTOGRAPHY & VIDEO RECORDING

Expertise in all media is essential, so if you're not fortunate to have someone help you out, try to get a good referral before you start soliciting these services. A package deal, by definition, can be a bargain because you get a bulk discount for a combined service contract. You'll want to capture images of the setup, signing books, shaking hands with guests, speaking, socializing and more!

(If you select a photo of yourself with a guest for public use, get permission to use it from the other person – in writing is best. Video record your event for your online press room or posting on your website, too. Don't forget BACKUP batteries just in case.

10. ❑ SUPPORT

Depending on the size of your party, you'll need help with planning, setting up and cleanup! It's best if you have a functional team to free you up to meet guests, sign books, work with the press, etc.

If you have other book selling ideas, include them in your marketing plan. Highlight the marketing tactics you'll put into action first and schedule other activities within a short period of time. Use the momentum of your party to catapult your stardom as an author!

Here are some photos of a book launch party that I helped to set up for a friend. Not only did I plan the refreshments and agenda for the book party, I also took photographs of the event that we could publish on her website, the local newspaper and share with others.

MY CHECKLISTS

Below, are a few of the photos from the book launch party. You see pictures of the author autographing books, talking to book fans, socializing, while readers are holding her book, etc. You can never take too many photographs. Post them to your social media accounts and share the fun online with others!

Register a great domain name for your book, business, or great idea at **www.ReallyCheapNames.com.**

BOOK MARKETING
CHECKLIST

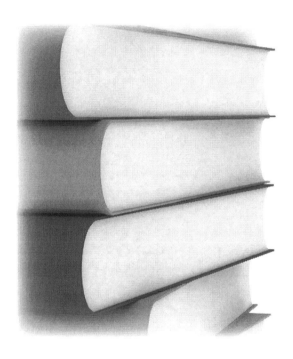

"Without publicity a terrible thing happens ... *nothing!*"

Legendary Publicist & Entrepreneur, P.T. Barnum

So, your manuscript is written, edited, and now it's in book form on Amazon.com and other online bookstore outlets as well as eBook formats ... CONGRATULATIONS! Now what? MARKETING …

For marketing any book, there are 15 KEY STEPS to check off your list as you accomplish them. Preparation and participating in all these areas (1) helps to ensure you sell books, (2) elevates you as an expert in your field/industry/genre, and (3) increases demand for your services and so much more.

Before hiring a publicist or even asking for assistance with marketing, be sure you understand essential book marketing components. This will enable you to better communicate your needs to a the professional who will assist you.

1. ❑ Turn Your Book Into An eBook

Turning your book into an eBook format is highly recommended to increase profits. eBooks are gaining momentum over hard cover and paperbacks books and you don't want to miss out on these digital sales. Submit your book to Kindle and SmashWords.com and/or BookBaby.com or others to tap into those markets where eBooks fly off the virtual shelf. One good reason to use a variety of eBook venues is because not all reading devices can accommodate all eBook formats.

2. ❑ Record Your Book In Audio Format

You might not think about recording your book in audio format, but this is another opportunity to sell most books. This will help you expand your market reach and make sales to those who prefer listening to reading. As a successful author of several books and CDs, there is a market for audio books. Make your own audio book and gain new readers. Frequently, the author is the best person to narrate a book because of familiarity with the topic, characters, words, etc. However, if you don't have the time or the skill for it, talent available.

3. ❑ Testimonials, Reviews & Endorsements

Strive to get at least 10 testimonials or more prior to promoting your book. One of the first things people want to know is WHO READ IT? WHO LIKED IT? WHAT ARE READERS SAYING? Reviews and testimonials serve as tipping points for any potential buyer. So, while you're hot to sell, share 20-50 copies of your book with family, friends and associates; people you can trust to give you an honest critique. Ask for testimonials within 10 days even if the reader can only comment on a few chapters and post them on your website. Give people the option to leave a voice mail or send an eMail. If you plan to use a testimonial, especially if you "tweak" it, get the reader's permission to publish it. Testimonials can do some of the marketing for you so be sure they are easy to find … within the first few pages of the book and/or on the back cover.

4. ❏ Author and/or Book Website

If you have a website, then you're ahead of the game. Ideally, you should have a separate website for each book you write. Purchase a domain name with the title of your book such as BSTheBook.com, MotivateYourselfToSucceed.com, MyNetworkingTactics.com, RichCoachBrokeCoach.com, etc. I have individual domain names for each book. Direct people to your book's website (not your business or personal web page) because selling big time is your new goal.

5. ❏ Press Room, Online Press Kit & Author Interview Questions + Web Training/Rehearsal

Here's the skinny on what your website should include:

❏ **Press Room** — The beauty of an online press room is that it's open to the public 24/7. It provides contact information, hi-res images, videos, logos, press/media notices, biography, awards, etc. Your press room should be a work in progress where you're always adding new and interesting content. Refer interviewers to your press room to familiarize them so their interview with you is spot on. Your goal with your own press room should be to provide an easy to locate, easy to use, and up to date and impressive face. You don't want to create a

press kit at the last minute.

❏ **Online Author Press Kit**—This kit is typically a downloadable PDF that includes your biography, a heads hot (or other photos), interview questions, and a press release or specific information about you, your book and/or other activities. It is particularly helpful to interviewers and bloggers who want to promote your book.

❏ **10 Interview Questions** — If you aren't using a Print-Ready PDF that the host of a radio or TV show can use to ask questions, then create a list of interview questions (and responses) about you and your book. Be prepared to share what makes you different from other authors because you'll need to convince your readers that your story is a best seller.

❏ **Interview Training/Rehearsal** — Whether this is your first interview or you're a pro and confidently can articulate compelling answers in an interview with flow and flair, do ask someone to role play with you prior to a scheduled interview. Take time to respond to questions. Pick up ideas and make mistakes. You're learning, rehearsing, and perfecting your skills prior to your broadcast. AND don't forget to breathe! You'll be glad you did.

6. ❏ Press Release Marketing Campaigns

With a well-written press release and ideal press release distribution company, precisely chosen industries to distribute your press release to, you should attract a fair amount of coverage. Often, this can lead to interviews in print, radio, television and more. Are you ready for the exposure? More and more marketers are engaging buyers with videos, articles, eBooks, and infographics because they are looking for insight. Who is their buyer? What are they thinking? What are they reading? Know your target audience before you launch your marketing campaign.

Before you launch your book, make sure you have all your social media account information such as photos, books, biography, etc. are up-to-date. The most popular social media outlets are:

☐ **Facebook.com** ... Create a fan page on Facebook for your book and name the account (URL) with the title of it. Engage discussions, post photographs and create video messages about you and your book. Facebook is a critical marketing channel for you.

☐ **LinkedIn.com** ... Announce that you have authored a new book to your contacts and that you're looking for people to review it.

☐ **Twitter.com** ... Twitter keeps book fans updated. If you don't have an account, set one up and customize it to display your book. Tweet something daily about your book or when you have an event/activity to promote your book.

☐ **YouTube.com** ... Did you make a video book trailer? You should! Post multiple messages recorded via video format with excerpts from book to inspire potential buyers.

☐ **What other social networks** are you a part of? Are you on Pinterest, Instagram, Google Plus, Vine and more? Sell your eBook on JVZoo.com, ClickBank.com, or E-Junkie.com. Take advantage of their networking channels!

7. ☐ Affiliate Program

Can sales from your book pay a legion of affiliates to promote it to their lists? Affiliate programs always translate to increased revenue. Consider recording your book, creating an eBook and offering a bundled product of print/eBook/audio to generate even more sales opportunities for your affiliates. Start your own affiliate program today and run it through your website. Work with experienced affiliates that will effectively promote and sell more books by linking these promoters to

your affiliate marketplace. You can't afford to pass up this winning opportunity.

8. ☐ Book Signings & Parties

Who doesn't love a party? People enjoy meeting authors. They're like an enigma because they've written a book. These kinds of events can be both fun and profitable. The venue can include new or used bookstores, companies, restaurants, residences, vineyards, theaters, organizations ... wherever you can get adequate space to talk about your book, autograph it and sell.

9. ☐ Virtual Book Tours

Who said you have to leave your house to promote your book? You can promote your book by phone or webinar with people who have lists of readers/ subscribers who would be interested in hearing about your topic. Prepare a mini-seminar about your book and pitch it to people who own websites, blogs, online radio shows, etc. They'd be very interested in giving you a stage to promote your book if it helps or entertains listeners. Create a concise 2-4 page handout with fill-in-the-blanks so your listeners can interact with you on the call. Of course, you can hire a company to assist you with this, but this is something you really can do yourself. No matter what type of virtual book tour you plan (at least 2 months in advance), organization and practice are critical to your success.

10. ☐ Public Speaking, Seminars & Workshops

If you choose to speak about your book real time, take that same fill-in-the-blank worksheet that you created for your virtual book tours and give it to your live audience. Speaking engages attention and when the media picks up that you're wowing audiences locally and/or nationally, they'll be contacting you. Count on it. Create believers and buyers with your live presentations.

11. ☐ Associations, Organizations & Societies

There are a multitude of groups, associations and organizations with open membership that might be interested in hearing about your book. Maybe you've written about a specific topic. Focus on these groups first. To find niche groups that might be interested in hearing you speak, search for:

your book's category + the word "associations"

OR

your book's category + "organizations"

Do the research, contact them, sign up for membership (if required), and/or ask to speak to their audience of members or be a guest speaker.

RECOMMENDED RESOURCES

❑ **Business Associations** — Online, conduct a search for organizations near you by city, county, state and/or neighboring state (within driving distance). Find any association that could tie in with your book's topic.

❑ **Listmania (Amazon.com)** ... is a free marketing Amazon tool for authors that lets people know about products you find interesting. It offers a perfect opportunity to cross-promote your work with best-selling titles that are in your genre. You'll want to create a book list that will attract your potential audience. You can also create more than one list, if you want to cross promote your work to different audiences.

Here are some **author-friendly websites** that can help get your book the additional exposure:

❑ AbsoluteWrite.com

❑ AddictedToEbooks.com/submission

❑ AskDavid.com/free-book-promotio

❑ Authonomy.com

❑ AuthorMarketingClub.com/members/submit-your-book

❑ AuthorsDen.com/visit/cat_articles.asp

❑ BiblioConnection.com

❑ BlackCaviar-Bookclub.com

❑ Blog.BooksOnTheKnob.org

❑ BookAndReader.com

❑ BookBrowse.com

❑ BookBuzzr.com

❑ BookHitch.com

❑ BookMooch.com

❑ Books.Google.com/googlebooks/tour

❑ Booksie.com

❑ BookTalk.org/authors-publishers.html

❑ DigitalBookToday.com/join-our-team

❑ eBooksHabit.com/for-authors

❑ Facebook.com/authorsbroadcast *(Video Trailers)*

❑ FlurriesOfWords.blogspot.ca

❑ Forums.onlinebookclub.org

❑ Freebooksy.com/for-the-authors

❑ GoodKindles.net

❑ Goo.gl/bM4BZK (Amazon.com Authors Forum)

❑ GoodReads.com

❑ JacketFlap.com

❑ Jogena.com/ebookdir/ebookform.htm

❑ Kindlemojo.com/info.php

❑ LibraryThing.com

❑ NothingBinding.com

❑ Scribd.com

❑ Shelfari.com

❑ TheBookMarketingNetwork.com/forum

❑ TheVirtualBookcase.WordPress.com

❑ WattPad.com

❑ WiseGreyOwl.co.uk

❑ Writers.net

12. ❑ Large Quantity Book Sales

Nothing beats receiving an order for 100 or more books from a single buyer. Large quantity book sales or bulk sales are especially lucrative! Who buys large quantities of books?

❑ Companies

❑ Associations

❑ Foundations

❑ Book Clubs

❑ Marketing Organizations

❑ Promotional Product Firms

❑ Network Marketing Companies

❑ Gift & Specialty Catalogs

❑ International Sales

Large quantity book buyers are everywhere. Offer a discount off the retail price of your book so these unique buyers can make a nice profit, too. Naturally, you'll gain from books sold in bulk, but imagine having 10 companies buying 100 books each! Depending on the price of your book, you might just make 10 x 100 x $5 profit for each book amounting to $5,000 cash in your pocket! Go after those special market sales by searching online so you too can sell your book in r large quantities!

13. ❑ Book Printing, In-Bound Order Taking & Fulfillment Preparation

It goes without saying, before you attempt ANY of the previously mentioned book marketing, publicity and promotional tactics, be sure you have a reliable fulfillment service system in place. Without it, you could receive 1,000 orders from one radio show interview only to have your merchant account provider tell you that they'll be holding your earned funds (from sales) for 90 days! How will you fill large orders or pay your bills? Check out your fulfillment center practices in detail.

14. ❑ High-Profile Publicity / PR Coverage

At this stage (assuming you followed many of the suggestions on this checklist), you're probably ready to take your book promotions and publicity efforts to the next level. More specifically, I'm talking about television, national radio and publications that reach millions.

"In publicity, contacts are everything."
— *PR Week Magazine*

KNOW THIS. If you're serious about reaching thousands, even millions of TV viewers, radio listeners and print readers, then contact my office. Some of my contact alliances may be of assistance to you such as:

• Strategic publicity and public relations with a focus on mainstream pop media ...

• Designing affordable and effective campaigns for personalities and businesses ...

• Negotiating with the media for maximum client benefit and promotional impact ...

• Publicist / broker on the sale of exclusive interviews, photos and news material ...

• Bankable publicity for national products such as a DVD, book or fashion line ...

- Matching up corporate brands with the right celebrity, spokes model or expert ...

- Advance / on-site PR for entertainment events, book signings and fund raisers ...

- Increasing demand for artists, speakers, authors, journalists, and air talent ...

- Helping clients network with talent agents, directors and speakers bureaus ...

- Lead publicists / PR management on political or cause-oriented campaigns ...

- Book publicist and PR counsel to traditional, independent and E-publishers ...

- Internet publicity and public relations counsel on web image / social media ...

- Creative director and publicist for photo / video shoots and marketing events ...

- Guidance and PR counsel on potential TV, book, music and business projects ...

- Publicist and initial spokesperson on news exclusives or entertainment items ...

NEED MORE WAYS TO PROMOTE YOUR BOOK?

As a member of MyTrainingCenter.com, you too can tap into my 120 ways to promote your book based on proven success.

121 WAYS TO PROMOTE & MARKET YOUR BOOK(S)

www.MyTrainingCenter.com/121-ways-to-promote-market-your-book

BOOK PUBLISHING
CHECKLIST

Do you want to write a book for publication? Have you chosen a book printer yet? If you haven't thought about using the company I use to print your book, you should.

I have written more than 10 books and printed all of them using the printer I use. I've also referred several of my clients to them with 110% satisfaction. Allow me to share the positives I've experienced publishing with my printer, over some others I have used in the past, and I'll get right into my checklist for how to prepare your written content for a printer.

☑ **Highest profits paid to you** for listing your books on Amazon.com through this printer and from wholesale purchases account.

☑ **24/7 telephone support** always available to answer questions or handle specific printing matters.

☑ **You can order one book or several books** and ship them to one or multiple locations.

☑ **Unlimited changes to your manuscript and covers.** Simply upload a revised version and submit it for a proof as often as needed at NO CHARGE!

☑ **Order as many proofs as you like.** My printer will charge you an inexpensive wholesale rate based on page count. For example, if your book has a page count of 136 pages, the proof might cost $2.36 times the number of proofs you require versus other printers that only give you ONE free proof and then charge you $30 for EACH proof thereafter! What if you have three people reviewing a proof of your book? You could be charged $90 for three books! What if you have multiple submissions and need more proofs? In my experience, no printer can compete with my printer when it comes to this small a quantity.

☑ **My printer's online digital proofing tool helps you proof your own books**, page by page, locate errors, and fix them. This gets your books approved faster for printing.

☑ **FREE ISBN#'s for your books** if you choose not to use your own. I say, "Save your money!"

☑ **With my printer's "FREE" EXPANDED DISTRIBUTION**, your book will be listed with Baker & Taylor, Ingram, bookstores, online retailers, libraries and academic institutions. My printer also lists your book with 20K+ outlets.

HOW TO USE MY PRINTER FOR PRINTING YOUR BOOK

1. ❑ **If you're currently with another printer, I would recommend that you terminate their services and allow my printer to print/distribute your book.** Notify the printer of termination in writing and request all book files that rightfully belong to you provided you don't already have copies of them on your own computer.

2. ❑ **Create a FREE account with my printer, which will hold ALL your book titles.** Don't create separate accounts per book title or break up your different book title royalties into different accounts. This is not good. If you work with clients, don't put their book titles in your account. Create individual accounts for their books. If you co-author a book, create a separate account for that book. Don't let other people into your personal CreateSpace account and don't mix royalty payments!

3. ❑ **Enter your first book title for print through my printer and follow all the prompts that direct you.** When asked, DO NOT select **AMAZON** and **EXPANDED DISTRIBUTION** until your book is ready for sale. You'll want to proof a hard copy of your book prior to any distribution.

4. ❑ **Prepare and upload your book to be printed with my printer by generating two PDF files (one PDF for the interior pages and another PDF for the back/spine/front cover files).** If you need help creating a book cover, you can download a cover template from my printer to help you design it. Caution: BOTH PDF files should be prepared by a professional skilled in working with book files and printers.

5. ❑ **After you upload your book files, proof them digitally online with their proofing tool.** Once you have fixed any errors and both files are uploaded, submit them for review. The review process takes about 24 hours.

6. ❑ **Once your interior and cover PDF files are approved for printing, you will be sent an eMail saying you can now order proof copies!** DO **NOT** ORDER A PROOF, because they only allow you to order a minimum quantity and the word "PROOF" is printed on the last page.

   APPROVE YOUR BOOK DIGITALLY and then order copies that can be shipped to one/more locations. If my printer finds mistakes and doesn't approve your book for printing, you'll be directed to fix them (such as alignment) and resubmit your PDF file(s) for another review.

7. ❑ **Once you have received your book proof in the mail, read it, review it, ask others to view it for obvious errors.** Make any necessary changes and resubmit the files for another review session.

8. ❑ **ONLY when you believe your book is ready for sale, activate the AMAZON and Expanded Distribution sales channels.** Finish any other sales descriptions, set your book price, and you're ready to unleash your written work to the world for sale!

9. ❑ **Start marketing your book and making $$$ as a new author through my printer!** Contact me online at MyTrainingCenter.com to find out who I use to print my books. You might be surprised, delighted, or assured who I'm using.

BOOK WRITING
CHECKLIST

This may not look like a standard checklist because I decided to incorporate my thoughts on writing a book in this section. Well, here are some stress-free writing tips to help you write a book, eBook, blog, article, etc. Every tip should have some kind of impact on the success of your writing. Hopefully, you find a few useful nuggets from my own experience as an author of more than 10 books, articles, blogs, and more.

❏ **Write daily.** Write as much as possible, as quickly as can, but with some level of detail. The purpose of this writing formula is to write anything down that comes to mind. Writing quickly keeps your thoughts flowing and your memory jogging!

❏ **Keep thoughts and ideas always flowing.** You can always review and rewrite later. It's better to have more content than you need, which is why you should keep it simple. Just sit down and write.

❏ Start writing with where you are at a given moment, not where you want to be or how you expect to end up. Stay in the present.

❏ Write 1-3 hours per day and continue writing on the weekend (3-10 hours) or even more. This may require some self-discipline, but the more you write, the more you can write.

❏ Never go to bed without writing something even it it's only one page or 10 minutes. Ernest Hemingway wrote, "There's nothing to writing; all you do is sit down and bleed." Now, I know he didn't mean that literally, but write something!

❏ Imagine yourself telling a story to someone. Write narratively; write how you talk. This will depend, of course, on the subject matter. If you're writing a technical piece, write what you know. You'll have plenty of time to research and/or rewrite later.

❏ Not everyone has a Notebook, mobile device, or mini-laptop that they can conveniently carry around with them. Get in the habit of carrying at least a small note pad so you can jot down ideas as they occur because you know you'll forget them.

❏ When writing, avoid outside contact. Turn the phone over to voice mail, shut off the radio, etc. This is a period of deep concentration. For some, music makes the whole process that much better. Avoid distractions, obviously, but establish an environment that stimulates your creative juices.

❑ Look around you for resources to help you such as libraries, bookstores, museums, meetings, etc. The more you read, the better writer you become.

❑ You've no doubt heard that everyone has a book inside of him/her. The challenge for any writer is to pull it out of you and put it on paper. It's a challenging, vulnerable journey for most; rewarding for many.

❑ Writing a book gives you a certain level of credibility, believability, and validation. You become somewhat of an expert on the topic you wrote about whether it's fiction, business, history, etc. Writing can be a great marketing tool when your content needs to be convincing, strategic, inspirational, and more.

TIPS FOR WRITER'S BLOCK

When you just can't think or know how to get started, here are seven sure-fire ways to help you out of your rut.

❑ **Keep the pen rolling!** It doesn't matter if you write junk, doodle, create nonsense; keep writing. Why? Because the magic comes when you go back to the beginning of your work and read what you wrote! You realize that you're on to something and cleverly start thinking of ways to improve on what you wrote. You will see it come together.

❑ **Take a break!** Walk outside. Step away from your writing so you can think clearly, refreshed and then regroup. You can't write when you're exhausted or burned out. Get some rest to get the blood flowing back to your brain. Don't feel overwhelmed. Try to dissect the cause of your writer's block so you can understand it and get past it.

❑ **Exercise!** It's important to realize that the brain can't just go on and on without stimulation so get up and move around. Sweat a little to get your body working in an entirely different direction. Do something different such as bake some cookies, seriously. Sometimes it's helpful just to step back and look at your writing later with fresh eyes. Don't be surprised if during your departure that you come up with more new ideas to develop. Write them on a note pad, if possible. In any case, collect your thoughts and look forward to writing again.

❑ **Read more material!** You can never run out of words to use, which is why reading is such a boon to good writing. It improves your vocabulary. Reading new material will definitely give you more thoughts, ideas, facts, experiences, names, places, dates, figures, statistics, truths, realities, etc. The same applies to listening to audio programs. Many writers claim inspiring books shaped their writing.

❑ **Collaborate with someone (part-time or full-time)!** Two minds work better than one. Work with a friend or associate on a piece you're struggling with. Just a few words fro another person can get the juices flowing again. Co-author with someone that has complementary skills or can bring a unique perspective to what you write.

❑ **Write what you know about!** Even if your writing fiction, you'll need relevant information to set the scene or environment or period in time. So your first step is the collect and read as much information as you can on your topic or story and then start planning. What resources will you need? Don't limit your research to the Internet. Developing a flexible outline will help you stay organized, focused, and free up your mind to write more effortlessly.

❑ **Interview others who can assist with your writing!** Take a class, attend a lecture or seminar, participate in a workshop, socialize with others about topics that relate to your writing interests. It's all about (1) pulling your thoughts together, (2) getting what's inside of you "out" and (3) putting it into a format that will sell a reader.

BUSINESS STARTUP
CHECKLIST

When it comes to starting your own business, working from home, being your own boss, making money and paying taxes (yes, taxes), there's plenty to learn to ensure that your business is a success.

Here's a quick checklist of things that you'll want to give serious thought to as they pertain to your business or start up. Learn more at MyTrainingCenter.com.

1. ❑ The Ideal Business

Read this first. Get your mind set on what the "ideal business" looks like to avoid traps and gimmicks to avoid going down the "wrong road." You've heard the saying that when starting something you, you must have a passion for it. Don't follow the money; follow your heart because any new venture is a lifestyle change! Steve Jobs once said, "The only way to do great work is to love what you do. If you haven't found it yet, keep looking. Don't settle."

2. ❑ Mindset of an Entrepreneur

To be an entrepreneur, you need to start thinking about being an entrepreneur and start living like one. This means hard work. This means believing that you can succeed and then putting all of your energy into it.

3. ❑ Products and/or Services

Before you do anything, research the market. What are people buying? What are people asking for? Whether you sell a product or supply a service, be prepared to solve a problem or satisfy a need and then with tenacity and determination commit to succeed.

4. ❑ The "Income Wheel"

Do NOT go into business for yourself until you learn about my "Income Wheel," a money-making strategy for growing, preserving and investing your income.

Many of **MY CHECKLISTS** have video tutorials that teach you more at www.**MyTrainingCenter.com**.　　**35**

5. ❏ Business Name + Domain Name

Brainstorm and list of names and then try them out on your friends and associates. Even look to your competitors for inspiration. Keep it short, easy to remember, and relevant to what you do. Once you have a business name, RUSH to your computer to register your domain name to protect it! The same applies to any business ideas, product titles, etc. you might have. You can register all of your domain names at:

www.ReallyCheapNames.com

If you intend to create other websites, manufacture more products, obtain trademarks and logos, copyrights for written, audio or video creations, and every money-making idea, register those domain names for future use to ensure that any name you create is not undermined or stolen. You might even purchase variations of a domain name to drive more traffic to your website.

6. ❏ Private Mail Box

Renting private mail boxes at a local mail box rental store guarantees that your business (and personal) mail is protected. You generally have access to your mail 24/7 and don't have to worry when you are off on a business trip or vacation. DO NOT GET A P.O. BOX. (See my report on Private Mail Box service at MyTrainingCenter.com).

The biggest reason not to use the U.S.P.S. is because they do not accept mail/packages delivered by any other service than their own such as UPS or FedEx. If you operate your business from home, do not want your customers to have your home address? For safety and professional reasons, use a private mail box service!

7. ❏ Business Plan

Now that you have a business name, your domain name is secured, and you know what products/services you will sell, your next step is to make a BUSINESS PLAN. Keep it simple and straightforward without the buzz. Using bullet points and lists are easy to follow. If you have metrics, charts, graphs, simplify them, skip the 3-D stuff, and be sure to reference the attachments in the text.

Write out your steps for PRE-launch and POST-launch. The physical look of your plan should be organized and transparent and then proof it. You'll be very surprised at how easy it is to "plan your success" with My Quick-Start Business Plan tool.

8. ❏ Business Structure

Now that you have a business plan, how will you structure your business? Much of your tax liability will be determined by the decision you make. For most, a sole proprietorship or partnership such as a spouse or even an LLC (limited liability company) is sufficient. Going the corporate route isn't always the most cost effective way to go unless you have several employees and deal with several clients, vendors, etc.

9. ❏ Tax Deductions

Before you hire an accountant to help you with your taxes and other business needs, familiarize yourself with business tax deductions so you can speak the accountant's language. Using an accountant is highly recommended to ensure that, at a minimum, you're deducting as many legal/allowable expenses to lower your business' and personal tax obligation annually.

10. ❏ Accountant

If you have income coming in from multiple sources or qualify for business deductions, hiring an accountant could save you money. Accounts must stay current with the tax laws, which could save you time. They maintain the records and are on top of when to file tax forms. Accountants are not as expensive as tax attorneys and they can assist you should the IRS contact you.

11. ❑ Tax ID or E.I.N. (Employer Identification Number) Issued by IRS

AFTER you decide on your business structure (Partnership, Sole Proprietor, LLC, etc.) and prior to opening a bank account, apply for a Federal Tax I.D. online. Your accountant can help your with this application and will know about any applicable sales tax laws on the sale of products in the state you reside in and others.

12. ❑ Attorney

Depending on the nature of your business, an attorney has expertise with contracts and can ensure that every "i" is dotted and every "t" is crossed. While your need for an attorney is be on a case by case basis, there is also FREE legal assistance for your business available online.

13. ❑ Bank Account

After you've consulted with your accountant, secured your tax I.D. number, and made copies of your business structure paperwork, now you can open your business bank account. Ask to speak with a new accounts representative to learn about the different plans for managing your business revenue and expenses.

14. ❑ Website

Doing business online is a big step for most. Depending on your budget, time and readiness, you will need a website for your business. Prior to building your website, consider having at least a brochure, postcard or marketing literature to advertise and market your business until your website launches. Social media accounts work much like a website such as Twitter, LinkedIn groups, Facebook fan pages and groups, etc.

The more you sign up for the more exposure.

15. ❑ Shopping Cart + Payment Processing

If you're going to sell products, services, training, etc., you should have a shopping cart to accept online orders. You'll also need a payment processor like PayPal or similar to process credit card orders from your website.

16. ❑ Product Duplication/Replication, Packaging, Publishing & Fulfillment

If you have a product in mind to sell, you will need to look at production, inventory, fulfillment and distribution in small and large quantity, which is where the real money is including overstocking. issues. Will you be operating all facets of your business out of your home or off sight.

17. ❑ Business Cards

Even if you're operating an online venture, business cards can be critical to developing your business. Your card should be make an impression and include your contact information, website address, domain name, and be highly personalized.

A few tips when ordering business cards: (1) Don't order 1,000 cards (versus 500) immediately unless you truly satisfied with the design. (2) Put your picture on the business card. When networking, people remember faces before names and what you do. (3) Put a call-to-action on the back of the card or list your products / services. Use of the back of your business card as a mini-billboard for what you do.

18. ❑ Marketing Plan

Why do you need a marketing plan for your business? Take adequate time to write the plan and get input from others especially if there is

---

more than one person involved in the business because you will depending that team to share your vision and help you implement it. The plan should cover one year, but you should check it at least monthly. Study my Daily/Weekly Marketing Checklists in this book.

Marketing means everything to a successful business! This means that you need to spend at least one-third of your day promoting your business to generate a consistent flow of revenue. Experts say that it's better to have a poor plan versus no plan and to put together a genuine marketing plan, you have to assess your company, top to bottom, and make sure everything is working in the best way possible. For more marketing strategies and tactics check out MyTrainingCenter.com.

19. ❑ Joint Venture (JV)

Marketing as a JV enables you to pool your resources and do much more advertising and promotion than you would independently. Joint ventures enjoy increased traffic to your website, blogs, etc. By joining forces with another marketer, you create more business opportunities and you're less likely to fail in a JV. Why not collaborate with your competitor? The more you can do with a partner frees up time to work on other aspects of your business (building your list, extending your reach, expanding your brand.) A JV can catapult you to your next level of success!

20. ❑ Virtual Assistant (VA)

Your business is booming and you could use an extra set of hands. Don't want to risk losing potential business because you are overwhelmed with administrative tasks. By prioritizing your business activities and then delegate some duties to a qualified VA to grow your business. Most VAs contract from home and provide their own office supplies and equipment. Review the OUTSOURCING CHECKLIST so you can take even more $$$ to the bank.

BUSINESS TAX
DEDUCTIONS
CHECKLIST

W hy should you learn more about legal, allowable tax deductions for your business? The obvious is to save money on your taxes. If you run your own business, as I do, or you are thinking about starting one, add learning about taxes, tax deductions, business structures, and tracking business income and expenses as major part a sharp learning curve for running a successful business.

For starters, read this tutorial on tax deductions. It should enlighten you on your business tax responsibilities and then talk to a CPA (certified public accountant) or tax consultant, which I strongly recommend you hire to help you with your business.

They can keep you on track, honest, and advise you on tax tips and pitfalls.

What tax forms will you need to file at the end of the year for yourself and your business? For starters, what state do you reside in? Are you required to pay income tax in your state? What type of business entity do you have? For the most part, you and your business should be filing the following tax forms, unless otherwise advised by your accountant:

PERSONAL TAX OBLIGATION

STATE TAXES ... unless you live in a state that does not require you to pay state income tax.

FEDERAL TAXES ... which most people pay, unless exempt and then are you paying your fair share?

BUSINESS TAX OBLIGATION

STATE TAXES ... unless you live in a state that does not require you to pay state income tax.

FEDERAL TAXES ... which most people, unless exempt and then are you paying your fair share?

Again, depending on the number of business partners you have and your business structure, you may be required to submit a minimum of four (4) sets of tax forms. This is why you hire a tax professional. It's risky to complete and file your own business returns unless that is your area of expertise.

What can you deduct when it comes to business expenses?

What kind of business are you operating? Your records should be showing expenses, profit and loss statements. Here are many of the allowable tax expenditures that the IRS allows a business to deduct from their gross earned income:

- ❑ Accounting
- ❑ Advertising, Promotion & Marketing Expenses
- ❑ Auto
- ❑ Cartons, Boxes & Shipping Supply
- ❑ Contributions (Certain ones, up to a certain limit.)
- ❑ Delivery Expenses
- ❑ Electricity, Electronics, etc.
- ❑ Entertainment (Meals, Events, etc.)
- ❑ Insurance (Certain types related to your business.)
- ❑ Interest on Loans related to your business.
- ❑ Internet-Related Charges
- ❑ Inventory, Merchandise & Materials
- ❑ Laundry/Dry Cleaning
- ❑ Legal Fees & Expenses
- ❑ Licenses
- ❑ Miscellaneous
- ❑ Office Expenses
- ❑ Office Supplies
- ❑ Postage, Stamps, Shipping Expenses
- ❑ Rent (100% of business office space, or % of your home use.)
- ❑ Repairs (Computer, Office Machines, etc.)

- ❑ Research Materials (Books, Magazines, etc., if related to your business.)
- ❑ Selling Expenses (Facilities, Training, Materials, etc.)
- ❑ Storage (Used for storing business supplies and inventory.)
- ❑ Taxes: Other, Local, etc.
- ❑ Taxes: Sales Tax You Collect from Customers
- ❑ Taxes: Social Security/Medicare
- ❑ Taxes: State U.I. (Unemployment Insurance)
- ❑ Telephone, Cell Phone, etc.
- ❑ Trade Dues, Membership Fees, etc.
- ❑ Training & Education (Classes, seminars, workshops, etc.)
- ❑ Traveling Expenses (Gas, lodging, meals, car rentals, etc.)
- ❑ Utilities
- ❑ Wages, Commissions & Bonuses
- ❑ Water Expense (If purchased for the office.)
- ❑ You may have other allowable expenses (directly linked to your efforts to making money with a real business) that only a qualified tax person will know.

COACHING BUSINESS
CHECKLIST

Rich Coach

Broke Coach

101+ Coaching Tactics To Start, Run & Explode Your Coaching Business & Your Income As A *"Rich Coach!"*

Bart Smith, TheMarketingMan.com
and Founder of MyTrainingCenter.com & BreakThroughBS.com

❏ Setting up your coaching business ...

❏ Further training, certification, etc. ...

❏ Building your coaching website ...

❏ Writing a book about your niche ...

❏ Preparing coaching forms/contracts ...

❏ Marketing your coaching services ...

❏ Speaking about your coaching niche ...

❏ Securing media about your services ...

❏ Finding clients ...

❏ Creating client successes ...

❏ Working with clients ...

❏ Closing clients ...

❏ Asking for testimonials ...

❏ Asking for referrals ...

D o you like helping people? Do you find that people come to you for advice on matters of importance whether it's business or personal? Then you, my friend, may have a calling to be a professional coach.

How do you become a great coach? Review this quick checklist and read Rich Coach Broke Coach.

1. ❏ Assess your strengths and weaknesses for coaching others or even starting your coaching business. These are some key components for any coaching business:

2. ❏ When you have doubts/concerns, address them with more information (education, training, practice, consulting) or hire a personal coach.

3. ❏ Pick your coaching niche unique to your skills, talents and abilities.

4. ❏ Define your ideal (paying) client. What qualities do you bring to the table that would prompt a client to pay you for direction? What pain or passion do they have that you can help with?

Many of **MY CHECKLISTS** have video tutorials that teach you more at www.**MyTrainingCenter.com**.   41

5. ❏ Prepare all the coaching contracts, forms, questionnaires, surveys and materials you'll need. Know when and how to use them. If you need help with such forms and agreements, my book, **Rich Coach Broke Coach**, addresses them and how to use them.

6. ❏ Set your fees, create your coaching packages and learn how to sell to prospective clients. Know how make money through coaching?

7. ❏ Set up your office or coaching zone. Where can you work with clients where you're not disturbed? Secure that place and treat it like Fort Knox to avoid interruptions whether you are couching by phone or in person.

8. ❏ Consider offering FREE sessions to perfect your selling approach for securing new clients and to get ideas on what works best with your clients. As your services grow in popularity, you can possibly bump up your rates and take on fewer clients.

9. ❏ What marketing tactics best suit you for finding clients? Is it networking, speaking, and asking for referrals, working with the media?

10. ❏ Build a website to promote your coaching services/packages.

11. ❏ Write a book about your coaching business with some success stories that might inspire new clients. Use your book to garner interviews and promote seminars and workshops and speaking engagements to grow your business. Imagine saying, "I don't have a business card with me, but I do have one of my books."

12. ❏ Read to learn about the coaching business and how you can continually improve your skills as a coach.

13. ❏ Get certified by one or more coaching certified programs that are offered online and/or in the classroom.

14. ❏ Stay current with news and updates within your coaching niche or industry to stay current on what's happening so you can share the information with clients.

There're even more great tips, advice and tactics in my book, **Rich Coach ◆ Broke Coach** … 280+ pages and one-stop shop for what you need to know, how to do it, and instructions you won't find in any other book.

You'll learn at least 150 mistakes coaches make, money-making ideas to promote your business, product ideas, how to find your ideal client, and so much more. Just head on over to:

www.RichCoachBrokeCoach.com

COMPUTER TRAINING
CHECKLIST

Computers are the lifeblood for many people and their incomes. What do you need to know about computers? LOTS! For starters, here's a quick checklist for the main skills you should know regarding computers so you can function in today's technology-driven society and make the most of it! The more you know about computers, the greater your opportunities to make money online and offline.

❏ **Computer Shopping Tips** – Do you need to purchase a new or upgraded computer? Before you shop, check out a few recommended computer buying tips at MyTrainingCenter.com.

❏ **Quick Keys Commands** – If you master any part of the quick keys I outline for you at MyTrainingCenter. **com**, you will save so much time because you aren't having to navigate with a "mouse" versus a few quick clicks on the keyboard to perform the same tasks.

❏ **eMail Types & Tips** – When it comes to eMail, what are the different "types" of eMail? How do you get a (FREE) eMail address if you don't already have one? How do you get a custom eMail address with your own domain name? I answer these questions at **MyTrainingCenter.com**.

❏ **Cords & Accessories** – You might think you have all the cords, cables and adapters you need, so why have extras on hand? You never know when you'll need one while working late at night, losing one forcing you to replace it, wearing one to an unsfe frazzle, etc. It's a fact of "computer life" that you will need extra computer cords and accessories so be prepared with spares.

❏ **Typing Skills** – How are your typing skills? Speed and accuracy are vital. You can test your typing skills online for FREE. The faster you type, the more you'll accomplish, giving you more momentum at work, on the job, in business, writing books, writing articles, writing speeches, etc. You can purchase typing software to help you increase typing speed and accuracy. If typing is your weakness, this will be one of the best investments you'll make in yourself!

❏ **Installing & Uninstalling Software** – When it comes to software, knowing "exactly" how to install/ uninstall software on your computer is a big plus! Master these skills so you don't have to hire someone to do it for you! I show you how to install/uninstall software at MyTrainingCenter.com.

MY CHECKLISTS

❏ **Installing & Sharing Fonts** – What are fonts? Good question! While you probably know what they are, (i.e., Times Roman, Arial, Verdana, etc.), do you know how to install new ones on your computer? Do you know how to send a specific font to someone else via eMail? Check out this very informative series of video tutorials on fonts at MyTrainingCenter.com.

Once you know what you need to know about fonts, look out! You're going to become much more confident about using your computer and working with fonts.

❏ **Computer Maintenance** – Do you know what to do when you're computer's "sick?" I have a series of videos at MyTrainingCenter.com on how to help maintain your computer and prevent all kinds of threats, viruses, and so forth from damaging your computer.

❏ **Troubleshooting** – What's going on with your computer? Let's check it out! I have a special report on what to do when "trouble" lurks and your computer seems to want to misbehave!

❏ **Internet Browsers** – While "browsing" is easy, there are several features associated with your Internet browser you might want to know about. Check out my helpful Internet browser tutorials I show you how at MyTrainingCenter.com so you can really master using your Internet browser when surfing the Internet.

❏ **Parts & Accessories** – It's one thing to know about software, fonts and other aspects of your computer (on the inside), it's another to know and/or become familiar with important "parts and accessories" related to your computer and using it. Check out my special report at MyTrainingCenter.com on computer parts and accessories.

❏ **Windows Explorer** – Wow, if there was one set of tutorials at MyTrainingCenter.com you should check out, it's this one! Windows Explorer is the program that comes with your computer that lets you move, rename, delete, copy/paste all kinds of files and folders on your computer. Lots to learn here, but once you do, you'll use these tricks forever!

❏ **Windows Operating System** – Here's a nice introduction to Windows 7, your computer and how to use many of the basic functions that come with Windows 7. If you have Windows XP, 8 or 10, you too, will benefit from these video tutorials.

❏ **Audio Essentials [Downloading MP3 Files, Playing MP3 Files, Ripping MP3 Files & More!]** – Wow, what do you know about "audio" and using your computer? In these video tutorials at MyTrainingCenter.com, you'll learn A LOT about audio and using your computer to listen to it, download it, rip it ... and much more!

❏ **Working with ZIP Files** – Wow, you've heard about them, but how do you "zip" files, send "zipped" files, "unzip" a file! Heck, what does "zip" mean, again? Check out my video tutorials regarding zip files at MyTrainingCenter.com.

❏ **Computer Graphics & Digital Design** – Learn a whole new set of design and graphic skills using the most popular digital design software on the market today. These "quick-start" courses will teach you what you need to know with regard to graphic creation; image editing and manipulation; even picture animation.

❏ **TeamViewer.com** – When you need to let someone access your computer or you'd like to access someone else's, the best program for this is TeamViewer.com. It's free, fast and easy to use. Download it today at TeamViewer.com and learn how to use it at MyTrainingCenter.com. Check it out!

CONTINUITY PROGRAM
CHECKLIST

Continuity programs are online training programs designed to teach a specific niche/topic over a specific period of time (one week, two weeks, four weeks, three months, etc.) to customers who pay a flat fee or make monthly payments to participate and access a training program.

Continuity programs are not designed to drag on and on. They are designed with specific start and end dates. Customers appreciate that! What's more, paying customers have the opportunity to cancel any time and have zero obligation to make any future payments if they decide to drop out of a continuity training program. Customers like that, too!

Continuity programs should not be confused with full-blown membership websites that allow customers to sign up and become members for several months or indefinitely. Continuity training programs offer membership access to exclusive articles, high-quality

video instruction, special reports and/or other unique training information that you create and customers pay for the use of your program for a specific period of time.

Continuity programs typically consist of multiple training lessons delivered in a consecutive order (daily/weekly/monthly) online, by telephone or tele-seminar. They are very specific in what they teach. For example, *Learn How To Start Your Own Coaching Business* might consist of 12 individual, weekly lessons over a period of 90 days. Another continuity program might last for 6 months, even 12, and focus on a different niche topic altogether.

Here's a money-making tip for you ... the more niche topic continuity training programs you create and automate, the more money you can potentially earn online.

Why do customers prefer the continuity "learning method" over others?

For the paying customer, what they most prefer about learning via the continuity method are:

1. Customers know specifically what they are going to learn because you provided a schedule and a detailed course curriculum.

2. Customers know how much they are going to be charged to learn because the payment obligations were explained up front.

3. Customers count on having a specific end-date for training to set goals. Short bursts of training can make a big difference in the long run. They get in, learn what they need to know, and get out. Time is money!

Customers today want to know they're getting real value out of what they're paying for and they want assurance they they'll be able to use what they learn once the training is finished. Some will want to know if they can opt-out of the training if they don't think they're getting what they paid for.

The real advantage of continuity programs are that they are short-term, pay-as-go programs that specifically spell out what they'll learn and for how much.

How do continuity programs deliver training material to clientele?

While the training is delivered sequentially online, it is also specifically designed to "drip" or deliver key nuggets of information in a specific order per week/month. In my continuity tutorial checklist, I'll go over this in more detail so you can effectively deliver a quality program.

Another benefit for continuity programs is that once you build it, you're done. You don't have to keep adding content to it such as a membership training website. This is a good example of "work once and get paid again and again" model for making money online.

Perfecting the "selling process" for continuity programs ...

With any continuity program, you can build a list of prospects and filter those prospects into potential buyers from those simply looking for free information.

That's one great thing about continuity programs. They divide those who really want to learn from those who really don't. What does that mean? It means, you have people separating themselves

into groups who are ready to pay you to teach them what it is they want to learn. continuity income (e.g., ongoing/passive/residual income) allows you to work once and get paid over and over again with solid results after launching your first continuity program.

Continuity programs can also help you generate more income for your business month after month when you learn specifically how to automate the selling-process. In this checklist, you will learn the specific steps to automate the selling process of your own continuity program, as well as any other product or service you wish to up sell or down sell to the customers who enroll in your continuity program.

What's the best way to sell continuity programs?

While there are several ways to promote your continuity program and the products and services you have to sell/up sell/down sell, the best way to promote your continuity program is to use a solid "automated selling process" you create (1) once and (2) use over and over again to enroll more and more potential customers into your continuity program.

Within this checklist, I've mapped out the "selling process" to sell your continuity program and any other high$-end/low$-end product/service you might like to sell to a qualified list of buyers.

I will take you through each step (i.e., box) you see below so you too can learn how to duplicate the selling process for what you'd like to sell.

What's the real SECRET to a really successful continuity program?

Know that every paying customer will expect to learn something from your continuity program because today's customer is weary of slick-selling gurus that promise knowledge but lack effective application.

Answer: Your content must have value, solid information that the market has decided people really want and need. If they are paying hard-earned dollars for your expertise, they don't want to have their time wasted.

You can check out my continuity training checklist, master the creation-process to build your own program, but if you don't have original, empowering content to deliver to the consumer, you'll find a vast majority quit before they get started. You want them to absorb as much as possible during your time together.

So, be sure when you embark on this journey, that the content and training material you have to sell is in demand. It's that simple. How important, intuitive and innovative your content is will determine the success and profitability of your continuity program.

What you train others on will depend on your areas of expertise from a hobby to some form of specialized knowledge, interest or skill you have acquired. If you are considering training a niche group of people, get their input. Ask questions. Find out what they need. If you have a specific topic in mind, survey your lists and get feedback. What training resources and materials do you currently have at your disposal? Whatever topic you decide on, interactive sessions will keep learners engaged in your training and make them more receptive to the new information your continuity program can provide.

CHECKLIST

1.0 ❏ TOOLS/SERVICES you need to create a Continuity Program ...

What are the tools you need to create a successful continuity program? Let's get started.

1.1 ❏ Website (your primary site or one with a domain name dedicated to selling your continuity program)

1.2 ❏ Landing Page + Sales Letter Page

1.3 ❏ Opt-In Form

1.4 ❏ Autoresponder

1.5 ❏ Video Camera (Optional)

1.6 ❏ Video Player (Optional)

1.7 ❏ Shopping Cart

1.8 ❏ Payment Processor

1.9 ❏ Fulfillment or Digital Delivery System

1.10 ❏ Audio Recording Software & Equipment

1.11 ❏ Membership Software

1.12 ❏ Content Drip Feature

1.13 ❏ Affiliate Program

2.0 ❏ STEPS to follow when creating your own Continuity Program ...

Once you know what tools and services you need to create a continuity program, roll up our sleeves because it's time to start building it! Will you create your own program or will you need help? With my step-by-step checklist, you'll save some time planning and designing it.

2.1 ❏ TOPIC: Generate a list of ideas that you can work from and choose a topic that you know will sell because it's what people need and are asking for.

2.2 ❏ DURATION / NUMBER OF SESSIONS: How long will your continuity program run and how many sessions do you plan? People learn best in short increments so don't overwhelm them.

2.3 ❑ CONTENT: What is your continuity program about? What can people expect to learn? Do you have a syllabus? Create one and use as a guide for the individual lessons you'll create.

2.4 ❑ PRICE: How much will you charge people to enroll in your continuity program? Will the cost be a single payment or multiple payment option? Can customers cancel anytime during the continuity program and cancel their payment obligation?

2.5 ❑ TOOLS: Get the tools you need to create your continuity program based on 1.0 on the previous page.

2.6 ❑ HELP: If you need help creating a continuity program, you can find help on Fiverr.com and other freelance websites.

2.7 ❑ LANDING PAGE: Create a landing page that will serve as a sales page to enroll people in a trial version of your continuity program. This FREE version should consist of 1-3 introductory lessons. Following that, you should charge for access.

2.8 ❑ SALES COPY: Write the sales copy for your continuity program that will go on the landing page.

2.9 ❑ DELIVERY: With your tools set up and content separated into individual learning segments, configure the membership (or "drip") software you'll use to deliver your training material.

2.10 ❑ TEST: Test your continuity program to see if it performs the way it should. (1) As a test, sign up for it yourself. (2) Does everything function as planned? Are you fully enrolled in the test version and receiving the eMail announcing how to access the material you've set up for delivery? If not, go back, review your work and test it again.

3.0 ❑ **MARKETING Your Continuity Program**

This is where the fun begins! It's time to market your continuity program. This can be done in several ways. Here are a several ways to approach marketing:

3.1 ❑ Paid Traffic / Pay-Per-Click Advertising

3.2 ❑ Affiliate Marketing / Affiliate Program

3.3 ❑ Tele-Seminars

3.4 ❑ Webinars

3.5 ❑ Your Own Website

3.6 ❑ Newsletter/Ezine Promotion

3.7 ❑ Podcast Show Promotion

3.8 ❑ Viral Video Promotion

3.9 ❑ Viral eBook Promotion

3.10 ❑ Blog About It

What other ways can you think of to promote your continuity program? Make your list and act on them! Some of the marketing tactics mentioned above are also discussed in my book **MY CHECKLISTS**.

The success of your continuity program will enable you to build a stream of ongoing subscription revenue into your business and then you can up-sell other products/services to your customers and create a potentially lucrative residual income.

CUSTOMER CARE
CHECKLIST

If you're in business for yourself, selling products/services, you know how important it is to provide excellent customer care and support. You also know if you don't, you might not be in business very long. We all know good news travels fast ... well, bad news travels faster! Here are a number of customer care and support ideas you can implement immediately to provide your clients with the kind of support and service they deserve!

1. ❏ Telephone Number

Put your telephone number on every page of your website. If someone wants to reach you for any reason, the contact information is available at a glance without having to scour your website. You can even place your telephone number in the tag found at the top of every page.

2. ❏ Support eMail

cPanel video tutorials allow you to have an eMail specifically created so customers can eMail you with their customer support concerns. That eMail might be called **Help**[at]YourDomain.com or **Support**[at]YourDomain.com. This will then forward to you or a designated person in your organization allcustomer inquiries. As questions come in, make note of them and post them on a (read on) page.

Depending on the hosting company that hosts your website, you might have access to a cPanel where you can create any number of eMail accounts. Be sure to check out my cPanel video tutorials and learn how to create eMail accounts.

3. ❏ F.A.Q. (Frequently Asked Questions)

Customers typically have the same set of questions when buying a new product or signing up for a service. Post those questions online on a FAQ (frequently asked questions) page so customers can learn and potentially have their questions answered. Education is key for any kind of success!

4. ❏ Video Tutorials

Posting any number of video tutorials on your website explaining different aspects of your product/service can be very beneficial. If your video tutorials answer 20% of your customer call-in questions, you just saved time and money fielding repeat calls. When calls are received, customers can be directed to videos specific to their questions to answer their question.

5. ❏ Support Ticket System

One way to provide an effective online customer support system is with a "support ticket system." Forget eMail. With a support ticket system, say goodbye to lost or hard-to-track eMails!

Support ticket systems are web-based, store correspondence between you and your client, and some systems such as Kayako combines ticketed support (via eMail) with live chat and an intuitive customer interface. Kayako is especially advantageous if you have multiple web sites/products/services.

A help desk ticketing system allows you to offer prompt and efficient support to your clients. RSTickets!Pro comes by default with an integrated knowledge base system. It allows staff members to decrease response time and improve efficiency. Customers can submit support requests without being logged in. It requires a name and email address only.

After submitting the information, an account is automatically created and the credentials are sent to the eMail address supplied. Along with each ticket, additional information about the customer is stored such as IP, browser used, referrals and whether the customer was logged in or not.

6. ❏ Toll Free Number

If you don't have a toll free number for customer support issues, I encourage you to get one that will accept telephone orders. Toll free numbers are easy to get and inexpensive to maintain. The toll free number should spell out your personal or company name, product name, website, nature of your business, etc. Make it easy to remember!

FYI: Any toll free number can be supported by any toll free service within the U.S. or Canada by filling out a Responsible Organization Change Form called a Respond form and it does NOT need to be carried by the company that provides the local line.

7. ❏ Answering Service

For a reasonable monthly fee, you can hire a professional company to respond to your calls when you're temporarily not available. When travel, meetings, or appointments take you away from the phone, an answering service is preferred to an impersonal voice mail system. Treat your clients to a friendly voice by employing an answering service if you don't someone to assist you with calls.

8. ❏ Virtual Office

If you're a one person show, consider giving the impression that your small office is staffed with a number of people that work in designated departments. In other words, set up a virtual office by asking callers to "Press 1 for (Your Name), press 2 to send a FAX, press 3 to leave a message or press 0 to hold for the next representative."

9. ❏ Help Desk Software

Help desk software usually provides you (and your customer support staff) with a wide variety of features such as escalation, automatic notifications, a knowledge base, and more to help improve your customer experience.

10. ❏ Customer Service Centers

Consider having the service center or agents who answer your calls sign a Non Disclosure Agreement if needed. You want to protect yourself and your ideas from your competitors. Maintain your own toll free 800 number versus having a toll free number assigned to you by a service center. It's better to customize your own toll-free number so your customers aren't reduced to calling the service center's number. Unique numbers are easier to remember, too.

11. ❑ Outsourcing

Chances are your competitors are outsourcing their customer support to save money and serve their customers 24/7 by using global call centers. TIP: When outsourcing your customer support needs to a call center, find out where your customers will call into. Just because the company you signed up with is in your "country," it doesn't mean that the support center is. Some companies today outsource support services to other countries where the operational expenses are lower. Before you agree to any type of outsourcing, determine the quality of the service you are considering. Clear, well-informed communication is key.

12. ❑ Virtual Assistant

Hiring a virtual assistant could be a positive step towards handling your customer support issues. Virtual assistants often work from home, can provide telephone support service and help troubleshoot customer service issues while you focus on building the business.

When your business takes off, hire more help, or outsource the entire customer care portion of your business to a quality customer care service center. Your virtual assistant can still work with you in other parts of your business such as growing your list, conducting followup calls, and more!

13. ❑ Automation

Customer service is one area that could be worth automating. Before customers reach you, direct them to a series of F.A.Q.'s on your web site,

video tutorials, forums or help guides. If half or more of your customers' questions can be answered with these automation tools, you'll free up more time to dedicate to the business. Automation works when customers are satisfied with the information they are getting from the system. If you survey customers and ask if the automated response system meets their needs, then you've got your answer.

14. ❑ Speed

Providing prompt, quality and caring customer service is essential to keeping customer loyalty and building trust with you and your company. Every second that goes by is one second a customer thinks that you don't care about them or their complaint. To avoid any ambiguity, answer the phone within 3 rings or reply to their eMail within 30 minutes of receiving it. The quicker you respond to their "hurt", the "better" they feel about you and continuing their buying relationship with you.

15. ❑ Customer Support Database

No matter how many customers you have, use a database to manage all of the information you encounter, learn, acquire from supporting your clients and customers. What questions do your customers continue to ask? What is the typical complaint/need? Document the information in a database that you can review easily and periodically to assess if questions are being answered, problems are being solved and customers are more than satisfied with your service.

16. ❑ Think Like Your Customer

You may recall the idiom, "The customer is always right!" Well, they are, for the most part! Put yourself in the customer's shoes. Anticipate the kinds of questions a customer might ask, what kind of support is expect and what improvements are need. You always want to be one step ahead of your customer and meet the customer eye-to-eye whenever possible. Be prepared to go the extra yard to maintain those valuable customer relationships. A happy customer is a referring customer!

17. ❏ Complaints

When you get complaints, address them immediately without getting emotional, accusatory or trying to prove (you're) right. Approaching complaints with clear logic and genuine concern goes a long way toward turning lemons into lemonade!

In the case where you receive an eMail complaint, step back, read it carefully and do reply, but give yourself time to propose a solid resolution. DO let the customer know that you received the eMail and that you're investigating the situation and will reply within a reasonable period of time (the end of the day, within 24 hours, etc.). Once you have the information or best answer, respond to the customer, honestly, constructively, and sensitivity.

Remember, complaints are chances for you to fix what's wrong with your product/service so others don't have the same complaints in the future. Always thank customers for contacting you immediately with their concerns and giving you the opportunity to rectify them.

18. ❏ Refunds

Don't be too quick to refund a customer's money on a first request. Instead of giving a refund immediately to resolve a problem, see what YOU can learn first. For example, the customer says, "I'd like a refund …" Your response, "Of course, but can you tell me what went wrong?" and then offer to do X or Y to fix the situation. Let the customers know that you value their business and your goal is for them to be highly satisfied with your services.

Ultimately, it can cost more money to issue a refund. It can cost your reputation. So, focus on providing added value to what the customer bought, so he/she is willing to give you another chance. Your goal is customer retention and demonstrating that you value their loyalty can go a long way.

19. ❏ Credit or Cash Refund

When given the option, opt for credit for another product or service you provide. If a customer insists on a cash refund, try offering something with added value to maintain the customer and their money. Statistics show that customers that use credit cards versus cash actually spend more. That's a plus despite the small percentage you pay in transaction fees.

20. ❏ Guarantees

Let's face it, solid guarantees make sales! How long should your guarantee last? 30 days? In most cases, 30 days is the norm. 60 days? Better. 90 days? Excellent! Six months to a year? Too long in most cases. The purpose of a guarantee is to get people to buy your product/service. Think about it. Most customers don't have enough time within the first 30 days of purchase to truly evaluate some products/services, whereas a 60 or 90 day guarantee provides ample time for most customers to sample your product/service. It's a reasonable cut-off time and reduces the number of returns.

If your product/service is strong, 60-90 day guarantees are perfect timing and will encourage more people to buy from you. One year guarantees? Lifetime guarantees? They work great for some products, but fortunately for most, it's unlikely that a customer will ask for a refund at the three year mark.

DAILY/WEEKLY
& MONTHLY MARKETING
CHECKLIST

H ere is the TRUTH about MARKETING and DRIVING TRAFFIC to your business, product, service or website:

■ Marketing **DOES NOT happen overnight.**

■ **Marketing DOES NOT happen as a result of one ad or one eMail or one blog post or one tele-seminar or one tweet!**

■ **Marketing HAPPENS through a series of steps and commitments to one's own marketing plan of action and then how do you accomplish this?**

■ **SCHEDULE your marketing activities to the HOUR!** When should you get started? If your product/service is ready to launch, then, now, you can begin to look into the competitive market scene for timing.

■ **DESIGN and LAYOUT your marketing plan to continually EXPOSE your business, product, service and website 24/7.** Documenting your marketing plan ensures that you don't skip a beat.

■ **PLAN your MARKETING SCHEDULE short-term and long-term goals (daily, weekly, monthly, annually).** Always, be planning ahead while you're WORKING TODAY. Identify the steps to grow your business including how you'll respond to market changes.

■ **ASSESS what you can spend on marketing and where.** What's your budget? Make a list of planned marketing activities that will return either LEADS or SALES! Know who your product will serve, where you will find your customers, and how will you maximize your reach given the resources you have.

■ **HOW WILL YOU INVEST income from sales?** The most critical path for your business should be growth. As sales really take off, know how you will continually improve and transform to keep up with demand? A good rule to follow is to fairly pay yourself, protect your cash flow, and put investment income back into the business to pay for innovation and expansion.

In summary, make a LIST of all the marketing activities you'd like to implement based on monies allocated, knowing your market and competition, how your business stands apart, which marketing steps you'll implement based on your timeline and then market accordingly. A worthy MARKETING PLAN takes patience to design and implement. Here are a few more tips:

- The FIRST STEP is always the HARDEST STEP.

- Only YOU can make the FIRST MOVE.

- The MINUTE YOU MOVE creates MOMENTUM and puts you in a good position to start marketing!

- Set achievable goals and work work smart (daily, weekly, monthly, yearly)!

- Promote your customized marketing plan enthusiastically. Be observant, persistent, committed, and determined to succeed!

- Identify your TOP 10 MARKETING TACTICS and pursue them.

- Your business should operate like a train taking off on the virtual success track:

1ST GEAR = A little slow moving; just starting ...

2ND GEAR = Going a little bit faster now ...

3RD GEAR = Building up a more steam ...

4TH GEAR = You're cooking so keep going ...

5TH GEAR = Now you're at *LIGHTENING SPEED!*

- AUTOMATE/DELEGATE the SIMPLEST ASKS!

- Be ORGANIZED and MAINTAIN it!

- DO SOMETHING EVERY DAY - ANYTHING!

The ONLY ADVICE I can offer is the same advice that I give myself: Test, try, fail, evolve, look, listen, learn, watch, grow, advance, survive, observe, monitor, record, persist, push forward, don't let up, never stop, keep going, follow-up, reward, enjoy success. The more experience you have with these stages, the more of an expert you will become.

When it comes to marketing, you must have a strategic plan to acquire new customers quickly and cost effectively. Be prepared to maintain your customers over the long haul and then start driving profitability with marketing tactics such as up-selling, cross-selling, inbound marketing, social media marketing,and other best practices to reach your growth goals. Remember, my sales and marketing motto:

EXPOSURE = LEADS = SALES

Have clear intentions about how you'll handle growth, exposure, leads, branding, sales and income and then turn those intentions into actions. Don't underestimate consumers! They no longer wish to be seduced or tempted to buy. They are turned on by branding and value propositions and status symbols; no accounting for a good deal!

DAILY MARKETING TACTICS

Consider implementing some of the following marketing tactics and planning activities into your strategy and conduct at least one of the marketing-related tactics daily! Plan then in advance if for no other reason than to keep ahead of the competition. Dare to be different and step up your marketing game by putting more effort to differentiating your product and telling people why they should buy from you. On an every day basis, maintain a consistent level of awareness activity to keep customers interested. The secret to success is a critical estimation of your resources, your commitment level and the support systems you have in place. More daily activities:

- **Protect your income-generating time.** This means you should be working on income-generating activities. Consider the opportunity costs of using precious time and resources on less profitable work. Play and socialize after your work is done.

- **Find prospects.** Be prepared to find prospects in a variety of ways and leave no stone unturned. Then, nurture your prospects into solid leads because they are the building blocks of for sales.

- **Spend a minimum of 20-40% of your time marketing daily.** A good plan of attack is to perform a thorough assessment of your market potential. Investigate needs, competition, logistics, and more.

- **Write a new blog article that you can post frequently.** Blogs help you gain visibility for your product/service.When you blog for business, you have a free hand to to highlight the complexion of your company and your brand. Always review and respond to blog comments to maintain that important dialogue.

- **Podcasts should be part of your marketing campaign**. It's easy to generate content. The editing process gives you quick turnaround and transcribing the audio of your podcast gives you rich content for your blogs and other articles.

- **Online videos are the present and the future of content marketing.** More than half of all companies are using videos. They are engaging, informative, entertaining, and bring faces, voices, and personality to leads, prospects, and valued customers.

- **Check all your social channels** such as Facebook, LinkedIn Group Discussions, YouTube, Twitter, Google+) for comments, updates, and tweets. Check for comments daily and reply to comments as appropriate.

- **The average frequency to post on social media follows.** Post daily on LinkedIn; one to two times daily on Facebook and Google+, and at least three times per day on Twitter.

- **The biggest challenge for social media sharing is to make sure your content is better than any others.** When sharing, stick to the "magic mix" formula: 60% of updates using third-party content; 30% original content; and 10% for your content with offers and links landing pages, for example

- **Audit your websites for problems.** You don't want to learn from someone on Facebook that you site has been down for a couple of days. That could be a costly mistake.

- **Review Google AdWords, Google Merchant Center, and Google Analytics accounts.** I adjust budgets, keywords, and check trends. I make sure that campaigns we've put in place are getting the results we expect and I determine what changes need to be made and make them happen.

- **Browse the Internet** within your niche/industry for interesting ideas and strategies and search for mutual or reciprocal business opportunities.

WEEKLY MARKETING TACTICS

Make a list of all the marketing activities you will perform this week and in weeks going forward. While the bulk of your plan should focus on the coming year, working in weekly increments to ensure that you are on track with knowing what you need to do and how you will do it. Following are suggestions for marketing your own business.

❑ **Get feedback.** This is especially important to get this realistic input on what's achievable, how your goals can be reached even if you are a one-person operation.

❑ **Browse your website for performance,** broken links, missing images, forms and product links that don't work, etc. Test your site at least weekly.

❑ **Contact one or more groups, companies,** speaker bureaus, and directories of people who promote speakers and secure their services. Speaking is an acquire skill and if you aren't talking about your business an what you do, you should be.

❑ **Introduce yourself to a new eZine publisher weekly.** Invite the publisher to be an affiliate for your product/services. They have endless lists of prospects.

❑ **Build a personal brand.** Getting your name out there can give you great connections, customers, and help you to succeed in the professional/business world.

❑ **Take advantage of networking events.** The more people you can connect with and with their people, the better for your business.

❑ **Participate in at least one webinar and/ or tele-seminar** weekly or bi-weekly. The possibilities are endless. They're easy to conduct and profitable. If you don't have immediate content, conduct a Q&A session where you can respond to questions and promote the benefits for what you offer.

❑ **Write a blog post** at least once a week.

❑ **Review your website traffic statistics. Where is your traffic coming from?** Study the keywords used by visitors that brought you to your website. Incorporate those key word search terms into your sales copy and meta tags to fine-tune your search engine optimization even further.

❑ **Speaking: Again, take some time to plan your speaking,** teleclasses or webinars.

❑ **Attend one trade show,** network meeting or expo one a week or once every other week.

❑ **Contact at least 1-5 new online/offline radio stations** per week (or every other week or so) and pitch them on an idea for their show based on your book, product, service, knowledge, etc.

❑ **Submit a press release to a variety of websites** each week (or every other week or so) that will distribute your press release for free or for a nominal fee.

❑ **Ask for a referral once per week** either from a colleague, client or another human being.

❑ **Attend a high-profile meeting** or social event once a week or every other week.

❑ **Weekly, analyze your income earned versus your expenses out** to conclude your weekly net income.

MONTHLY MARKETING TACTICS

Consider implementing some of the following marketing tactics into your MONTHLY marketing strategies.

While you're managing the day-to-day business, you must identify and keep two or three high priority marketing activities at the top of your project list each month. Once you have your monthly focus you can develop projects, resources and business relationships relative to a theme or action plan. Marketing should be habit-forming. At a minimum, consider these monthly activities:

❑ **Give a presentation, teleclass or webinar** to showcase what your company does and its benefits.

❑ **Make follow-up calls** to contacts you met at networking events.

❑ **Attend one or more trade shows or expos** in your field of interest every month; more contacts; more leads; more sales.

❑ **Ask for 1-5 testimonials per month** from loyal, satisfied, even new customers and post these on your website.

❑ **Speak to one or more groups** in the community about a topic in your area of expertise to promote your business.

❑ **Spend 1-2 hours online, at the library or book store**, etc. performing research on your profession. Stay abreast of current technology especially as it relates to your business and website.

❑ **"Spy" on the competition.** What are they doing that you should be doing? Learn how to respond to rival marketing campaigns.

❑ **Short videos for your business can be just the ticket.** Why not produce a monthly video of 3-5 minutes that viewers can depend on and look forward to. Think of all the possibilities.

❑ **Are you an author or think about writing a book?** To gain credibility, draw attention to your company, set aside time to focus on writing content that will expose you as an expert in your field.

❑ **Grow an affiliate program.** Affiliates are your sales force that promote your product/ service for a commission who anticipate recurring monthly checks for their efforts.

❑ **Make one new alliance (at least monthly) with another business** or individual who will swap leads with you.

❑ **Submit 1-5 new articles per month** to at least 1-5 eZines and/or websites or better yet create your own monthly eZine.

❑ **Host 1-4 affiliate tele-trainings per month.** Affiliates need guidance, training and motivation and need to be aware of changes in product/service.

❑ **Host 1-4 free tele-seminars and/or webinars per month to promote your products or services,** your new book, or to build your list by making presentations to other lists.

❑ **Host your own "prepaid" webinar and/ or tele-class/eClass** series or in conjunction with other professionals.

❑ **Send out thank you cards (at least monthly)** to clients who bought products or services and to top affiliates who generate sales for you.

❑ **Can any monthly tasks be outsourced?** Do you need a virtual assistant or freelance service provider so you can focus on driving traffic and sales and MAKING MONEY?

❑ **Send updated information about your product/service to all old, new and current clients** via an online newsletter or other communication.

❑ **Add a new product** to your online

merchandise store to enhance your brand.

☐ **Join clubs and associations related to your business.** Ask to attend a meeting as a non-member to see if it meets your needs.

ANNUAL MARKETING TACTICS

Your marketing plan should have at least a 5-year trajectory with the goals to grow and expand your business. Consider these annual marketing strategies:

☐ **Attend at least one annual convention** in your industry, and speak at one too!

☐ **Revamp your website at least once a year.** Technology changes every six months. Be prepared to change with the times and add new features, bells 'n' whistles as needed.

☐ **Review your marketing materials,** update your forms, postcards, flyers, and other marketing literature if it needs updating.

☐ **Revisit all your video and audio and redo them,** if the material on them is out of date.

☐ **Conduct at least one or two major seminars,** workshops or boot camps in your chosen field of expertise.

☐ **Be a guest speaker at seminar,** workshop or boot camp for brand exposure to get your message out there.

☐ **Keep photographs current** especially if you have a press room/kit, update your bio, etc.

☐ **Have an annual business party** to show appreciation for loyalty and support!

☐ **Celebrate your highest earning affiliates** and promote them on your website!

☐ **Engage a joint venture partner** or create a new project to add to your income stream.

With clear objectives and measurable goals, your marketing plan should span the full mix of marketing activities. These might include new products, building your distribution network, pricing strategies, or more efficient customer satisfaction to ensure success.

DOMAIN NAME

REGISTRATION
CHECKLIST

H ow do you register, transfer or forward domain names to a website hosting server such as FatCow.com)? There's a lot to learn about domain names that you might not be aware of.

Look no further than the awesome checklist I've prepared for you! Read through the topics for new information about domain names. The checklist was designed to teach you the most important aspects for searching, registering, transferring and working with domain names.

CHECKLIST

1. ❏ WHAT IS A DOMAIN NAME?

A domain name is a unique website address that helps identify where your website or blog is. For example, "MyTrainingCenter.com" is a domain name. I know, you knew that, right? Of course, you did!

2. ❏ WHERE DO YOU REGISTER DOMAIN NAMES?

You register domain names with a company such as ReallyCheapNames.com that works with companies for individuals interested in building a website for any purpose. Companies that register domain names are also called domain name "registrars" because they "register" domain names.

3. ❏ CHOOSING GREAT DOMAIN NAMES

When deciding which domain "name" to register, there are several things to consider. Above all, make sure the name describes what you do, that it is easy to say and it doesn't include any quotation marks ("..") or hyphens (-) in the domain name! Check out MyTrainingCenter.com for ideas when generating domain names.

---

4. ❑ REGISTERING DOMAIN NAMES

When registering domain names, never pay more than $10 per domain name per year. Keep them registered under one "roof" meaning one domain name registration company! A really great place to register domain names is ReallyCheapNames.com. Check out the special report on registering great domain names at MyTrainingCenter.com.

Can you register more than one domain name? Yes, you can! Why would you want to do that? For example, register the name of your company in the form of a domain name, titles of your books, product names, service description names, etc. Domain names are like real estate on the Internet. You can purchase multiple domain names to build your brand and expand awareness of you and/or your business.

5. ❑ BULK DOMAIN SEARCH

Rather than search for a single domain name, you can perform "bulk searches" when you are looking for more than one domain name. Type in more than two domain names and press the search button and see what comes up.

6. ❑ BACKORDERING DOMAINS

What if a domain name that you want to register is owned by someone else. Can you still buy it? If the domain name is expiring soon (within a year or less), you can "backorder it!" That means, if/when it becomes available for purchase and the owner chooses not to renew it, a company like ReallyCheapNames.com can "reach in" and attempt to purchase it on your behalf.

Typically, there is a fee for this, but it's nominal. Is it worth it? Yes, if you really want a particular domain name. Does it work? Yes, about 90% of the time. It comes in handy when you really want a domain name that's about to expire and you want to register

it before anyone else gets the chance.

7. ❑ PRIVATE REGISTRATION

If you don't want your personal contact information to be listed "publicly" in the WHOIS database for global viewing, you can purchase a service called "Private Registration" that most domain name registration companies offer. When you do this, the domain registration company places their business contact information in place of yours to protect your identity. Any and all correspondence will be sent to the registration company and forwarded to you. Is this necessary? Yes, in rare cases.

8. ❑ WHO OWNS A DOMAIN?

To find the owner of a domain name, you can look it up in the WHOIS database. Nearly every domain name registration company has a search function to help you locate a domain name owner. Check out who owns MyTrainingCenter.com using the WHOIS function at ReallyCheapNames.com. You can expect to find the owner of a domain name, address, usually the phone number, eMail address, when the domain name was purchased, expiration date and the nameservers. This is valuable information to keep on file when interested is a special domain name.

9. ❑ TRANSFERRING DOMAINS

Having the flexibility to transfer domain names is very useful should you need to move a domain name from one registrar (e.g., GoDaddy.com) to another domain name registrar (e.g., ReallyCheapNames.com). Why would you want to do this? You might want to transfer one or more domain names to the same registrar to consolidate multiple domain names under one umbrella. It's easier to manage them if when they're all registered at one location. Should you decide to sell a domain name, transfer a domain name to a new owner, it's easy to do once payment for the domain name is received.

10. ☐ ADMINISTRATIVE CONTACT

This is THE MOST IMPORTANT PERSON to contact when purchasing, transfering or making changes to any domain name. Make sure that the ADMINISTRATIVE CONTACT EMAIL ADDRESS is YOUR eMail address and no other. If the address is incorrect, or the telephone number changes, that won't matter. It's the EMAIL ADDRESS that is the most important factor for controlling the destiny of a domain name! If you change your eMail address, update the ADMINISTRATIVE (ADMIN) CONTACT eMail address for your domain name. If you don't, you won't receive renewal notices. You could potentially lose your domain name if you aren't notifed that it is about to expire. KNOW THIS ... you have about a .000000000001% chance of ever getting your domain name back if it expires and someone else buys it. ALWAYS, keep YOUR contact information current.

11. ☐ LOCKED / UNLOCKED STATUS

To prevent a domain name from being transferred to another domain name registrar without your knowledge or consent, LOCK YOUR DOMAIN! This prevents anyone from initiating a request to transfer IT when you haven't authorized it. When you decide to transfer it, UNLOCK YOUR DOMAIN and you're free to transfer it with ease.

12. ☐ DOMAIN EXPIRATION DATE

The NEXT MOST IMPORTANT ELEMENT of a domain name is to monitor it as diligently as you Administrative Contact eMail address. Every domain name expires on an annual basis. It's your job to keep track of your domain names and renew them prior to expiration.

Your domain name will expire exactly one year from the date it is registered. Now, if you registered a domain name for 2, 5, or 10 years, it will expire on the anniversary date for that period of time.

If you're not sure when your domain name will expire, how can you find out? There are two ways:

(1) Log into the domain name registrar company where the name. is registered to view the expiration date. Is it set for an automatic renewal? If so, make sure your credit card information is current. If your domain name is expiring this week, renew it NOW!

(2) Perform a WHOIS data search for your domain and then check the expiration date on the results page. This information is so valuable.

What if your domain name expires and your website disappears? TIP: If you DON'T renew your domain name and it expires, you have **2 weeks** after the expiration date to SAVE YOUR DOMAIN from falling into public domain or being snatched up by a backorder domain registration service! Login to your account and renew it ASAP. If you need help, contact the domain name registrar's customer service for assistance.

13. ☐ AUTO-RENEW (ON/OFF)

This feature is helpful when renewing a domain name, automatically. Keep the credit card information that you have on file with your registrar so the name can be renewed seemlessly.

Should you lose your credit card or report it stolen, register the new card number with your domain name registrar ASAP. Don't lose your domain name because you forgot to update their records. Obviously, this applies to any vendor or business that automatically charges payments to your credit card.

14. ☐ DOMAIN NAMESERVERS (DNS)

When you want to "host" your domain name with a website "hosting company," you need to "point" the

---

"nameservers" associated with your domain name to the "nameservers" the website hosting company gives you when you initially set up website hosting.

If you don't change the nameservers correctly, your domain name won't point to your website hosting company. This isn't good, but it can be easily fixed!

Every domain name has its own set of nameservers. They're easy to change/update. Simply log in to your domain name registrar, look up your domain name, click on the mameservers option, and proceed to update the nameservers as instructed by your hosting company. Should you move a different hosting company, you'll probably need to change your nameservers again.

15. ❑ FORWARDING DOMAINS

Once you register a domain name, you don't need to order website hosting services to point or redirect your domain name to a website. You can simply "forward" it to an existing website. It's easy done and you can change the website you're forwarding it to anytime.

16. ❑ EMAIL ACCOUNTS

With most domain registrars, you can set up either an eMail alias that forwards eMail to your newly registered domain name or to your main eMail address. For example, yourname123[at]yahoo.com or you can setup POP3 eMail accounts to use eMail software programs on your computer such as MS Outlook, Mozilla's Thunderbird, Eudora, etc. to collect eMails that will use your newly registered domain names.

17. ❑ SSL CERTIFICATES

An SSL (Secure Sockets Layer) certificate is an electronic key that encrypts transmissions between two computers on a public network providing privacy and security to the session. The certificate key is issued by a third party. They are used for secure e-commerce communications, protecting information such as credit card numbers and personal data.

FYI: You'll probably never need to deal with SSLs. If your site needs to provide a secure (https://) connection for your visitors, then you might need to purchase a SSL certificate. They're inexpensive and renewed annually.

18. ❑ WEBSITE HOSTING

Website hosting refers to "hosting" or "storing" website files on a server so people around the world can access your website! For example, you registered your domain name and now you're ready to build your website. You'll need to obtain a reliable website hosting company such as HostGator.com.

How much does it cost to host a website? On average, it costs about $7-10 per month to host a simple website. More complex sites requiring lots of storage room for files and bandwidth can cost $20-$200 per month.

How do you pick a good website hosting company? Ask for a good referral from someone you trust. For example, my website (MyTrainingCenter.com) is hosted by HostGator.com. With 400,000+ web clients, 24/7 telephone support and great pricing, I value the services of HostGator.com.

19. ❑ DOMAIN NAME MANAGEMENT

Who manages your domains? You? Your webmaster? Your assistant? If your domain name expires and the company neglects to tell you, you can lose big time! Think of the impact on your business! Realistically, you will need to register a new domain name and change your eMail address. This is why you need a reliable company to manage your domain names to prevent problems.

You can easily learn how to maintain your own domain names by watching the video tutorials inside MyTrainingCenter.com. We offer a variety of video tutorials even if you don't use the same domain name registration company we do. The information is universal. The tutorials will introduce you to the functionalities associated with domain name registration companies. Once you see how it's done, you can duplicate the process with another company.

20. ❑ INTERNATIONAL DOMAINS

International domains are simply domain names that are registered in specific countries around the world. Depending on where you reside, you might be required to purchase a domain name unique to your country of residence. For example, in Australia, your domain name would end with ".com.**au**" or ".com.**uk**" if you live in the United Kingdom.

21. ❑ SELLING DOMAIN NAMES

Selling domain names can be profitable if you know what you're doing. Here are some good tips for selling domain names:

SELLING: If you're selling a domain name, the best way to price it is to determine its "value" in the eyes of a potential buyer. You can also precheck to see what it's worth by using an online URL appraisal service such as URLAppraisal.net. This site is easy to use. Check it out before you sell a domain name.

For example, let's say you're selling a domain name for $1,000 and the buyer says, "No way, I could have bought that name for $10 ..." Well, your reply might be, "Of course, but since I sell a product through that domain name, and you want to buy it ... you need

to know that I generate about one sale per day using that domain name, which brings me about $500 per month in income. Now, would I sell a piece of real estate on the Internet that was bringing an income of $10? NO. In three months, I earn $1,500 with that domain name so I need to sell it for a price that fairly compensates me. Surely, you can appreciate that the domain name has value for both of us. Are you still interested?"

22. ❑ SELLING DOMAIN NAMES

Typically, the interested buyer will respond with (1) "Yes. Thank you for sharing that information with me. I understand why you're charging $1,000. How can I pay your for this transaction?" or (2) "I understand why you are charging $1,000, but it's out of my price range. I'll have to pass on this." You can always negotiate, but be sure that you are getting value for the domain name you plan to sell.

BUYING: If you're buying a domain name, here are a few tips ... (1) Definitely tell the seller that you're interested in working with him/her on the price. (2) Try to reach them on a personal level especially when dealing with family or friends. You might be inclined to reduce the price and cut yourself short. (3) Offer something of value in exchange for the domain such as your products or services.

Finally, when it comes to buying and selling domain names, I recommend using a (third party) Domain Name Escrow Company to handle the transaction between you and the prospective buyer/seller of the domain name in question. This protects you from losing your money (if you're selling a domain) or securing the domain name (if you're the buyer).

SAFEGUARDING
CHECKLIST

I've been registering domain names for more than 20 years and over that time, I've learned a few things that will assist you when registering any domain name. **If you anticipate using a domain name for a long time, register if for several years when you first purchase it.** You can feel reassured that your domain will not expire every year because you've locked it in for 2+ years. With domain names so cheap, it benefits you to purchase other domain names to preserve and prevent losing them even though you have no plans to use them now.

1. ❑ **Know WHERE your domain names are registered.** If in doubt, you can go to **WHOIS.net**, enter the domain name you own, and search for the company name on the line that reads, "Registrar URL:." Call the support department for that company for any assistance. If the company is unable to help you, check your eMail records for a domain name purchase receipt. By the way, never delete any domain name purchase eMail receipts ... EVER!

2. ❑ **Know WHEN your domain name(s) will expire.** When it's time to renew a domain name, don't hesitate and re-register it ASAP! If you lose your domain name because it expired it becomes available for real estate for anyone to purchase before you can renew it again. Don't risk losing your web business by neglecting to re-register your domain name.

3. ❑ **Know that there is a 2-week GRACE PERIOD once domain names expire to re-register them without penalty.** The best advise is to re-register your domain name(s) before it expires to avoid the grace period, which is not always guaranteed. There can be an estimated $80 fee per domain name if you seek renewal for a domain name AFTER the grace period and, again, a higher risk for losing it altogether.

4. ❑ **If you lose a domain name, quickly BACK ORDER it on your domain registrar.** ReallyCheapNames.com (my domain-selling company) allows you to do that. This gives you the best shot at being the first person to purchase an expired domain name, particularly your own. Although it works 99 percent of the time, don't delay or count on this.

5. ❑ Look through all the domain names in your account, monthly, to REVIEW ones you want to keep or cancel. Make note of all expiration dates for renewals.

6. ❑ Make sure all your domain names have your CURRENT contact information. Don't risk someone claiming ownership to your domain name.

7. ❑ Make sure the ADMINISTRATOR contact information for every domain name has YOUR current contact eMail address. You don't want to lose your domain name due to bad information.

8. ❑ Turn all your domains on AUTO-RENEW. This ensures that your domain names get renewed automatically even if you forget to do it. When you review your domains, you can uncheck the auto-renew option for any domain you plan to expire.

9. ❑ TRANSFER all your domains to one single registrar. This is important! It's hard to manage them when they are scattered among numerous registrants. Transfer all of them to a single domain registration company for the price of one year's registration per domain.

10. ❑ Keep your domain name in YOUR NAME, not your webmaster's name. Webmasters have a tendency to want to control all files and information. What happens if the webmaster deserts you? How will you recover your domain registration or renew them if there're not registered in YOUR name? If a company or webmaster asks you to point your nameservers to them, DO NOT DO IT.

11. ❑ DO NOT register your domain name with the same company that hosts your website. Why? If you ever have problems with the hosting company or decide to terminate services, you'll feel relieved that you didn't register your domain name with them. For example, register your domains at **ReallyCheapNames. com**, but host them with another company such JustHost or HostGator. It's a good business to keep them separate.

12. ❑ Make sure your eMail contact information is UP-DATED for you so you can get eMail receipts so expiration notices can reach you.

13. ❑ MAINTAIN current credit card information wherever you register your domain names. You don't want to lose your domain names because your credit card expired and your domain names weren't renewed.

14. ❑ **Know where to get help with domain names as needed!** For example, if you register your domains at ReallyCheapNames.com, you can call (480) 624-2500 for 24/7 support with any of your domain names.

WARNING

WATCH OUT FOR ANY REGULAR MAIL REGARDING THE RENEWAL OF YOUR DOMAIN NAMES! Usually this is a SCAM by some unauthorized company claiming to be your domain registration company where you originally registered your domain name. Over time, you may forget where you registered your domain names and these predators count on you to perceive their notice of renewal is legitimate. They are counting on you to be a victim of their SCAM and pay their fee.

Scammers want you to believe that by authorizing them to renew your domain names , you will be transferred to original place where you registered

SAMPLE WORDING FROM SCAMMERS

DOMAIN NAME EXPIRATION LETTER:

As a courtesy to domain name holders, we are sending you this notification of the domain name registered in your name. It is about to expire. When you SWITCH today to the Domain Registry of Scammers, you can take advantage of our best savings. **(Which is B.S.)** Your domain name registration will only cost $35 per year. **(Instead the $9.97 you paid at your current registrar.)** Please detach and sign the stub saying you approve the transfer, and send us your money .... LOOSER!

your domain names. THIS IS NOT TRUE AND CAN BE DANGEROUS!

The company where you originally registered your domain name will rarely, IF EVER, send you a renewal notice through the U.S. mail service. The registration company will only use eMail to communicate with you. If you receive a notice of domain name renewal and receive a request for money via the postal system, you should report it as fraud for further investigation.

If you are uncertain about who your registration company is, search your eMail records to verify it.

SUMMARY / RECAP

When securing a domain name, thoroughly check it out through www.whois.net to ensure that there is no bad history associated with it. For example, suppose you select a name only to learn that it was previously used by someone who was banned from Google searches.

Take responsibility for your domains names -- where they are registered and when it's time to renew them!

As a convenience, set them up on auto-pay when you initially register your domain name so you don't have to worry about them expiring and losing them. Remember, they are the lifeblood of your business and making money online!

EBOOK CREATION
CHECKLIST

An eBook is a great way to make money, get your work to market faster, expand your brand and deliver content to your target audience cheaper than any other "publishing" method to date! Why do you want to create an eBook? What do you want to publish in eBook format? How will you generate the eBook? How will you introduce it to the market? In this checklist series, you'll be prompted to answer these questions and more as they relate to your eBook project.

1. ❑ What is the PURPOSE of the eBook you want to create?

1.1 ❑ A GIVEAWAY (Viral Marketing Purposes) — The term "viral marketing" is simply a fancy way to say "word-of-mouth" marketing. You allow people to circulate your eBook around or give it away as a bonus when other people's clients purchase product from their site, for example.

This is one of THE BEST ways to get lots of FREE EXPOSURE for your business, your products and/or services. Create an eBook and distribute it for FREE for recognition and speed to market worldwide. Link the eBook back to your website for bumper to bumper and never ending traffic. It's so easy and so affordable!

Many people will create any number of eBooks and then distribute them on KINDLE UNLIMITED, which allows Amazon customers to read up to 10 Kindle eBooks for free at any given time once they sign up for a $9.95 per month membership. Publishing your book via Kindle Unlimited is a great way to upsell your readers to other products and services you might offer.

You can write an unlimited number of eBooks and post them on Kindle Unlimited. For every eBook that you write, take excerpts from them and create viral marketing campaigns. Why not take advantage of a feature that increases brand awareness to achieve whatever your marketing objectives such as product sales?

1.2 ❑ FOR SALE — You might create an eBook containing the details for a unique product that you intend to sell. Do you have a shopping cart to deliver your (digital) eBook product? If not, there is a number of shopping cart systems that can do that for you. Consider uploading your eBook into digital delivery networks like JVZoo.com, ClickBank.com, E-Junkie.com and others. They process payments and pay you a large percentage of goods sold, minus their nominal processing fees (5%-10%).

2. Who will write your eBook(s)?

❑ **2.1 YOU?** — Whatever your writing style, you can't lose by writing an eBook or converting your books in print to eBook format. Getting started is the hardest part. So, start small and then start building. Some find it easy to write in a narrative style (writing how you speak) while others prefer to record their stories and transcribe them later. Writing is something that you can only learn by doing so pick up that pencil or open your laptop and eventually you'll start developing a sense of how the words should flow, express your feelings, and then when you have a body of work that you'll feel confident with, share it with others for comments and honest reviews. The more you write the better writer you become.

❑ **2.2 YOU + CO-AUTHOR?** — Join forces with another writer and collaborate on a book. Two heads work better and faster than one! Each person brings a certain value to the content while both are usually involved with and attached to the outcome of the project. Another advantage is if both writers are using the same software, it makes it easy to contribute from anywhere in the world and your book can benefit from the inclusion of different perspectives.

❑ **2.3 GHOSTWRITER?** — Maybe you don't have the time or interest in writing a book, but you have the idea and scores of details. Maybe you need material on a topic where you lack expertise. It's not unusual for published authors to use ghostwriters. This is a person whose job it is to write material for someone else who is the named author. Sometimes the ghost writer's contribution is acknowledged and sometimes it's not.

3. Who edits eBooks?

❑ **3.1 YOU?** — Did you write your eBook? Then, it's wise to turn your work over to a trusted person who will look at your book objectively and will identify obvious mistakes in spelling, punctuation and grammar. If you hired someone to write your eBook, then yes, you can edit their work if you have the skill. Print it and review it on 8.5" x 11" paper. It's a whole different reading experience versus picking up mistakes on the computer. Otherwise, secure a competent editor.

❑ **3.2 EDITOR?** — Good decision. If you write your own eBook, definitely have someone else proof and edit your work. They'll catch things you couldn't! A mistake that many writers make is publishing without a thorough proofreading. That goes for blogs, eZines and newsletters, etc. The self-publishing business has been a boon for writers, but you want your book to compare favorably with commercially published books … use an editor.

❑ **3.3 FRIEND/COLLEAGUE?** — If you can't afford an editor, at least ask someone else to read it in order to pick up bloopers and errors you'll miss. When you're too close to the forest to see the trees, as another writer, a teacher, someone with a good grasp for spelling, grammar and syntax and then ask a few good readers to read your work before you publish it.

4. Who enters the corrections?

4.1 ❑ **YOU** — As the author, you maintain full control of your work. Some editors will make corrections and clarifications with expressed permission from the author and others will communicate suggestions for corrections/changes that you might enter. Ultimately, you approve/disapprove all changes/revisions.

4.2 ❑ **ASSISTANT** — Save yourself some time and for help to enter corrections/changes in your book especially if it is in excess of 100 pages. Any rewrites should be done by you.

5. ❑ What FILE FORMAT is best for eBooks?

When it comes to producing eBooks, you have several options. Which format will depend on (1) the purpose of your eBook and (2) the preferred format you choose to sell in? Here are some suggestions:

5.1 ❑ **PDF FORMAT** — PDF format is the de facto standard for secure and reliable electronic document that is acceptable worldwide. This means, you can create an eBook, print it to PDF format and it's protected from anyone altering your content in any way. That's a good thing.

The PDF eBook version can be read by both Mac and PC. PDF eBook are great for viral marketing and promoting material you know will not change in a long time. Promoting excerpts from your main book is a good example. PDF documents can even be read on most smart phones.

Conversely, if you publish your eBook to PDF format and you want to make changes to it later, it's TOO LATE! Your eBook is ALREADY OUT THERE and the only way you can deliver an updated version of your (PDF-format) eBook is to republish a new version of it.

While you can insert links to websites in your PDF document, the features for publishing in this format are limited. If you plan to give away FREE copies of your eBook for promotion purposes, delivering it in PDF format makes sense.

5.2 ❑ **KINDLE, EPUB, SMASHWORDS & BOOKBABY EBOOK FORMATS** — Kindle.com, SmashWords.com and BookBaby.com are the largest eBook distribution companies. With Kindle and SmashWords, you can upload a basic WORD file. With BookBaby.com, you need to convert your material into an actual .EPUB file. Do you know how to generate an EPUB file? If not, there's software you can download or you can pay BookBaby to do it for you for a fee. My personal preference would be to create a simple WORD document, submit it to Kindle and then to SmashWords for further distribution. SmashWords will convert your WORD document into an EPUB file that you can submit to BookBaby.

5.3 ❑ **MEMBERSHIP WEBSITE FORMAT** — A viable alternative to PDF or any other file format for your eBook is to store your eBook online within your website or the website exclusively dedicated to selling your eBook.

In this way, the eBook content is protected within the walls of your membership. Customers pay online at your website to access your eBook. Depending on the membership software you use, the reader is prompted to log in with an assigned username and password to access your eBook online. The document is protected and customers simply scroll to read from front to finish.

On a positive note, your content IS protected. Customers pay for their own membership account to access your membership site/

eBook. If a user shares his/her username/ password with others, the member can be removed from the system completely. You can change/update content in your membership site/eBook at any time. You can easily incorporate video and audio because you're dealing with web pages and not PDF file formats or EXE, etc.

On the negative side, it's not viral! The website just sits on a server. People must go directly to your site for legitimate access. On the other hand, affiliate programs work well here. Some authors will publish a table of contents and a chapter or two to promote the paid version of an eBook.

The better alternative to PDF and EPUB file formats for generating eBooks is to place your content on a membership website for sale and promotion instead of within a PDF or EXE file. If you like the idea of passive and/or residual income (such as affiliate programs), then obtain the software recommended below that generates membership websites for eBooks and the like that you'd like to sell online! All you need is membership software and a website to store your eBook content in.

6. ❑ **How will you promote your eBook?** — Marketing an eBook is similar to promoting a print book in many ways. The only difference is the distribution and format your customers will use to read your eBook. Check out my *Book Marketing & Promotion Checklist* for book marketing ideas you parlay into eBook sales as well.

7. ❑ **What will you do after you write your first eBook?** — Write another one, I hope. The more you write the more your work gets recognized. Putting your words in an eBook and selling virtual copies of it online is an

effective, low cost way to self-publish. The checklist above should help you choose the right purpose, publishing platform, direction and actions to take prior to launching your next eBook.

I can't emphasize enough that once you've written your awesome eBook, share a few copies of the proof with trusted readers. Ask open ended questions prior to publishing. Ask, "What did you like most about the book? What did you not like? How can I improve it?" When you're ready for publication, Kindle and SmashWords will handle all of the distribution to every major eBook selling company online.

EMAIL BROADCAST
CHECKLIST

An eMail broadcast is an activity where you send an eMail message to a list of contacts. While the eMail marketing service provider you choose (Aweber.com, GetResponse.com, MailChimp.com, etc.) may have different requirements to send eMail broadcasts, in principle, the steps are very similar. So, before you start blasing your eMail lists, here are a few things to consider and check off your list.

1. WHAT are you sending? What is its PURPOSE for the eMail blast? Define the details.

a. ❑ **Are you sending a newsletter?** Many eMail broadcasting systems come with templates. Experiment until you have created the ideal look for your newsletter. Save the template as a DRAFT so you can use in future eMails. By changing the date, issuing a new number, revising any content, you're ready to send out your next newsletter with the same look and feel as the previous one.

b. ❑ **Are you promoting a special offer?** Are you promoting a product/service? This could be a brief eMail with a simple message and a link to a website with more details. Use a powerful topic to grab the reader's attention and use it to inspire readers to click on the link, learn more, and ideally BUY!

c. ❑ **Do you have a training announcement?** Do you conduct tele-seminars or webinars? Maybe you have a live workshop to announce. If you have a web page that shares details (time, date, topics, training, etc.), include that information in your eMail so prospective customers can read it quickly and make a decision to register for your event.

d. ❑ **What will it cost?** Email marketing is significantly cheaper and faster than traditional mail. When compared to standard eMail, direct eMail marketing produces a higher response rate and higher average order value for most businesses.

MY CHECKLISTS

2. ❑ WHEN do you need to send it?

a. ❑ Within the next 24 hours? Immediately? This is doable, but don't rush the process. Rushing leads to mistakes and you can't afford them.

b. ❑ This week? Planning ahead for your eMail broadcasts is the best measure. Allow a few days to create it, review and test it prior to launching it.

c. ❑ Weekly? Effective eMail marketing can boost profits by 40%. It's smart, easy to use, can expand your reach, and engages prospects and customers immediately.

3. ❑ What MISTAKES should you avoid?

a. ❑ Misspellings in the subject or body of your eMail ...

b. ❑ Incorrect dates/times included ...

c. ❑ Poor alignment of issues with your text or images ...

d. ❑ Embedded images/graphics can't be viewed by most ...

e. ❑ Links that don't work properly ...

f. ❑ Subject line is incorrect ...

g. ❑ Greeting reads reads as, "Dear $!FIRSTNAME!$" versus "Dear Bart"

h. ❑ Unwanted text or coding that appears at the bottom of the eMail message ...

4. ❑ What FORMAT are you sending it in?

a. ❑ Text? This is a clean format for eMails. Without images or formatting to worry

about, you need only edit thoroughly.

b. ❑ HTML? While this is an attractive way to send an eMail, when sending HTML eMails in color, these messages can't always by viewed by the myriad of computers, mobile devices and digital readers.

5. ❑ Preparing Your eMail ...

a. ❑ Write a brief, concise message on one page if possible. Paragraphs should consist of 2-3 sentences max. Sentences should consist of 5-10 words max. Write the text in short bullet format especially if you have more than three points to make. Add clickable links in your email to make it easy for your list to learn more about your products/ services or take advantage of your offers.

b. ❑ Proof It. Read it before you test it. No one person should proof his/her own work so ask for assistance with proofing. Every time you send an eMail, you have to prove your value. Make sure you aren't wasting your subscribers' time with cookie-cutter messages and automated greetings. Your eMail is one way of talking to your customer directly so be yourself. Make It personal.

c. ❑ Test your eMail by sending it to yourself, first. No matter how many times you have to test-send it to yourself, do it! You want the assurance that all the elements of your eMail look good and everything is working the way you expect it to. Check for:

i. ❑ Subject line reads well and there are no misspellings.

ii. ❑ Salutation (Dear ____,) reads correctly with your name, and not the [short code] for $FIRSTNAME$ is in its place.

iii. ❑ The body of your eMail message makes the point. You've used sensory and emotional words to attract attention and your subject line pops.

iv. ❑ Do your (optional) images display correctly? Images should be uploaded to a server whether it's yours or a media library the eMail broadcasting service company provides for you inside your account to ensure readability.

v. ❑ Do your links take you directly to intended websites?

vi. ❑ Do the website links all function properly?

6. ❑ Send Your eMail To Your List

a. ❑ WHO are you sending your eMail to? Make sure your lists are clean and all subscribers have properly opted in. Typically, you can choose between customers, affiliates, specific subscribers, autoresponders, unconfirmed, unsubscribed, etc. Your biggest mistake will be not knowing who your audience is.

b. ❑ MAKE SURE you don't send your eMail to the WRONG list! If you don't do this right, you could find yourself faced with a decrease in your open and click rates and an increase in your SPAM and unsubscribe rates. You don't want to hear, "I never signed up to receive information about XYZ. Unsubscribe me, immediately!" Most will say they get too much eMail, which is even more reason for your eMail to stand out in their inboxes.

c. ❑ When you send your eMail, watch for it to arrive in your own inbox. It would be helpful if you had a couple of eMail addresses to test when sending eMail to your lists. It's one thing to test-send the eMail to your address. It's worth it to find out how it appears on other eMail platforms such as gMail, Yahoo, Hotmail, etc.

7. ❑ Check Your Statistics

a. ❑ Open Rate - How many people actually opened your eMail? It can be useful to know what the open and click through rates are when sending broadcasts. If you have less than a 5% open rate, that's a red flag. Email metrics can determine the effectiveness of your communications and identify areas to improve efficiency.

b. ❑ Bounce Rate – This is the percentage of visitors on a particular website who navigate away from the site after viewing only one page. Other reasons eMails bounce back is because they were undeliverable due to an incorrect address? Audit your lists so you're always operating with accurate information.

c. ❑ Unsubscribe - How many people chose to opt out of your list after receiving your eMail? You can delete these people for future eMail broadcasts or you can maintain them on your list in the event they choose to sign up at a later date.

d. ❑ Sales - Email marketing is the most effective online marketing tool and the top factor in influencing sales and repeat business. With 44% of eMail recipients making at least one purchase based on

promotional eMails and 4.3 billion eMail accounts, how many sales could you make from an eMail broadcast?

ACCOUNT CREATION
CHECKLIST

> **After** your **hosting is set up,** quickly **create** these specific **eMail accounts.**

As soon as you set up hosting for your website and update the nameservers for the domain name, you might quickly set up a few eMail accounts so you can start receiving eMail through your new domain name and through the new hosting company as soon as the nameservers propagate. With every website hosting account, you have the option to set up two kinds of eMail:

POP EMAIL ACCOUNTS

A couple of worthy eMail programs are Microsoft Outlook and Mozilla's Thunderbird. These eMail accounts are easy to create. Simply assign a username and password to the account name, then configure the eMail program so you can check eMail with your new account off the server. You can begin receiving eMail once your domain's nameservers become effective.

FORWARD EMAIL ACCOUNTS

This is my favorite type of eMail to setup and use. I don't create/use POP email accounts often. I prefer to have all my eMail forwarded to a web-based eMail service such as Gmail, Hotmail, Hushmail, Yahoo, and others.

Gmail, for example, does require that you create a POP eMail account on your server for authenticity, but that's okay. It doesn't mean you have to load up your server with eMail, as it all gets forwarded to your GMail account.

Forwarding eMail accounts simply redirects all incoming eMail to a specific eMail address that you create or to another eMail address that you assign! For example, you might want to set up any or all of the following eMail forward accounts:

MY CHECKLISTS

CREATE ANY OF THESE FORWARD ACCOUNTS THAT YOU NEED:

FORWARD EMAIL ACCOUNT:

☐ **affiliate**@youwebsite.com
☐ **alert**@youwebsite.com
☐ **billing**@youwebsite.com
☐ **donotreply**@youwebsite.com
☐ **ezine**@youwebsite.com
☐ **help**@youwebsite.com
☐ **info**@youwebsite.com
☐ **mail**@youwebsite.com
☐ **member**@youwebsite.com
☐ **order**@youwebsite.com
☐ **news**@youwebsite.com
☐ **newsletter**@youwebsite.com
☐ **paypal**@youwebsite.com
☐ **service**@youwebsite.com
☐ **support**@youwebsite.com
☐ **yourfullname**@youwebsite.com
☐ **yourname**@youwebsite.com
☐ **yourinitials**@youwebsite.com

FORWARDS TO:

(YOUR MAIN / BUSINESS EMAIL ADDRESS)
(YOUR MAIN / BUSINESS EMAIL ADDRESS)
(YOUR MAIN / BUSINESS EMAIL ADDRESS)
(YOUR MAIN / BUSINESS EMAIL ADDRESS)
(YOUR MAIN / BUSINESS EMAIL ADDRESS)
(YOUR MAIN / BUSINESS EMAIL ADDRESS)
(YOUR MAIN / BUSINESS EMAIL ADDRESS)
(YOUR MAIN / BUSINESS EMAIL ADDRESS)
(YOUR MAIN / BUSINESS EMAIL ADDRESS)
(YOUR MAIN / BUSINESS EMAIL ADDRESS)
(YOUR MAIN / BUSINESS EMAIL ADDRESS)
(YOUR MAIN / BUSINESS EMAIL ADDRESS)
(YOUR MAIN / BUSINESS EMAIL ADDRESS)
(YOUR MAIN / BUSINESS EMAIL ADDRESS)
(YOUR MAIN / BUSINESS EMAIL ADDRESS)
(YOUR MAIN / BUSINESS EMAIL ADDRESS)
(YOUR MAIN / BUSINESS EMAIL ADDRESS)
(YOUR MAIN / BUSINESS EMAIL ADDRESS)

In this scenario, all of these eMail accounts forward to a specific Gmail account. What's great about Gmail is that it allows you to create specific accounts within your Gmail account so you can send out eMail that looks as if it came from a specific eMail address. Another reason for using web-based eMail accounts ... if your computer crashes or you lose data on your computer's hard drive, you'll never lose your eMail account data because it's stored ONLINE! It's easy to set up and I recommend it.

 WATCH VIDEO TUTORIALS ON CREATING FORWARD EMAILS:
http://MyTrainingCenter.com/email-forward-creation-checklist

EMAIL LIST BUILDING
CHECKLIST

WITHOUT A LIST of prospects to sell to, your chances of making money are nearly impossible. It's much easier to sell to people who know you, know about you, hear from you, and trust you. How do you attain that level of trust with people so they remain loyal customers? You build that relationship by building a solid eMail list!

What software tools do you need to build a list?

Before you can "build your list" however you need the right software that will perform the following functions:

❑ OPT-IN BOX FORM CREATION SOFTWARE: You'll need the ability to create the essential "opt-in boxes" (online forms) that collect specific information (first name and primary eMail address) from those who visit your website to express an interest in your eZine or newsletter, reply to free information giveaway, purchase your products/ervices and participate in your affiliate programs.

❑ ONLINE DATABASE / LIST MANAGEMENT SOFTWARE: You'll need the ability to sort, track, add and edit the names of people in your ever-growing database of new contacts, prospects, clients and affiliates.

❑ EMAIL BROADCASTING SOFTWARE: You'll need the ability to communicate to your list by eMail without being labeled as a spammer by your local Internet service provider. To do this, you will need to use a third-party, commercial eMail broadcasting service that is highly functional. This online marketing service should enable you to communicate to your lists through a variety of eMail communications such as eZines, online newsletters, special eMail announcements and autoresponders.

To perform these essential eMail list-building functions, you cand use MailerLite.com. You can learn more about them and sign up by going to:

www.MailerLite.com

Of course, there are other eMail list-building services, and I have used them before. If you're just starting out, use MailerLite.com.

When building an eMail list, consider enticing people to join your subscription list by offering a FREE gift such as:

- ❏ Offer a FREE NEWSLETTER/EZINE ...
- ❏ Offer a FREE REPORT ...
- ❏ Offer a FREE AUDIO ...
- ❏ Offer a FREE VIDEO ...
- ❏ Offer a FREE MINI-ECOURSE ...
- ❏ Offer a FREE WEBINAR ...
- ❏ Offer a FREE TELE-SEMINAR ...
- ❏ Offer a FREE PRODUCT (just pay shipping) ...
- ❏ Other offer _____ ...

Once you determine what you'll offer in exchange for names and eMail addresses, follow these steps with Aweber:

- ❏ **Create an autoresponder to assign those names and eMail addresses.** You can always assign those who opt-in to your list to another list, perhaps a primary list, should you decide. Create individual autoresponders for each list you build.

- ❏ **Create an "opt-in" (subscription) web form, assigned to this autoresponder and then add it to your website.** Place this form on your website in any one of the following areas:

  - ☐ Sidebar ...
  - ☐ Header ...
  - ☐ Footer ...
  - ☐ Via popup window ...
  - ☐ At the end of a page or an article ...
  - ☐ At the beginning, in the middle and/or at the end of a video ...
  - ☐ Before visitors can access a private page ...
  - ☐ Other placement ideas _____ ...
  - ☐ All of the above!

- ❏ **Test the form to be sure it works**. Do you see your name and eMail address appear on your list? Did you receive the "Confirm your eMail ..." letter in your inbox?

Encourage others to opt-in to your list by engaging in some of these activities:

- ❏ **Use webinars and tele-seminars to spread your message, knowledge, expertise among to audiences that own lists of all sizes!** Conduct these tele-seminars weekly in the beginning to gain momentum and then conduct them for FREE and invite listeners to sign up at your website in exchange for a FREE gift.

- ❏ **Co-market your eZine on websites that compliment your own.** If your business is already registered with your local Better business Bureau, you're already co-marketing. Check with your affiliations, certifications, and associations to stretch your income and enhance your credibility.

- ❏ **Create a FREE, viral product such as an eBook that others can give away for FREE on their websites.** Imagine if 100 websites gave away a small eBook that you authored. "To get this FREE eBook, provide your name and eMail address ..."

- ❏ **Create a web page dedicated to marketing your eZine.** The eZine can provide more details and inspire readers to sign up for your eMail/products/services.

- ❏ **Create autoresponder lists for the different products/services you sell.** "Are you interested in learning more about product X, Y or Z? Sign up to receive tips, promotions and products ..." You could create separate autoresponders per product. To ensure people stay on your lists, your discovering where their interests are regarding your products/services.

- ❏ **Create products that others can sell for 100% profit.** Many people are looking for products to sell from their websites. This is how this works. You create the products, someone else sells it for all the profit, but you collect on all future sales, because you have people selling for you, circulating your name, and introducing you to new/future business.

❑ **Encourage people to "forward" your newsletters by using the word "FORWARD" in your request.** Why? It's psychological! Just seeing the word "forward" induces others to do exactly that ..."forward your eMail" to others! Select the "Forward" button/ feature in your eMail program and (at the top and bottom of every eMail you send out) use phrases like "Feel free to forward this eZine." or "Please forward this eMail."

❑ **Everywhere you go, always be promoting your newsletter, eZine, eCourses, etc.** Whether you're on the phone, eMailing a new friend or associate, you need to sell yourself and your business.

❑ **Collect business cards when networking offline, then personally send each person a copy of your most recent newsletter or eZine or blog when you get home.** "Dear _____, it was a pleasure meeting you today. I thought you might enjoy a copy of my recent newsletter. To continue getting it for FREE, click on the sign up link on my website. I look foward to speaking with you again, soon! Best wishes," (Your Name)

❑ **If you have a table at live events or trade show, collect business cards or create a 2-column name/eMail form where people can write down their name/eMail address. (Not everyone has business cards.)** Always provide pens, clipboards and a FREE gift for signing up for your flyer, postcard, eZine, etc. to show your appreciation for the information.

❑ **Insert a quick "benefit-driven/call to action" statement right above the "opt-in" box to explain the value for giving names**

and primary eMail addresses. For example: "FOR A LIMITED TIME: GET YOUR FREE _____ TIPS!"

❑ **Put the "opt-in" box in your eZine!** If you encourage your eZine subscribers to forward your eZine on to their lists, wouldn't it be super-convenient to have the "opt-in" box inside your eZine? Make it easy for people to sign up!

❑ **Give an opportunity to subscribe to your eZine in every eMail your business sends.** These eMails include product order receipts to customers, order confirmation eMails, thank you web pages, product shipping notifications, customer service auto-replies, account management messages, survey pages, affiliate web pages, and more.

❑ **Run ads online and offline that encourage people to sign up for your newsletter.** Magazines and newspapers do it all the time. Advertise so even more people can subscribe to their publication.

❑ **Sell products directly to people. That's another way to easily add them to your list.** When they people from you, they expect to hear from you. They might be inspired to buy from you again because you followed up with them, which opens the door to upsell and resell to them again and again.

❑ **Exchange adds with other eZine publishers.** You can also create reciprocal promotional banners so you can help each other.

❑ **Think "quality" over "quantity" every time.** The more you qualify your prospect and others who want to subscribe the better. Don't focus on building a large list just for the head count. Target your list so that you attract qualified prospects who have a genuine interest in what you have to offer now and in the long run.

MY CHECKLISTS

❏ **Assign a dollar value to your FREE offer.** People will more often accept a FREE copy of an eZine subscription when they know the cost for a subscription or anything for that matter. FREE must have a value. Funny how that works!

❏ **At the onset of your campaign to build your list, just ask for people's FIRST name and primary eMail address.** You can get their last names LATER. Data proves that more people will respond positively when you ask for first name only.

❏ **Co-market your eZine in other eZines.** Swap FREE ads with others. Increase exposure for your eZine and your brand by providing a link to your website so people can sign up for ongoing communication.

❏ **Co-registration: When people agree to sign up for your eZine, add them to your list.** Ask if you can add their names to someone else's list or give them the opportunity to sign up for another eZine list when they arrive at your "thank you for subscribing" web page. Ask other eZine owners to return the favor.

❏ **When you promote yourself on the radio or TV, invite listerners to visit your website to sign up for a FREE report, eBook, audio eCourse or eZine.** Don't focus on selling. Focus on providing great content and useful information in exchange for names and primary eMail addresses. You can sell later with greater influence having developed trust and a relationship with your prospects.

❏ **Create a "name squeeze page."** People are then obligated to provide their names and eMail addresses to gain access to your website or other information they seek.

❏ **Sell only when you've established credibility, reliability and trust!** You can do this by teaching, training and informing about topics people are interested in. Impress them with your knowledge and expertise and then introduce products/services you know they will benefit from.

❏ **Keep it FREE!** Offer free reports, free eBooks, free software, free services, free memberships, free resource links, etc. Offering FREE merchandise gets people's attention. Offering FREE gifts with a purchase is a proven way to drive customer retention while building your business or brand.

❏ **Let other website owners advertise in your online newsletter at no cost.** You can do this with several web owners while continuously expanding your reach.

❏ **Place testimonials near your "opt-in" box to inspire potential subscribers to sign up for your product/service.** Testimonials are proven social evidence that give value and legitimacy to what you offer for sale and instantly builds rapport with people.

❏ **When you network with others online, have your eMail/website in your signature file.** This is true for forum postings. Depending on the forum's settings, users can register for a specific forum topic and then subsequently log in to post other messages.

❏ **Offer people the option to give you their eMail addresses so they can receive alerts** and other information related to an online article that you write or your website that promotes specials and opportunities. Place these at the bottom of every article on your site.

❏ **Build your lists with social media.** Trust me. People are talking (online) and if you don't engage, you risk losing potential customers.

EMAIL MINI-ECOURSE
CHECKLIST

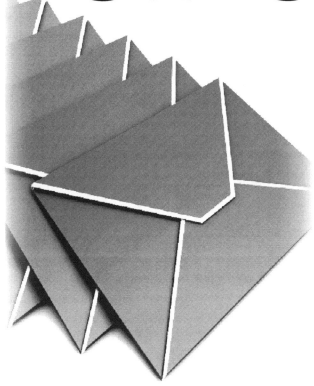

The best way to send out an eMail mini-course is to use an eMail marketing service provider such as Aweber.com, GetResponse.com, MailChimp.com, etc. These services come with autoresponders and can help you design and deliver your eMail in a text or HTML formatted email. Following are some steps to get you started.

1. ❑ **WHAT will you send?**

   a. ❑ If you're offering a mini-eCourse, your topic should educate and simultaneously engage subscribers via a set of emails (5-10) that are linked to teach a specific subject matter. You want to be sure that people will want to buy what you have to offer and the lessons are practical and easy to implement. If you've done your homework and surveyed your list, you'll have a better chance of having a successful launch.

   b. ❑ The purpose of any mini-course should be to tempt your prospects with just enough information that will ultimately influence them to buy what you offer. Mini-courses are a simple and yet highly profitable way to make money. Once you have the attention of your subscriber list, you can upsell (suggest) other products/ services. This works well when it is done at the point of purchase, for example, when the person registers for your mini-course. Cross-selling another product after an initial sale is another tool widely used in mini-courses.

   c. ❑ Are you struggling for content? You could make a mini-eCourse out of a book or eBook you wrote, a seminar, webinar or tele-seminar you conducted.

An eMail mini-course (or eCourse) is a series of eMails sent to a subscriber delivering a regular eMail message perhaps daily, weekly, etc. You determine the content and the duration. Many people prefer to send messages daily until the eCourse or campaign is completed. The subscriber ultimately emains on your list to receive future announcements and other special offers as they occur.

Similar to sending out an eMail broadcast message, an eCourse requires just a few more steps in the process. Maybe you already have a series of articles that you can convert into some easy lessons. The purpose of an eCourse is to help the subscriber learn a new skill, tackle obstacles, enhance what they already know about a topic and more. So, your goal is to share valuable, useful, appropriate information and develop ongoing relationships with your customers.

Turn a product into an eCourse by demonstrating benefits and useful tips. With enthusiasm and high energy, you can entice people to get in on something really good for them when you create a sense of urgency. In other words, "Hurry and register today for my eCourse to take advantage of discounts on all of my products."

d. ❏ How will you design your eCourse? There are instructional design experts that can help you. They will advise you to create an outline, organize your materials, choose the appropriate information and structure for your course. Having done that, it's best to divide your content into mini components; no more than one page of text or 2-5 minutes of audio or 1-3 minutes of video. All eMails should contain actionable, awe-inspiring content that will help your prospect meet a need and look forward to learning more. If you inundate your prospects with content, you will lose their interest.

2. ❏ HOW much content should be deliver and how often?

One day? One week? Begin by dripping content to your subscribers and pay close attention to their feedback. How long is it taking your subscriber to digest the content you're sending? If you are considering a 5-day mini-course, you might want to send out a daily eMail daily for continuity. Once per week for five weeks could discourage interest. Know what your subscribers hope to accomplish and don't hesitate to give away some of your best tips to keep them coming back.

3. ❏ HOW will you deliver your mini-eCourse?

a. ❏ You can deliver your eMails via text or HTML format. For example, post the eCourse on your website and send a teaser eMail with a link to where they can access each lesson and then forward subsequent eMails.

b. ❏ You'll need an autoresponder service such as Aweber.com, GetResponse.com, MailChimp.com, etc., to send your mini-eCourse. This will enable

to you reach more subscribers, automatically, and save time in delivery. You can have your eMails forwarded, followed up on, and tracked for performance with these services.

c. ❏ You'll need the ability to create an opt-in form that links to the autoresponder you select so people can sign up at your website. The eMail autoresponder service companies have easy to use tools that will help you implement your opt-in forms.

4. ❏ WHEN should you send your eCourse?

a. ❏ To keep subscribers enthused, sent your first eMail immediately after a subscriber signs to it.

b. ❏ Send the eCourse content regularly and reliably every few days once the first email was sent and while the content is still fresh. The objective is to warm up your audience and get them excited about your eCourse.

5. ❏ What mini-eCourse MISTAKES should you avoid?

Some of these many seem minor, but if you're wanting to make a dynamic impression, check for:

a. ❏ Misspellings in the subject line or body of ALL eMail messages ...

b. ❏ Incorrect dates, times and other facts ...

c. ❏ Poor alignment (left, right or justified) issues with your text or images ...

d. ❏ Images not coming through or showing as broken in your eMail letter ...

e. ❏ Links don't connect to the proper website as intended ...

f. ❏ Subject line has mistakes in it ...

g. ❑ Greeting that reads, "Dear Bart," and not "Dear $!FIRSTNAME!$."

h. ❑ Unwanted text or coding appearing anywhere in your eMails ...

i. ❑ Selling too soon. Building trust takes time.

Don't overlook metrics. If you notice that many prospects are unsubscribing, you need to review your content and change it until your unsubscribe rate diminishes. If you're not sure what the problem is, ask! In fact, to "unsubscribe," make feedback a part of the process to stop receiving future eMails.

6. ❑ What FORMAT will you use?

a. ❑ Text. This is a clean form for sending any eMail. Without images or text formatting to worry about, you're pretty much just proofing a simple letter.

b. ❑ HTML. This may be more attractive to send versus your basic letter, but there are a few details to consider when sending out colorful HTML eMails.

7. ❑ How should you prepare your Mini-eCourse eMail messages?

a. ❑ Create brief, well-crafted content. If your business caters to different types of customers, you might customize your material. Each lesson in your mini-eCourse should remain under one page. Paragraphs should consist of 2-3 sentences max. Sentences should consist of 5-10 words max. Provide links throughout your content. TIP: Draft the entire mini-eCourse in Microsoft Word or other word processor and then copy it to your eMail. Each lesson could start on its own new page (CTRL+ENTER). In this way, you can view each lesson in sequence, which is how your subscriber will view it.

b. ❑ Proof It. Read each eMail message in Word or other word processing software before you load it into your eMail autoresponder system.

c. ❑ Set up autoresponders and assign a catchy name such as, "7-DAY MINI-ECOURSE ON _____ (SUBJECT)." You could repeat this step for all of the mini-eCourses you publish. Start with one, perfect it and then duplicate it for future use.

d. ❑ Load each lesson into a separate eMail message using one autoresponder and then choose the period of time that works best for your content and your audience.

e. ❑ Create the opt-in form so your list can enter names and eMail address when they subscribe to your mini-eCourse.

f. ❑ Test-send your mini-eCourse to yourself, fir, to ensure it appears per your expectations. After placing the opt-in form on your website, test the opt-in form. Enter your own name and eMail address. Did the mini-eCourse arrive properly? Do you see any mistakes?

g. ❑ I recommend that you send it to two or three others as a test. Ask them to share their experience (good and bad). If possible, test it on other eMail programs such as gMail, Yahoo, Hotmail, and more. Look for errors.

   i. ❑ Is subject line enticing and without misspellings?

   ii. ❑ Does salutation (Dear ____,) read correctly or does it have short codes ($FIRSTNAME$)?

   iii. ❑ Does the body of your eMail message align properly?

   iv. ❑ Do your images display effectively? Images should link to actual images that are uploaded to aserver, whether it's yours or a media library the eMail broadcasting service company provides.

   v. ❑ Do your links work properly and/or direct the subscriber to intended websites?

vi. ❑ Do the websites they link to function properly?

8. ❑ How do you promote mini-courses via your website?

a. ❑ With your mini-eCourse tested, it's time to promote it! Provide an opt-in form throughout your website:

    i. ❑ In the header of your website.

    ii. ❑ In the footer of your website.

    iii. ❑ In the sidebar of your website.

    iv. ❑ At the end of pages and posts/articles of your blog.

    v. ❑ Inside videos you might play on your website.

    vi. ❑ In between paragraphs of an article on your website.

b. ❑ MAKE SURE your opt-in form is connected to the right autoresponder mini-eCourse. TEST each form on all pages to ensure they work.

c. ❑ When you do test your mini-eCourse live on your website, watch for it to arrive in your own inbox as expected. Subscribe to it and double check every aspect for operational efficiency.

9. ❑ What statistics should you check?

a. ❑ **Open Rates** ... How many people opened your eMail? The rate should be high for a mini-eCourse because most will be guaranteed subscribers looking for all the bells and whistles.

b. ❑ **Unsubscribers** ... How many people opt out of your mini-eCourse, how quickly and why? Your eMail autoresponder company can provide you with this data. It'd be interesting to know at what point in the course your subscribers opt out. If a large number of unsubscribers

opt out, then review your content. Change the copy, headlines, subject lines, etc. When people unsubscribe, you can either delete them from your list or keep them on the back burner should they decide to sign up for another course. If they bought product from you in the past, you definitely should not delete their account information.

c. ❑ Sales ... How many sales did you make based on your mini-eCourse? What percent of people who bought compared to the total number of contacts that signed up for your eCourse? If 1,000 people subscribed to your mini-eCourse and only 100 people bought your $50 product, that's a 1% return. Look at pricing.

Can you improve your sales pitch? When you identify areas for improvement, make them and then try again. If your sales rates are satisfactory, create a second and a third mini-eCourse for your next topic, product or activity. If subscribers like what you're doing, keep it up. There no limit to revenue you can generate.

Before you get started with your eCourse campaign, here are a few final tips:

(1) Never attach documents or files to your email blasts. Many people are reluctant to open them because of viruses and there are some who don't know how to open an attachment or even download one.

(2) Avoid using email lists from third parties or unrelated entities.

(3) Sending email blasts of any kind to people who don't ask for it by opting in is considered illegal and your messages may be automatically earmarked as SPAM.

EZINE PUBLISHING

CHECKLIST

S ending out an eZine or magazine is a powerful marketing tool, a great venue to create lists of prospects, customers and affiliates and to make money! Creating content may seem intimidating for some, but there are plenty of ways to pull content together. Ezines are one of the these most effective ways to promote products/ services on the Internet and they're very popular. What better way to promote website traffic. So, let's get your eZine in front of thousands of viewers and start growing your lists of prospects because want to hear from you right now. A potential customer today could easily become customers for sure tomorrow through the power of ezine marketing.

Here's my checklist for publishing eZines:

1. ❑ eZine Theme

The first step for creating an eZine is to develop a theme or topic for it. What topic peaks your interest or in what field do you have expertise? Keep your eZine targeted and focused on serving one niche audience at a time. You'll have more success that way. Do you see it in the list?

- Animals/Pets
- Personal Development
- Games
- Business
- Coaching
- Self-Help/How-To
- Science & Technology
- Sports/Athletics
- Money/Finance
- Travel/Vacation
- Consumer-Related
- News & Politics
- Other: _____

- Film & Animation
- Autos/Vehicles
- Relationships
- Health
- Comedy
- Children
- Internet
- Marketing
- Parenting
- Music
- Education
- Entertainment

2. ❑ eZine Title

One of the most important decisions you'll make is creating a title. It must grab the attention of the reader immediately. You only have one chance to entice a reader so be creative and make it easy to remember! The title should relate to what you do, what your product/service is about or convey a topic that is in popular demand.

Check out the special report on naming eZines at MyTrainingCenter.com. The sample titles in the list are designed to show you a few of the successful ones and inspire you to create something unique and eye catching. Consider making a list of several titles and then bounce them off of others for their feedback.

3. ❏ eZine Publishing Schedule

How often will you send your eZine? Be consistent with the schedule you select and don't miss sending an issue. Here are your best options:

3.1 ❏ Daily — If you have a large audience, plenty of material AND you believe your topic is worthy of communicating on a daily basis, then that's your schedule. TIP: Sometimes a daily magazine can be too much. Survey your readers for their reactions to receiving a daily eZine and then listen to what they tell you.

3.2 ❏ Weekly — Your best option is to send a weekly eZine. Your regular contact is appreciated and readers don't feel deluged.

3.3 ❏ Bi-Weekly — This has proven to be one of the better options … not too much and not too little.

3.4 ❏ Monthly — When you publish an eZine on a regular monthly basis, it gives you plenty of time to produce a well-thought-out, quality magazine.

4. ❏ eZine Content

4.1 ❏ Find content for your eZine is not as tough as you think. Did you write a book? You can borrow chapters or excerpts from your book. Why not elaborate on a topic from your book and expand the content into an eZine?

4.2 ❏ Do you write articles? Compile a series of articles for an easy eZine!

4.3 ❏ Do you podcast or have your own radio show? Transcribe it and publish segments in your eZine.

4.4 ❏ Read other eZines for ideas and articles that express your own thoughts and ideas and share them.

4.5 ❏ Write book reviews on a specific topic and you have good opy for an eZine.

4.6 ❏ You can interview experts, authors, speakers, and hobbyists for more content for your eZine.

4.7 ❏ Maybe you have cooking tips for a starving market or travel advice you can share from your expriences.

4.8 ❏ Maybe you're a problem-solver or handyman who can help others fix their every day problems. What questions do your clients have? What to they complain about?

Personalize your content. If you write like you speak, your personality will come through. Keep it informal. You should, however, have your work proofed be another person to avoid obvious mistakes and for clarity. Another great tip regarding "content" is the more content you have the easier it will be to publish an eZine.

You also don't need to be the sole writer for your eZine. You can invite a guest to write an issue to bring in a fresh perspective or hire a writer periodically (especially when you're short on time) or use content written by others. Just be aware of copyright laws when using material that is not yours.

5. ❏ eZine Format

When creating a format for your eZine, you have three options:

5.1 ❏ TEXT — This is the simplest format to send an eZine. It looks clean, straight-forward and gets to the point. It is received well by every eMail program on the planet. To send your eZine in TEXT format, all you need is a word processor such as Microsoft Word or a plain text editor like NotePad or TextPad. Simply type your eZine, proof it, test-send it to yourself, and you're ready to eMail it to your list.

5.2 ❏ HTML — If your eZine will include images, graphics, pictures, colorful headers, etc., you MUST use HTML and not TEXT format. HTML is the preferred choice for most eZine publishers because it's the most professional-looking and influential form of eZine publishing. To send your eZine out in HTML format, you'll need to design and proof it, preferably within your eMail broadcasting software program such as aWeber.com, GetResponse.com, MailChimp. com, etc.

5.3 ❏ WEB PAGE — Your eZine could actually take the form of a basic web page. Why not? Post your eZine on your website. Create a category (if you use WordPress) called Newsletter or a similar term. Every time you have a new issue to publish, create it in WordPress. Once you publish the page, eMail your list with a short message such as this example: "Learn about _____ in my new eZine issue. Click here to read it at my website ..." This works great every time.

6. ❏ eZine Tools & Software

When it comes to publishing your eZine, you will need a small variety of special software programs, services and eZine broadcasting tools to help publish it professionally. Here's what you'll need:

6.1 ❏ List Building Software — You'll require software to build your list of subscribers. For that, you can use MyMarketingCart.com that you'll find at MyTrainingCenter.com.

6.2 ❏ eZine Broadcasting Software — You'll need a built-in service tool to send out your eZine. For that, you can also use MyMarketingCart. com at MyTrainingCenter.com.

6.3 ❏ "Text" Editing Software — This is optional, however if you plan to send your eZine in "text format," you'll want a simple text editor software program such as NotePad or TextPad, which is my favorite.

6.4 ❏ "Image" Editing Software — If you decide to include images/graphics in your eZine, or even on your website, it might benefit you to learn an easy-to-use image editing software program called Inkscape, Artweaver or my favorite ... Adobe Fireworks.

7. ❏ Building Your eZine

Now that you've (1) decided on a theme and (2) a title for your eZine; you know (3) when you'll publish it, (4) how you'll generate content, (5) what format you'll use and, (6) the software you need to build it. Let's get started with the building process.

First, determine WHO will design your eZine:

7.1 ❏ You? — If you are confident in your computer/web/graphic design skills, you absolutely could design your own eZine.

7.2 ❏ Web Designer / Virtual Assistant? — If you need to hire someone to create your eZine, then ask for samples of their work before you make your final decision.

Secondly, begin the DESIGN phase:

7.3 ❏ eZine Templates — Your eMail broadcasting

software/service usually has templates to choose from. Pick one and stick with it for a consistent look and feel every time.

7.4 ❑ Section Headers — Determine what elements you want to cover in your eZine. A typical eZine has several section headers.

MUST-HAVE

❑ Table of Contents to give a quick preview of how the eZine is organized.

❑ Featured Article that offer real value to your readers.

❑ About US that identifies your name, company, etc.

❑ Contact US shows how to reach you and where (address, phone number, eMail address, web address, etc.)

OPTIONAL / RECOMMENDED

❑ Personal Note/Message that describes what the eZine is about.

❑ Promote Your Free _____ such as tele-class, audio course, etc.

❑ Featured Product or Service showcases something you offer.

❑ Featured Resource/Vendor Profile for an advertiser.

❑ Upcoming Events such as seminars, tele-classes, etc.

❑ Image Gallery such as photos of you, your products and/or satisfied customers (with permission).

❑ Recommended Resource Links such as recommended services.

❑ Affiliate Program with details for training, enrolling and log in links.

❑ Marketplace Ads for paying advertisers.

7.5 ❑ Content — Once you've collected content for several issues of your eZine, you're just about ready to launch. TIP: Always be accumulating material to publish in your eZine so you don't disappoint your subscribers.

7.6 ❑ Graphics — Make sure you have the rights to any graphics you plan to use in your eZine and then use only a few to add color and spice, especially if publishing in HTML format. If you're publishing an eZine in TEXTformat, you CANNOT insert pictures/graphics in a TEXT eMail.

There are several places online where you can obtain FREE images for commercial use and other sites where you can purchase them for as little as $1 each. My favorite site is YayImages.com ($9.99/month = unlimited image use).

7.7 ❑ Marketplace (Special Offers) — Do create a special place at the bottom of your eZine to promote special offers to earn extra income with your eZine. Over time, as your subscriber base increases, you can offer advertising opportunities to others for a fee ($20 to $250 or more) per ad depending on demand. Offer a minimum of five day advertising slots per eZine. Talk about passive income!

8. ❑ Test-Send & Proof It

Before you send your eZine to your entire list, send it to a select few and to yourself to see how it looks. Make changes if needed to ensure that you are satisfied when you send to everyone. Should you modify your eZine, retest it. Make no assumptions. Feel confident when you hit the "send" button.

9. ❑ "Officially" Sending It Out

At this point, you and a few people you trust have reviewed your eZine and it's ready to fly. What's next?

9.1 ❑ Select the list of subscribers from your database. Be careful to select the correct list. Sending it to the wrong group could be disastrous.

9.2 ❑ Enter the time/date when you'd like to eMail your eZine. Will you send it immediately or on a scheduled future date?

9.3 ❑ Enter your name, eMail address and an appropriate subject line for your eZine. Be creative!

9.4 ❑ Choose either TEXT or HTML format when prompted.

9.5 ❑ Save your first eZine as a draft as a work copy for future eZines. When you save your eZine the first time, it will grab the subject line as the name for this draft, which will help you identify it.

9.6 ❑ When you're ready to send your eZine to your chosen list of subscribers, click the "Continue Broadcast" button.

9.7 ❑ Preview your eZine a final time prior to clicking the button that reads, "Send Broadcast" or a similar button.

9.8 ❑ When you click on the "Send Broadcast" button, you have just a minute to CANCEL this action if necessary. Check with your eMail broadcasting provider about the option for your system. Otherwise, hit the send button and wait for the information that confirms how many eMails addresses received your eZine and how many opened your eZine.

10. ❑ Promoting Your eZine

Now that your eZine is created and sent, it's time to GROW your list! You should always be looking for new ways to add new subscribers. For tips and list-building techniques, see my report called **Learn How To Build Your List Of eZine/eMail Subscribers For Profit!**

With your eZine, you can continue to grow the trust and confidence of thousands of people who have subscribed to it. With that trust, you can strategize offers and promotions to confidently grow your income with your eZine.

Retaining customers is not easy for most businesses. While eZines give owners a way to communicate with customers with ease, flexibility is another advantage the eZine affords subscribers. They can decide if and when to read your eZine and generally appreciate the convenience and options.

FACEBOOK MARKETING

CHECKLIST

We all know that Facebook is a great way to expand a brand, find new customers, survey fans to see what you should Surprisingly, I know some small business owners who aren't on Facebook yet. Well, for them, and those who are active on Facebook, here's a reminder checklist of things we ought to be doing on Facebook.

CHECKLIST

❑ If you're not active on Facebook, sign up. Facebook is a great way to reach your audiences with targeted ads and help your business grow. Now, check this out ...

❑ Make sure you're using a Business Fan page builder, which is an extension of your business. Use your personal profile page to for personal use. You can still use your personal profile page to promote what you do, but your business fan page has several features that you don't want to miss out on.

❑ Once you setup your Facebook business fan page, create a custom "vanity" name URL for your Facebook business page. Choose wisely because once you set it, it's concrete. You can't go back and change it. For example:

www.Facebook.com/**bartscookies**

❑ Celebrate moments and achievements.

❑ Update your Facebook fan page at least every few months. Freshen up the background, logo/ headshots, etc.

❑ Add photos regularly.

❑ Post information weekly.

❑ Post videos. It's all about visuals, today.

❑ Post links to your articles and other resources.

❑ Comment on what others are doing.

❑ Study other Facebook pages for creative ideas to enhance your fan page.

❑ Don't post too often. Daily is good, but 15 times a day is too much. If your business is running a special or you've expressed some call to action, post it and monitor. Facebook has a monitoring tool to help you track clicks, likes, shares, etc. You can track trends, demographics and generate comprehensive reports.

❑ Respond to Facebook inquires within 24 hours at the latest. Social media has opened up avenues for customers to reach companies with their questions, beyond the simple *Contact Us* online form. If you don't reply quickly, you could get some bad press such as, "Hey, I think this company is dead. They haven't answered my question (on Facebook)." Keep your eye on your eMail notices via Facebook. Better yet, have an automatic message that directs all inquires to our website.

❑ Complete your *About Us* section and keep it updated. Link to other social media profiles if you have them. Update your logo and other profile images and backgrounds every few months or immediately as changes occur.

❑ Advertise on Facebook. Set a budget and commit to running some ads directed at your target markets. Track their progress. You can create sets of ads to connect with a variety of audiences. You create ads in the admin panel of your page using Facebook's ad creation tool. It's easy to do.

❑ Once you've built a community around your page, use the ad creation tool to expand your reach to lists from others who "like" your page.

❑ Create a Group on Facebook for your current clients or paid customers and refer them to a membership club. People already socialize on Facebook. Having a Group gives them more reason to comment. No Group, no talk/mention.

❑ Study your Facebook stats and see how your page is doing. Where can you improve? Make notes and work on it.

❑ Keep your posts short and to the point (under 80 characters).

❑ Post videos or visual tutorials. People will stop for a good video. Your videos should inspire viewers to read your posts and direct them to your website.

❑ If you send coupons to your eMail list, post the same coupon on your Facebook page don't forget to delete it as soon as it expires.

❑ Build your facebook following with "likes" organically. You do need to earn them. For example, Facebook won't allow you to "require" a viewer to like your page to enter a contest. Yes, you can run contests, but you can't manipulate likes on your fan page ... per Facebook terms.

❑ Push to get your likes up over 10,000. Likes don't always translate to sales, but they do give new visitors and customers to your website an idea of how many people have stopped by and expressed their quasi-approvals of what you do, and to some extent, establish trust. Imagine going to a website where they claim to be the best at what they do, but their "like count" is only at 185. On the flipside, someone could have a "like count" in the six digits, but beyond that, they may lack real content.

What's the real value of likes on a fan page? Only you can do the math for your business. Ideally, the more likes a brand gets, the more prominently its search results will be.

FTP (UP/DOWNLOAD)

CHECKLIST

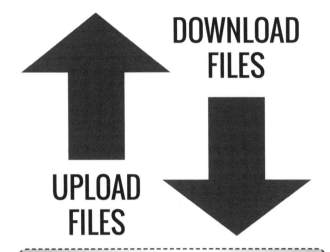

FILES + FOLDERS ON YOUR WEB SERVER

DOWNLOAD FILES

UPLOAD FILES

FILES + FOLDERS ON YOUR COMPUTER

AN FTP ALTERNATIVE

An alternative to using an FTP program is to move lots of files on your website server is to use the File Manager feature found in CPANEL. This is normally provided when you ordered website hosting. I prefer File Manager for several reasons:

1. You can MOVE, COPY AND DELETE several folders and thousands of files in SECONDS. This makes it easy to clean your server.

2. You can COMPRESS (ZIP UP) one or more files and folders into a single ZIP file. This is great if you want to make a complete copy of a website, download it to your computer and then upload it to the next website hosting account you might move to at a future date.

3. You can UNCOMPRESS (UNZIP) files that are ZIPPED up, which contain either software, files, folders, images, you name it. This is a powerful tool for File Manager that is not found elsewhere with standard FTP software programs.

If you build websites, work with WordPress or need to upload any kinds of files to your website server, use an FTP (File Transfer Protocol) program to do that.

An open source FTP software program that you can upload, download and/or manage files on your website hosting server account is called FileZilla.

FileZilla is a cross-platform program, which means it runs on both Windows and MAC computers. What do you need to do (and learn) about FTP programs?

❏ Uploading
❏ Downloading
❏ Renaming Files & Folders
❏ Moving Files & Folders

Check your hosting package to see if you have CPANEL and FILE MANAGER. You can find out quickly by going to http://yoursite.com/cpanel. If you don't have it, contact your hosting company for assistance. They can tell you and advise you with your user name and password.

Check out these screen shots to get familiar with FILEZILLA and FILE MANAGER, as well as my favorite

FTP program, FTP VOYAGER. I have video tutorials for all these three methods of uploading/downloading files to your computer at MyTrainingCenter.com.

cPanel's FILE MANAGER

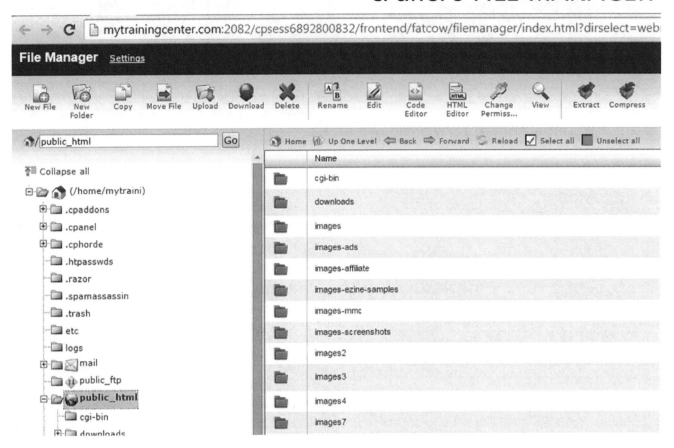

FILEZILLA

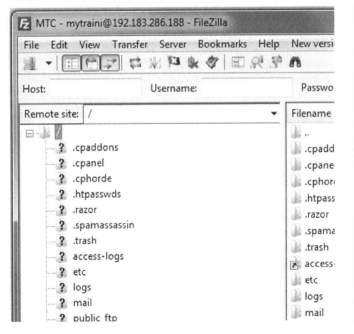

FTP VOYAGER

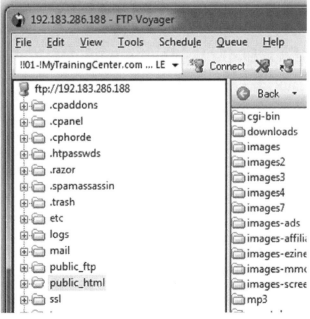

FULFILLMENT CENTER

CHECKLIST

Are you responsible for fulfillment from your home/office? It's wise to keep ample supplies on hand for shipping moderate amounts of product to your customers. I recommend you work with a fulfillment company and outsource shipping of much larger orders.

Here's a quick checklist of supplies and some tips on processing orders professionally and efficiently. While mailing product may sound simple, you need a system in place to ensure you don't waste your time or money. The following list should help you organize the ideal fulfillment center and keep fulfillment supplies and materials in-stock when needs arise.

Depending on your situation, consider the following suggestions:

❑ **Envelopes** — What kind of envelopes do you need? Large envelopes to slip a book or other product into and/or padded envelopes depending on the product? Search online for the lowest prices and buy in bulk.

The costs for mailing different types of envelopes will be based on what you are shipping such as a book or two books. If your package exceeds a certain weight, look at the different postage pricing options provided by the USPS or UPS.

❑ **Boxes** — Depending on (1) what your needs are, (2) what you're shipping, and (3) where you buy your postage from, you have several options. You could order custom made boxes online in bulk and store them at your home/office or you could order free boxes from the USPS if you plan to ship priority mail, Express Mail, Flat Rate or Regional Box A, B or C.

I found using the USPS Regional Boxes A or B serves many of my shipping needs. USPS flat rate boxes are a good deal too because no matter the weight of the items you ship, if you can pack them into a flat rate box and you will always pay the same rate.

❑ **Bubble Wrap** — What are you shipping? It's always good to have a large roll of bubble wrap on hand to protect whatever it is you're shipping.

❑ **Packing Peanuts** — These are a must when you are packing most items. You can shop Walmart, your local mail box service retailer, or online for good buys. Most of the office supply stores charge more for packing peanuts not unlike movie theatres that charge a few dollars for the movie and $25.00 for snacks. Your best bet is to shop online and have them delivered to you.

❑ **Packing Tape** — My favorite is DUCK EZstart. I don't like using tape guns and most other tape dispensers are too flimsy and fall apart in use. (Besides, tape guns are noisy.)

DUCK EZstart tape rolls can be bought at virtually any Walmart. It's strong and inexpensive tape. You may prefer other brands, but this one works for me.

❑ **Paper Cutter** — This comes in handy when you need to cut a clean edge so it looks professional. I use cutting boards to cut precise measurement, even bubble wrap strips for lining boxes. When you are mailing a variety of boxes, you don't want to be cutting anything manually.

❑ **Sharp Scissors** — There are few business/work tasks that don't require a good pair of scissors. Restrict a designated pair of scissors to the office and/or shipping area to avoid their misuse or damage.

❑ **Box Cutting Knife** — How many times have you searched for something to open a box such as the kitchen knives or that pair of scissors. Having the right tools to do a job saves time and wear and tear.

❑ **Assembly Table** — It's much more efficient to fulfill orders on a long folding table opposed to working out of the kitchen, dining room or the floor. Depending on the volume that you are shipping, you might want to invest in several tables. They are highly portable and very affordable. Compare prices from $25-$50.

❑ **Digital Postal Weight Scale** — Depending on how you calculate your postage, invest in an official postage weight scale to help you determine the weight of your envelopes and/or boxes. This will determine postage and allow you to print accurate mailing labels.

USPS postage weight scales can be purchased for $25-$40. You can find them online at Amazon.com, Staples.com and even Walmart.

❑ **Mailing Labels** — What are you shipping? Envelopes? Boxes? Depending on what you're shipping, you might choose from a variety of mailing label sizes to meet your label printing needs. Again, how are you paying for postage? UPS? Are there machines that print postage only? Yes. They can run between $100-$500.

Before you buy, determine how you will be printing, where you'll be printing it from, and then find the exact printer that will print postage on peel-and-stick labels. Peel-and-stick labels on a full 8.5" x 11" sheet allow you to peel 2, 4 or more labels from one sheet.

You might purchase peel-and-stick labels on a roll depending on your printer. For example, the Zebra LP2844 Thermal Label Printer is a perfect printer for printing USPS or UPS labels on a roll.

Search Amazon.com, online printer stores, even Ebay.com for best buys. Most companies sell inexpensive printer labels cheap when you buy in bulk. I have a supplier on Ebay.com that takes care of my label needs.

❑ **Postage Purchasing Account** — Who enjoys standing in line at the post office or UPS store? I prefer to drop off my packages for mailing and walk away. To do this, decide where you will buy your postage.

I'm not a big fan of Stamps.com, per se. There's a monthly fee or they don't generate labels for all of their USPS boxes, and I found out they don't handle USPS Region Box A, B or C. That might have changed as of this writing. Those box types are a tad smaller than USPS Priority Medium and Large boxes. This is important if you want to save money shipping items in those boxes within regions closer

to you. You can save as much as $5 (or more) on a single shipment.

USPS® Click-N-Ship® offers a free account where you can purchase (and print) postage labels for any package provided you ship Priority or Express mail. You cannot use USPS® Click-N-Ship® for First Class mail.

Other options include postage meter companies such PitneyBowes.com (http://goo.gl/6qqbPA), a competitor of Stamps.com. Compare rates, fees and printing solutions.

❏ **Postage Label Printing Machine** — Again, this is based on your shipping needs. If you do a lot of shipping, it might be worth investing in a postage label printing machine like the Zebra LP2844 Thermal Label Printer. Having a hassle-free machine to print postage labels is well worth my time and money.

❏ **Storage Cabinet or Rack** — To secure your shipping supplies, store them in an accessible locations where you can maintain an adequate supply and they are dust-free such as a large storage cabinet. A good one might cost you $100-$200.

❏ **USPS Drop Off Points / Hours** — If you ship packages via the USPS, here are some need to know tips: (1) the hours of operation during the week and

on Saturday) and (2) the last pick up times during the week and on Saturday. This applies to domestic (USA/CANADA and International shipments). Identify the locations for at least five postal locations near you. Not all offices have the same open/close times, weekend hours, and last pick up hours. Keep the information handy including the phone numbers for each location.

Another good idea is introduce yourself to each post office manager/director (and the counter employees) particularly if you plan to ship a lot of product. Whenever you need help or have questions, you can go to someone specific for assistance especially when dealing with a lost or stolen package.

Even though the USPS might direct you to call-in service centers for such matters, it's always good to have a contact on the inside. I've personally given the staff my world famous chocolate chip cookies to show my appreciation for their good service.

❏ **UPS Drop Off Points / Last Pick-Up Hours** — Know where the UPS drop off locations are even if you use USPS to ship your packages.

❏ **Fed Ex Drop Off Points / Last Pick-Up Hours** — Know these times so you never have to waste time researching information when you need it and to avoid missing deadlines.

❏ **International Shipping** — This is a tricky one. Are you using USPS, DHL, etc. to ship internationally? My suggestion is to use quality packaging materials due to excessive handling prior to reaching final destinations.

Light-weight, thin, flimsy boxes and envelopes are risky. Stuff envelopes inside of other envelopes for extra protection and use sturdy boxes that will withstand heavy wear and tear due to weight from other packages, mishandling, and travel mishaps by train, truck and air.

Review the checklist above and make note of what's missing for your particular needs! Never be caught without the supplies you need to manage your home/office effectively.

HUNGRY?

TIME FOR A BREAK?
SNACK ON SOME
OF THESE ...

Milk Chocolate Chip

Dark Chocolate Chip

Milk/Dark (Combo)

White Chocolate Chip

White Chocolate Chip & Macadamia Nuts

Peanut Butter Flavored & Milk Chocolate Chip

HEAD ON OVER TO:

www.BartsCookies.com

GMAIL SETUP
CHECKLIST

Do you have a Gmail eMail account? Are you taking full advantage of it by customizing it to serve all of your needs?

What's so great about Gmail? Here are several reasons why you should have a GMail account for your business:

☑ **Your Gmail account links to your YouTube account.** If you plan to host videos on YouTube, YouTube now asks that you link your account to a Gmail account.

☑ **Your Gmail account links to your Google+ account.** If you want to "hang out" with Google, you'll need a Gmail account.

☑ **Your Gmail account is web-based and doesn't store all your eMails on your computer**. Should your computer crash and you lose data, your eMail and contacts are safely stored online with Google.

☑ **GOODBYE SPAM. Gmail has THE BEST anti-spam sorting feature**! There's no need to set up spam filters as Gmail automatically isolates

SPAM in a SPAM folder. Check the folder regularly for any legitimate eMails that slipped through and move them to your inbox.

☑ **Built-in chats via text, voice, and video.** Gmail packs in the tools to communicate with clients and colleagues with texting, voicemail, video and chat features.

☑ **Loads of storage space**. I previously used Outlook on my computer, until the PST file, which used to store everything Outlook collected, FROZE when I hit a 2GB file size and locked me out of Outlook. All of my eMails, notes, contacts, etc. were GONE. With Gmail, you get 15GB of storage and if that's not enough you can order 100GB for a mere $1.99 per month.

☑ **Access Gmail on your phone with an "app."** When you return to your office, you don't have to check eMail because you already did it while on the go.

☑ **Labels, filters, and stars** help you label, filter and identify important eMails as you should expect from any eMail program.

☑ **Access to other Google tools such as Google Voice, Drive, Blogger, Calendar, Forms, Docs and more.** You can't run a successful business without tools! Gmail is essentially FREE.

HOW TO SET UP YOUR GMAIL ACCOUNT FOR EFFECTIVE USE

Here are the steps that anyone can follow to set up Gmail with confidence and ease.

1.0 ❑ **Under SETTINGS > GENERAL (Tab)**

MY CHECKLISTS

Settings (... for GMAIL)

General Labels Inbox Accounts & Import Filters Forwarding & POP/IMAP Chat Labs Offline Keywobard Shortcuts Themes

☐ Maximum page size: Show 100 eMails
☐ Undo Send:
☑ Enable Undo Send
☐ Send Cancellation Period: 20 seconds
☐ Stars: All Stars
☐ Keyboard Shortcuts: On
☐ Button labels: Text
☐ Signature: (Add your contact info, social media info, product or service info, your photograph, etc.)

2.0 ☐ Under SETTINGS > LABELS (Tab)

☐ Starred   show
☐ Important   hide
☐ Chats   hide
☐ Sent Mail   show
☐ Drafts   show
☐ All Mail   show
☐ Spam   show
☐ Trash   show

Create these labels and more ...

☐ $ Order (New)
☐ $ Order (Pending)
☐ $ Order (Processed)
☐ Clients
☐ Domain Name Activity
☐ Purchase Receipts
☐ Travel Plans
☐ Vendors

I make great use of LABELS to identify incoming eMails by title and color. I have 1,000+ labels segregating vendors, client names, domain name transactions/activity, affiliate companies, and much more. My Gmail video tutorials on creating labels offers more details for using labels to keep you organized.

3.0 ☐ **Under the ACCOUNTS & Import Tab,** I prefer to set up my own domain name eMail accounts and hide the fact the **From:/To:** when using Gmail.

4.0 ☐ **FILTERS** ... I use hundreds of filters to label incoming eMail automatically. You can also create filters for incoming mail by clicking *Filter Messages Like This* option within an eMail.

5.0 ☐ **KEYBOARD SHORTCUTS** ... Specifically, I reset just three functions: A=Archive, D=Delete, Z=Undo.

6.0 ☐ **Under SETTINGS > LABS (Tab)** I activate all of the following: Custom keyboard shortcuts, Mark as Read Button, and Google Voice player in my eMail account. There are other options, too.

7.0 ☐ **Google Voice Telephone Number** ... Do you have one? Why not give that number to the general public and then forward it to your cell phone so your cell phone number remains private to the world. A mobile "app" for this allows you to call out with your Google Voice Number and displays the Google number on caller ID and your cell number is protected.

To learn more features and benefits for having a Gmail account, go to MyTrainingCenter.com.

 WATCH MY **GMAIL VIDEO TUTORIALS** AT ...
MyTrainingCenter.com/gmail-video-tutorials

HTML BASICS
CHECKLIST

<h3> </h3> **Level-one heading** *to t*

<b> </b> *Bold*

<strong> </strong> ***Strong emphasis***

<i> </i> *Italics*

<u> </u> <u>Underline</u>

NOTE: When designing websites, installing opt-in forms, working with Joomla or WordPress, and other web design-related tasks ... knowing these very basic HTML commands will assist you with your digital projects.

<h1> </h1> **Level-one heading** to be used to enlarge titles and headings of web pages.

<h2> </h2> **Level-one heading** to be used to enlarge titles and headings of web pages.

<h3> </h3> **Level-one heading** to be used to enlarge titles and headings of web pages.

<b> </b> **Bold**

<strong> </strong>	**Strong emphasis**
<i> </i>	*Italics*
<u> </u>	<u>Underline</u>
<sup> </sup>	Superscript
<p>	Starts a new paragraph, with a line between paragraphs.

	Starts a new line without a blank line in between. Use two of these if you want a blank line between paragraphs or other objects.
<hr>	Draws a horizontal line across the web page.
	Non-breaking "space." This means you can place a space on the same line as other text. It's like hitting the spacebar. The more of these you use, the more spaces appear.
<center></center>	Centers text, images, video embed code, etc.

WORKING WITH <u>FONTS</u> AND CUSTOMIZING WEB TEXT

To customize the style, size and color of text for display on your website pages, I recommend:

<font face="Arial" **size**="3" **color**="#000000">Text<**/font**>

face	=	specifies a font (or a list of fonts) to be used
size	=	specifies a size to be used; 1-7; regular is 3
color	=	specifies color to be used; six-digit color codes are called hexadecimal numbers.

Another way to format text (instead of using <font></font> tags) is with the <span></span> tag commands such as:

<span style="**font-size**:33px; **font-family**: 'Oswald', sans-serif;">Text<**/span**>

font-size	=	specifies a size to be used; for examle, 33 is very large

font-family   =   specifies a font (or a list of fonts) to be used

Check out **http://Google.com/fonts** for more ideas and <span> code for great fonts.

INSERTING <u>IMAGES</u> INTO YOUR WEBSITE PAGES/DESIGN

If you need to insert any kind of image into your website design,
inside a WordPress widget or Joomla module, shopping cart, view
cart or check out page, or inside autoresponders, use this code:

<**img src**="images/bart.jpg" **height**="100" **width**="60" **alt**="Bart Smith">

src	=	URL source file for the actual image
height	=	number, percentage (pixel size or % of page)
width	=	number, percentage (pixel size or % of page)
alt	=	helps search engines; shows if no image appears
align	=	top, middle, bottom, left, right
border	=	border="0" means no border
title	=	this is the "title" tag for images, which causes a popup to appear showing a text description of an image when you mouse over the link

INSERTING <u>HYPERLINKS</u> INSIDE YOUR WEB PAGES

To insert links into your web design or other design instance, use this link.

<**a href**="http://bartscookies.com" **target**="blank">Bart's Cookies</a>

href	=	URL source file for the actual image	
target	=	"blank"	opens link in a new tab or window
		"parent"	opens link in current tab or window
		"#top"	takes visitor to the top of the page

WHAT **OTHER** BASIC **HTML** COMMANDS SHOULD LEARN?

This overview is basic HTML. I'd also like to encourage you to learn about:

LISTS = Being able to add and customize ordered and numbered lists is very useful when laying out text on a web page.

FORMS = While most forms today are generated with form-building plugins, it's nice to know how to customize fields and replace a default form button with the custom image button.

PAGE BUILDING SOFTWARE = Do you use WordPress? Have you ever heard of Visual Composer? It's a plugin that helps you build web pages on your website with ease. Check it out at MyTrainingCenter.com/visual-composer

The video tutorial(s) I have on HTML cover a little more details that what I've gone into in this section, and demonstrates how to customize HTML virtually anywhere on your website, especially, using WordPress. Check out those tutorials at:

www.MyTrainingCenter.com/videos

IMAGES/GRAPHICS
CHECKLIST

W hat's a PNG, JPG, GIF, TIF and what's the difference when it comes to these and other image file formats? You'll want to know the difference between these particular file formats especially when you're working on projects or getting help from others!

Many of my clients have a difficult time working with IMAGES whether they are using them, creating them, locating them, and what software programs work best. Here's my checklist for learning everything you should know about images, graphics, graphic design software programs and more.

IMAGE FORMATS

1. ❏ **GIF (Graphic Interchange Format)** format is one of the most popular digital formats used for displaying small and animated graphics. GIF files support a maximum of 256 colors, which makes them very practical and fast loading for small images with very few colors such as a banner or button that has only 1-2 colors in it. Generally, GIF files should be used for SMALL logos, text image buttons, and icons.

   Avoid using GIF formats for photographic images. Photographic images and those with millions of colors are best viewed in JPG format. GIF is also best used on the web.

   Yes, you can use GIF's in your brochures or flyers that you print from your computer. However, if you're going to use a professional printing company to print "mass quantities" or "high-resolution" print materials, the company will require that your images be in .TIF format.

2. ❏ **JPG (JPEG)** format is best used for anything photographic in nature where there are thousands of colors in the photograph, such as pictures of people, landscapes, buildings, food, animals, etc.

   The JPG file format supports millions of colors (not just 256 such as GIF formats). As a rule, JPG format should be used for photographic images and images that don't look so good in GIF format and only 256 colors.

JPG is best used on the Web. You can use JPGs in your brochures or flyers you might print from your computer. Again, if you're going to use a professional printing company to print "mass quantities" or "high-resolution" print materials the company will most likely require that your images be in .TIF format UNLESS you can send them a high resolution JPG file format.

3. ❑ **PNG (Portable or Public Network Graphic)** is a great image file format to use for the Web or for working on (and saving) vector art and other images collectively as a whole in graphic design programs like Adobe® Fireworks. While PNG images can be used on the Web as an image, it's better to use a JPG, UNLESS you need a transparent background. In this case, save your image(s) as a PNG 32 with a transparent background and the image will appear on top of your desired background perfectly with the background in place.

4. ❑ **PSD (PhotoShop Drawing)** is a file extension associated with Adobe® PhotoShop™. These files can only be opened in PhotoShop. They cannot be used online or displayed on a website.

5. ❑ **TIF (Tagged Image Format File)** images are primarily used for printing high-quality, high-resolution images on print materials such books, book covers, postcards, flyers, brochures, manuals or anything a professional printer will produce for you in mass quantity. Remember, GIF and JPG formats are best suited for the Web and printing from your home computer. DO NOT give JPG or GIF files to a professional printing company. Provide TIF files ONLY. Almost any image editing program such as Adobe PhotoShop™, Adobe Fireworks™,

etc. can be saved in TIF file format. Other features include:

❑ **Transparency**: Another nice feature of a GIF or PNG 32 files is that they support "transparency." This means you can make the background of the GIF or PNG image "transparent" or invisible. When you do this, the image itself will appear nicely against any colored background you select.

❑ **Image Optimization:** This is a method for reducing the size of GIF, PNG and JPG files for the Web so they download faster. Programs that optimize graphics are simply reducing the number of colors within the image, which makes downloading faster. Note, the more colors you remove from an image, the fuzzier it may appear. So, use your best judgment when optimizing graphics for your website. You should optimize them so your site downloads quickly, but not at the expense of making the images look distorted or unclear. Also, you don't need to optimize .TIF files because you won't be removing any colors from them. You want them to remain as crisp and sharp as possible when they go to your printing company.

❑ **Interlacing:** Interlacing is simply a feature in GIF files that creates the illusion of faster loading graphics. While the image is downloading, it appears in your browser window through a series of several steps.

At first it will appear blurry and then as more of the image is downloaded from the server, the image becomes more and more defined until the entire image has fully downloaded. At that point, you see the whole picture clearly!

It's important to note that interlaced GIF files will usually be a bit larger than non-interlaced ones. In modern terms, a similar effect is called LAZY LOAD. This occurs when the image(s) on your web page aren't fully loaded, that is until you actually see them in your viewing browser window.

IMAGE SOFTWARE

FREE GRAPHIC DESIGN PROGRAMS

1. ❑ **Artweaver** – These FREE image editing programs are very similar to Photoshop. The Pro version is only $40 est. I recommend you purchase it if you plan to regularly work with graphics and hi-res (300dpi) images.

2. ❑ **Inkscape** – This FREE vector program is great for designing headers, banners and buttons with text and stock photography. It is NOT to be used to check image file sizes, saving to different formats or editing images.

PAID PROGRAMS

1. ❑ **Adobe Photoshop** – This image editing and graphic design program by Adobe is used to edit images and more. Note that you can use Artweaver in its place for 80% of what you'll need to do in Photoshop.

2. ❑ **Adobe Fireworks** - My favorite graphics design and editing program is Adobe Fireworks! If you have this program, tune into my video tutorials and learn more. You won't regret it. I've used every program on the shelf for more than 20 years and this one blows away the competition. Don't think twice about buying it if you're not using it.

3. ❑ **Adobe Illustrator** - I frequently also use this program when I need to create posters, postcards, book covers, etc. I'll use Fireworks, but Illustrator has design advantages that other programs don't have.

ONLINE RESOURCES

- ❑ Aviary.com/tools/phoenix
- ❑ Lunapic.com
- ❑ Picnik.com
- ❑ Pixlr.com/editor
- ❑ SumoPaint.com/web

IMAGE STOCK PHOTO WEBSITES

PREMIUM PROGRAMS

- ❑ YAYImages.com (MY FAVORITE!)
- ❑ 123RF.com
- ❑ Pond.com
- ❑ GraphicStock.com
- ❑ Crestock.com
- ❑ CanStockPhoto.com
- ❑ Fotolia.com
- ❑ Dreamstime.com
- ❑ PeopleImages.com
- ❑ StockLib.com
- ❑ PhotoDune.net
- ❑ DollarPhotoClub.com

Find more at MyTrainingCenter.com.

FREE STOCK IMAGES

- ❑ Pixabay.com
- ❑ PicJumbo.com
- ❑ FreeImages.com
- ❑ ImCreator.com/free
- ❑ MorgueFile.com
- ❑ SuperFamous.com

- ☐ Unsplash.com

Find more at MyTrainingCenter.com.

IMAGE ICON WEBSITES

- ☐ FindIcons.com

- ☐ IconFinder.com

- ☐ IconArchive.com

LEGAL ISSUES USING IMAGES

- ☐ **DO USE ONLY** those images that you PAY for or have the exclusive right to use because you took the photograph yourself or you created the image using a graphics design program.

- ☐ **DO NOT USE** any image that you find by just searching the Internet and downloading it. It's illegal to break copyright laws and companies will find you and prosecute you for fraud.

First, you'll receive a letter advising you that you have infringed on a copyright law by using an unauthorized image on your website that you or your webmaster placed on your website. No excuse is acceptable. You will then be advised to pay $1,500 (+/-) immediately to avoid a lawsuit. It's risky not to respond to these requests. Just a heads up that, without any warning, you could also receive a phone call regarding the alleged theft.

Keep this information in mind when tempted to grab an image without verifying ownership or paying for it! Be certain that you understand and honor usage terms for every image.

INCOME PROCESSING
CHECKLIST

Money, money, money! When it comes to getting paid by your clients, customers, vendors and suppliers, there are a number of things to consider. In this checklist, I'll cover some of the essentials for getting paid, accepting payments, handling refund requests, fraudulent orders and more!

1.0 ❑ Establish A Strong Relationship From The Beginning!

Before You Ask For The Money — Before you ever talk money, price or ask for payment, etc., establish a strong relationship with your client/customer by spelling out all terms up front, in writing, and preferably with a signed contract. Two people operating on the same

page with full understanding of expectations is a secure relationship. Without trust, you can expect problems!

1.2 ❑ Pour On The Value — Customers and clients will sense that you care, that you'll put in extra time and guarantee that they get their money's worth from your products/services. Make yourself available by accepting their calls and returning them shortly, replying to their eMails promptly, and treating them with respect. Strive for excellence when dealing with them.

1.3 ❑ Become A Regular In Their (Business) Life — To keep clients/customers coming back for more product/service, check in with them, periodically. Ask how they are enjoying the product/service you provide. By demonstrating genuine interest in them by phone, eMail or even regular mail, it says that you value their patronage. What a novel concept in our busy world.

1.4 ❑ Be Likeable! — Customers that like you will gladly pay for your products/services! This relationship is especially valuable when a customer experiences of problem with your product/service and hesitates to tell you or is unable to pay the bill on time. If they know that they can approach you with problems, they are more inclined to contact you to work on a solution with you.

2.0 ❑ Getting Paid [What you need to know!]

2.1 ❑ Deposits Up Front — Depending on the kind

of work you do, being paid up front or collecting a deposit is the first step in ensuring that you get paid. I don't bake my world famous cookies or ship my books without payment in full up front. It's just good business and most clients/customers expect to pay.

2.2 ❏ Collecting Payments

If you provide a high priced service such as website design, I recommend you ask for a deposit to begin work. If it's an on-going project, you might require regular payments weekly or bi-weekly. Then, before you turn over the remaining work, ask for the balance of payments due prior to releasing the files and passwords for all work performed.

2.3 ❏ Cash Payments

• If you accept cash payments, be sure to issue a receipt to your client/customer and "report it" as income on your taxes. Otherwise, you might be targeted for an audit any time. Audits and unexplained "missing" income on your return is challenging at best. These errors can generate penalties and interest. Always keep good records including receipts. You can't fool Mother Nature or the Internal Revenue Service.
• It's advisable that you do NOT accept cash payments when you can avoid it. It's must easier for you as a professional to track of your income via credit card and payments by check. Even PayPal.com payments can be difficult to track. I would never refuse cash. Cash is king! Utilize a sales receipt booklet purchased at your local office supply store or eMail one that you create. The buyer may need the information for tax purposes. It's the right thing to do for both you and the other party.

2.3 ❏ Payment By Check

• While accepting manual checks for payment gives customers the flexibility to pay in this manner, you, the merchant, take a risk that the customer's check might bounce. Many companies have stopped accepting checks altogether.
• Depending on your history with a certain client, or if you accept checks daily in your business from customers, deposit the checks immediately. If you have concerns about a check, you can contact the issuing bank (bank, branch location and phone number on the bottom of the check) to ask a bank representative if there's enough money in the account to cash the check in question. If the teller says, "No," then call the customer immediately to say, "I checked with the bank and there isn't enough money in your account to cash the check you gave me. Do you have another form of payment you can use?"

• Further, for any check over $1,000, do NOT deposit via ATM; walk it in to the bank and deposit it in person. Lastly, make COPIES of all checks you receive from clients/ customers. If you keep individual files on your clients, you have a great place to file these copies to ensure you have a record of the transaction.

• Lastly, if you're expecting a substantial payment for service provided, you might ask the client/customer to send the check to you by an overnight mail service or a reputable overnight courier service. You don't want to risk losing a check in the mail, endorsed via forgery and cashed leaving you with nothing. The $17-27 cost to overnight a check should be worth the protection for you and your client/customer.

2.4 ❏ Credit Card Payments

• The best way to increase sales and your income is to accept credit card payments from your customers and clients both online and offline.

• The best way to accept credit card payments is through your own merchant account or any online credit card processing account such as PayPal.com, Stripe.com or SquareUp.com.

• If you need a merchant account, you could apply for one at MyTrainingCenter.com. I work with credit card companies that specialize in merchant accounts. With your own merchant account, you can accept Visa, Master Card, American Express, Discover and other credit. While the merchant company will charge a small fee (about 2-3% depending on provider) to process every credit card transaction, the money you collect is deposited directly into your bank account.

• Now, if you are accepting payments via credit card that exceed $1,000, consider asking that client/customer to pay by check to avoid the 2-3% fee charged by merchant account companies. Note that the fees are charged per transaction. If you have five transactions in one day, you will be charged a fee five times. So, ask your clients to write a check or (at your discretion) tell the client/customer that YOU must charge your own fee of 2-3% to cover YOUR cost for the fee the credit card company will charge (2-3%). In most cases, these fees are tax deductible.

• Is a merchant account that allows you to accept credit card payments still worth it? Just know that there are many competitive merchant account companies that want your business. Stripe.com is one example. You need only sign up, order your mobile phone credit card swiping equipment, swipe your first credit card transactions and within days the money will be in your account. Stripe.com offers a customized payment flow that works great at your desk or on your mobile device. They securely transmit card details into their system and take care of the annoying processing and compliance issues.

2.5 ❑ PayPal.com Payments

• This is a great way to get paid by some clients. PayPal.com processes payments for millions of customers worldwide. That's a pretty good track record. It's free to set up a PayPal account and you can start accepting payments almost immediately. I have used PayPal.com for years and can attest to its security and simplicity.

• PayPal works like a bank, although it's not a bank.

PayPal customers are free to buy and sell with ease whenever products/services are rendered.

• You can also accept payments from YOUR website using PayPal. The Standard version allows you to accept credit card payments plus PayPal.com payments. Their "Pro" version allows you to process credit cards through a virtual terminal, and when accepting payments through your website, your customers never have to leave your site to make a payment.

• Does PayPal accept phone/fax/in-person payments from customers? Yes and no. YES to credit card payments. NO for PayPal payments where the customer's PayPal username and password access is needed. If you take orders via phone/fax/mail and collect a customer's credit card billing information, you could conceivably create a BUY ME button inside your PayPal account for these transactions. With the customer's billing information, you can proceed to the checkout page, complete the fields with their information, insert their eMail addresses, and click the PAY button. You'll know immediately if the credit card payment is accepted or not. Processing credit card payments online can save you the expense of having to get a merchant account or virtual terminal.

2.6 ❑ Other Payment Methods

• If you sell digital products (i.e., eBooks and other downloadable products and you're not shipping product), you might want to sell via JVZoo.com, E-Junkie.com or ClickBank.com in addition to your website. These website companies have smaller communities of sellers and affiliates and they're lucrative!

• When you sign up to sell digital products through any of these sites, they will handle all aspects of the sales transactions for you. They can accept a wide range of payments and will issue a monthly statement of transactions that include 3-7% (+/-) fee for their service.

• The good news? You too can accept a wide range of payments, but a fee up to 7% can be a stiff share of your profits.

• Consider selling your digital products directly from your own website. What's the advantage? You don't have deep fees dipping into your pocket. You have full control over marketing, advertising, selling, and product fulfillment. You have a seller-centered, customer-first marketplace in every niche out there. Build your own online store to sell you digital products and services.

• There are many online companies that specialize in high volume sales of digital products and services and that's all they handle (digital). The great thing is that you do have many options and there is one that will best suit your needs. Test a few of them and base your decision the size of your operation, whether you need a shopping cart/website/online store, exposure and cost for services. (For tangible product sales, you'll need a merchant account and the ability to accept credit card payments.)

2.7 ❑ Recurring Billing

• Who doesn't want to get paid on time every time? Set up a regular payment system (bi-weekly, monthly) for the duration of the amount owed to you! Most customers prefer payment plans versus having to pay for a large ticket item or large order in full.

• Recurring billing is a payment method that charges your customer once a month, for example, or a prescribed period of time until their bill is paid. You might advise your client of the value of making payments on time to avoid penalties or fees over the agreed upon period of time. It's unwise to manually charge credit cards to ensure timeliness and accuracy. Automate your billing process with recurring billing.

• Some shopping cards allow for recurring billing. Check with your shopping cart provider. PayPay.com allows you to create recurring billing product buy

buttons. Simply add a product/service description in the account, determine how many payments are needed (i.e., 1 monthly payment, 12 months in a row, for the exact same amount, etc.), and enter the clients credit card information and your payment system is automated. You'll know when to expect payments and how much you'll be paid every time.

• Update client/customer credit card information when the need arises. In the course of making payments, credit cards can expire or require replacement due to theft or loss. Even though you have good service automating your willing, don't look at the system as a hands-free operation. Stay on top of things and don't let past due payments accumulate. It's much easier to go after one overdue payment versus several.

2.8 ❑ Banks, Bank Accounts & Banking Tips

• If you're in business, it's wise to keep your personal income and expenses separated from your business income and expenses primarily for tax reporting purposes.

• Also, save time making deposits at the ATM machine, if those dollar amounts are under $1,000. Your time is money and don't waste your time standing in line, unless you can slip into the "Merchant (only) Line." Make the most of online banking, mobile deposits, direct deposits, etc.

• If you need a merchant account, I DON'T recommend that you obtain one through your bank unless they truly beat all the competitive fees, services, performance features, etc. Banks typically don't handle all the merchant account features for either offline or ONLINE transactions. If you are uncertain about your bank, ask your bank this question: "Is your merchant account compatible with my shopping cart? I use _____, and need a payment gateway." If there is any hesitation in the bank's response, go! Check out a few of the merchant accounts such as PayPal.com. PayPal.com works well for most merchants, unless you want the monies transferred directly into their bank account. PaylPal is an independent account (not unlike a debit card) where funds are immediately available.

2.9 ❑ Bank Deposits by your Clients!

• Another way to get paid by clients/customers is to simply ask them to deposit their checks directly into your bank account. If you are comfortable with this procedure, the one paying only needs the name of your bank, your name and account number. This works effortlessly for me and some clients/customers prefer it to mailing checks or using credit cards for products/services.

• How does this work? At the bank, the person paying need only fill out a deposit slip with your name and account number. Be sure that you designate how you want your name or company name to appear on the check. The payer should write the name you provide on the front and the back of the check (on the endorsement line). If the client/customer has blank deposit slips from your bank, he/she can use the drive-through window to make the deposit. It's as easily done as, "Hello, I'm making a deposit for another person." It's advisable for the payer to tell the teller this especially if you or the payer requires a receipt. The teller will issue a receipt for the deposit ONLY without disclosing your bank balance.

• Don't shy away from this payment option too fast! It's NOT a big deal for your clients to have your bank account number. It's always printed on the backs of their checks once they're deposited. The account number is public information. Look on the backs of checks you've deposited and you'll see the other person's bank account number.

• For your security, no one can ask for a bank balance, unless he/she is the owner of the account. Withdrawals or making changes to an account requires key information that only you (and your bank) possess such as the secure pass codes you assigned to the

account to safeguard it against fraud or loss. Don't rely on your tax ID or the last 4-digits of that tax ID or your SS# to protect you. Some clients will ask you for your tax ID number for their tax reporting records. They do this (by law) so they can report all the money they paid you that year so this is public information. So, if you haven't already, create a unique password on every bank accounts and securely protect the information. Do not use the same password for all of your accounts. Big mistake!

• Benefits for asking clients/customers to deposit their checks into your bank account on your behalf are: Convenience! Time! Availability! Do you always have a postage stamp when you need one? It takes less time to make a deposit than a drive to the post office no accounting for the check getting lost in the mail. And, funds are available the same day in most cases. You can't put a value on the assurance of getting paid.

2.10 ❑ Billing Address vs. Shipping Address

• If you accept credit card payments from your clients and customers, you might experience a blip or delay in the system when things go wrong that are out of your control and the customers.

• Payments are often delayed when "life happens." People move and delay making address changes with all of their accounts, experience life-altering challenge and chaos, and sometimes, they just forget to make that payment you are eagerly awaiting. We're human! Very often mailing addresses, billing addresses, and shipping addresses are not the same by design. Be sure that you have all the information and it's maintained up to date.

• If a customer's credit card is declined, you might ask them to confirm all of their addresses for mailing, billing and shipping. Hopefully when these kinds of changes occur, you have one or two phone numbers (better) where the individual can be reached to reconcile the problem.

Many of **MY CHECKLISTS** have video tutorials that teach you more at www.**MyTrainingCenter.com**.

• When it comes to fraud and bogus orders, look for wide discrepancies in billing and shipping addresses. For example, the billing address is in the USA and the shipping address is in Africa. This order should be frozen and investigated further to ensure you have a bona fide order and method for payment. Communication is key! Call the customer and follow up with an email and/or letter. Know the dangers for fake checks and face money orders.

For example, a customer sent a money order to me in payment for a large order of product. The amount I received was much more than the cost, which raised a red flag. The customers called me immediately to ask for a refund of the overpayment he claimed was a mistake on his part. I took the money order INTO my bank, which coincidently was the same bank that issued the money order (I believed). The reality was that the bank confirmed that I was being SCAMMED. The bank recognized the fake money order and turned it over to their legal department. Fortunately, I had (1) not mailed product when I received the money order or (2) made an ATM deposit of the money order and (3) blindly refunded the overpayment. You can imagine the potential loss!

• More often your bank or credit union can't tell if there is a problem with the check or money order until it has gone through the system of the person or company that supposedly issued the bogus funds. That can take weeks. By that time, the fraud is discovered and the offender has pocketed the cash. To avoid SCAMS, go to www.consumerfed.org/fakecheckscams and www.fakechecks.org for information to help you and others avoid losing money to fake check scams. (I was very fortunate that my bank was aware of the money order abuses and immediately recognized the fake.)

3.0 ❑ Merchant Accounts [What you need to know!]

3.1 ❑ What is a merchant account?

• This is an account with a bank that allows you to accept credit cards (Visa, Master Card, American Express, etc) as a form of payment, over the web, from your customers.

• NOTE: Traditional Merchant Accounts, those used in face-to-face transactions as in brick-and-mortar businesses, are generally NOT authorized for online transactions.

• If you want to accept payments via credit card from your customers, you will need your own merchant account via companies such as Stripe.com, PayPal.com, and SquareUp.com. Every business that accepts payments via credit card from their customers has a merchant account.

3.2 ❑ What is a Payment Gateway?

• Payment gateways are online systems for real time charging/processing of credit cards for customers that place online orders through your website. The company that issued the payment gateway processes those credit card charges and deposits the monies collected from your customer's credit card into your bank account within 2-3 business days.

• If you already have a merchant account, but not a payment gateway to accept credit card payments through your website, then contact your merchant account provider. If it didn't already come with a payment gateway, you'll need to order it separate or you can use PayPal.com to process your online shopping cart payments.

3.3 ❑ Offline Payment Processing

• You may wish to accept credit card payments for orders placed by the phone, in-person, by fax or by other means other than the Internet. If you do get your own merchant account, you might also receive a "virtual terminal" that will allow you to turn your computer into a credit card processing terminal in which to handle these types of transaction 24/7/365.

3.5 What is a Virtual Terminal?

• A virtual terminal allows you, the merchant, to authorize, process and manage credit card transactions manually from any computer in the world that has an Internet connection and a web browser.

For example, PayPal.com and Authorize.net both offer "virtual terminals" for a monthly fee. You can charge customers' credit cards manually online. All you need is a computer, an Internet connection and your username and password to access your account and process customers' credit cards, manually.

• With some systems, you can manually void credit card charges, refund monies to customers as needed, run special reports, and much more on your computer.

4.0 ❑ Rent A Private Mail Box (Not P.O. Box)

Are you having your business mail delivered to your home address? Unless you live in a gated community or your mailbox is locked and secure, STOP! Either have your business mail sent to a private mail box (at a minimum) or have all of your personal/business mail forwarded to a secure box that you can rent for a nominal fee.

I CANNOT recommend a USPS mail box. NOTE: The post office will NOT sign for any packages from UPS or FEDEX or DHL. Their rates might be a bit cheaper versus private box rental services, but you could potentially miss out on mail sent to you by UPS or FEDEX or DHL. You'll find that private companies also offer more services that could be beneficial to your needs.

A good reason to rent any mail box is to keep your business life "public" and your personal life "private!" Seriously, do you want your clients, vendors, and others to know where you live? Suppose you change your residence within the area or take a vacation? You can no doubt maintain your rental mail box without having to notify scores of people that you've moved. Rent a mail box! You can check it at your convenience and you have the assurance that your mail is secure.

5. ❑ Invoicing Strategies

• Invoicing is a very important element for collecting payment from clients/customers. If you don't invoice, how will they know what they're paying for or the amount owed? Here are some helpful tips:

(1) You can send your invoices via eMail or by regular postal mail or both. Your choice.

(2) If you eMail an invoice to your client, send a copy to yourself and, when you receive it, file it in your eMail program in a sub folder you create called "Invoices" and a sub-folder with the client's name. This gives you a record of every invoice you eMail plus you have information for generating the next invoice.

(3) There are several ways to generate invoices. You could use a word processor like Microsoft Word, Excel, eMail, text editor, etc. You can also view sample invoice layouts online by just searching for "sample invoices." Customize your invoices based on your research and needs.

(4) Do you have a PayPal.com account? They have a great invoicing system. When you click on REQUEST MONEY, click on the link that reads, "Create an Invoice." Check out my PayPal Video Tutorials to see how you too can use this feature to send out simple invoices so your clients can pay you accurately and on time.

There are several online companies to help you generate invoices, such as FreshBooks.com. They offer a host of other services and benefits, but not without an affordable monthly fee. Check out Invoiceable.com. They offer a FREE online service that lets you keep all your clients in one place, track/manage your hours, and create invoices.

6.0 ❏ Guarantees & Return Policies

If you sell PRODUCTS, it's a good idea to post your "Refund/Return Policy" and all the rules and regulations so customers know what to expect should they choose to return merchandise to you for a refund, whether in full or minus a restocking fee. Some important points regarding "Return Policies" include:

❏ "You may return most new, unopened items sold and fulfilled by [YOUR COMPANY] within 30 days of the date of delivery for a full refund." [MODIFY AS NEEDED.]

❏ "Merchandise should be returned in their original product packaging." [MODIFY AS NEEDED.]

❏ "If packages are opened, seals are broken, packaging shows wear and tear, merchandise cannot be returned and monies cannot be refunded." [MODIFY AS NEEDED.]

❏ "Please call our office to request a refund/return." [MODIFY AS NEEDED.]

❏ "You should expect to receive your refund within 30 days of the date merchandise is returned to us." [MODIFY AS NEEDED.]

Remember to post comments like these and others on the "Terms & Conditions" page on your website. Make it clear up front, and on your site in writing, what you do and do not allow. Always include a copy of your regulations in any order you fulfill.

It can't be said enough, STATE EVERYTHING IN WRITING ONLINE OR OFFLINE TO PROTECT YOURSELF!

7. ❏ Bogus Orders, Fraud, International Orders & What You Should Know

• If you conduct any business online, you can easily become a victim of fraud and bogus orders because in today's global economy, we all have access to every website. It's critical that you know what to look for when suspect orders show up in your shopping cart. Here are some examples from my research and experience:

• If an order shows up SEVERAL TIMES with DIFFERENT EMAIL ADDRESSES of CREDIT CARD NUMBERS, it could be fraudulent order. Don't charge the credit card (or even attempt to), but do try to contact the potential customer directly by phone or eMail. Note, while eMail is one means of communication, the phone should be your FIRST means of contact! If the customer doesn't return you call, then I would definitely not fulfill the order. If that "customer" doesn't get the merchandise, he/she will either contact you or will move on to the next victim. At that point, don't delete the order, but archive it for future reference if need such as reporting it as SPAM.

• If an order comes in from AFRICA, EASTERN EUROPE or ASIA, be very cautious of completing these orders. Why is that? In many of these cases, web savvy "culprits" are testing any number of stolen credit cards to see if they'll work for them. They may be using your shopping cart as a test to see if they can use the card by using a bogus billing address. If they succeed, they will then place an order for a more expensive product which is then mailed to them. When they receive the product, they'll usually sell it for cash while the credit card holder gets stuck with the bill and you get stuck with a charge back.

• A word of advice: "Don't be so quick to get the money!" An order from Nigerian for 10 of a product that sells for $100/each adds up. Fraud is more prevalent in specific foreign countries such as Nigeria. This country is notorious for making fraudulent deals.

In fact, depending on what you sell and who your primary customer is, I would not accept any order from a non-English speaking country. Ask yourself why is someone from a foreign country ordering my product/service? BEWARE.

• One way to protect your business/company against credit card fraud is to check for this information on all orders. The credit card owner of the card processing an order must be able to give you two pieces of information to help combat fraud: the 3 or 4-digit "security code" and an AVS (Address Verification System) response. If someone has stolen credit card information electronically, this information would not normally be available a thief.

• I've even gone so far as inserting a string of code in my .ht access file on my website to BLOCK any traffic from specific countries that I deem commit the majority of fraudulent orders. Those countries include, but are not limited to: China, Russia, Nigeria, Iran, North Korea, etc. You get the idea. WHY should those countries be contacting you about anything? Don't give anyone an opportunity to defraud you.

• In some shopping cart systems, you can disallow accepting orders placed by certain countries or restrict buying to certain countries. I typically only include the USA, UK, Canada and Australia. If someone from any other country REALLY wants to order from me, I can be reached via the contact information on my website.

• You can also call your merchant account company's customer service line to verify if a credit card is valid, stolen or other! They'll advise you and appreciate your help in fighting fraud.

• Here's a sample letter you might send to someone who is continually trying to send "bogus" orders, testing numerous credit cards and each order shows up declined for one reason or another:

Hello _____,

We're sorry, but our system has declined your order. Please call our office to place your order by phone. We look forward to speaking with you.

Regards,

YourCompany.com
Billing Department
(000) 000-0000 TELEPHONE

• Your message is simple and gets to the point. If the order is not fraudulent, obviously, process it. It's doubtful that you would ever hear back from a thieving customer. Can you report them? Perhaps, if the credit card company is reachable, however, if the perpetrator is in another country, forget it. There's no international authority that tracks down these "crooks." You can stop them at the front door when they try to use a stolen credit card to transact business.

• Another area of fraud to be aware of are people that sign up for your affiliate program and make bogus sales with bogus and then expect to receive a fraudulent commission. Personally, I am in favor of affiliate programs as they have proved to be very reliable and profitable. I caution you to validate every affiliate candidate.

• Remember, all orders should be verified prior to paying commissions. If you see a number of orders come from an affiliate and those orders happen to be coming from ASIA, EASTERN EUROPE or AFRICA, research and investigate the orders to protect yourself and your business.

• Do you really expect a criminal to answer the phone? Does the telephone number even work? Have you received a reply to your eMail requesting more information from the prospective buyer? If not, you have your answer. Cancel these orders to avoid paying any commission, immediately. If any affiliate refers even one bogus order to you, you have the right to decline that affiliate's relationship and you shouldn't hesitate to do so.

• The primary message here is to keep your merchant record clear of charge backs, bogus refunds, and the like, trust your instincts and take action when you expect fraud. By doing so, you'll enjoy a prosperous relationship with valid customers as you carefully observe transactions for them, the banks, the merchant account company and your security.

8.0 ❑ Accepting Payments Online (Pros & Cons) Security & Encryption

When asking for credit card information on your website, make sure your clients and customers are entering their private and personal information should provide such secure technology.

8.1 ❑ Payments via eMail

Never ask a client to eMail their credit card information to you via eMail. At least suggest they break up the information into separate eMails. An eMail is NOT a secure method of transmitting high confidential information and can easily be hacked via cyberspace. I recommend you send the first 8 digits of the credit card number in one eMail, the last 8 digits in another, the expiration date in another and the billing address in another. This might sound tedious, but it's worth the effort to protect you.

What I like to do is send an eMail with a payment link within the eMail. When clicked, it will take the customer directly to a secure checkout page where billing and credit card information can be entered.

8.2 ❑ Payments via Phone

Collecting the information you need by phone is trustworthy. I caution you not to delegate this responsibility to someone else unless that person is

a trusted associate, employee, etc. operating on your behalf. Then, keep the client/customer on the phone while the credit card is processed through your virtual terminal or other payment processing tool. If there's a problem, you can resolve it while the other person is still on the line. "It seems the card didn't go through. Can you repeat the credit card numbers again? Do I have your current billing address?"

9.0 ❑ Collecting Past Due Balances

Do clients owe you money? Here are a few methods to help you get paid:

9.1 ❑ First, speak to them about their situation.

Ask the customer why he/she is unable to pay you. Find out when payment can be made. If the client/customer needs a little time, agree to a specific date. Don't stretch it out more than 60-90 days and then don't forget about it. A reminder is sometimes helpful and some will appreciate it. Above all, you have a business to run and you should expect to be paid for services or a product that you delivered.

9.2 ❑ Offer payment arrangements.

Utilize the power of recurring billing to put clients/customers on an automatic payment plan that will charge their credit card each month the amount that you both agreed on. Send regular (monthly) itemized invoices and record and track payments as you get paid. Provide your payment policy, PayPal eMail address, credit cards you accept, and your physical mailing address. This will help them stay on track with payments and keep you in the know as to what's owed and when you can expect payment.

9.3 ❑ Small Claims Court for Uncollected Debts
You always have the option to take someone to Small Claims Court when monies are due and unpaid. To ensure a positive outcome, you should mail a monthly invoice for three consecutive months. Mail each invoice to the residence or business mailing address via Certified Mail. This gives you an official record of

mailing monthly invoices once over a 90 day period. If you question whether the person will sign for the certified mail, send your invoice via UPS or FedEx. Most people are more inclined to sign for these. Some mistakenly associate certified mail with the IRS or bad news in general and they can refuse to sign for it.

Following the three month timeframe with no payment, you have a strong case in Small Claims Court to demand the money you are owed. The dollar amount one can claim in Small Claims depends on your state standard; $7500 to $10,000 in most states; more and less in a few others. You may wish to speak to an attorney for advice otherwise an attorney is not required representation in this court.

In Small Claims Court, you are encouraged to represent yourself. Be prepared with a copy of the contract between you and the person owing the money (is possible), evidence of work completed, copies of invoices and mailing receipts. The judge will ask to review all of your evidence and if all of your ducks are in order, the judge will invariably rule in your favor. At this point, the client now has a judgment against them to pay all monies due. Perhaps, that motivation will encourage the person to either pay you in full or ask to for payment arrangements. A judge can issue You might also ask the judge to issue a warrant for their arrest if they don't pay. Or, you could contact any number of collection agencies to see if they'll take your judgments and try to collect for you on your behalf for a fee. You could also call your client to let him know you are going to sue him/her after sending those letters and they could be arrested for not paying. Anything (legal), to help you get paid, is what I think you should do. It's what I'd do if someone owed me money.

I've also just sent gifts, like my world famous chocolate chip cookies, to those who owe me money. They feel so guilty when I send them the gift and a bill reminder that they call me up to say, "Bart, we feel so guilty. How much do we owe you? I'm writing the check right now and mailing it today. Your cookies are out of this world. Thank you for your patience, and we're very sorry to keep you waiting for your payment."

Another client paid me the $1,000 she owed me a year later. I have a saying, "I'll always need money, today, tomorrow, next week, next month, next year ..." So, why not give clients the time they need to pay you back. You come across as someone so sweet and nice to work with, and as long as you keep sending them those invoices monthly, they know they have a bill to be paid from you. Just, they might really need the time. I've worked with clients who ran out of money to pay their own bills. Well, I wasn't going to take the roof over their head or food off their table. I stayed in contact, asked monthly. Then, one day, I found $1,000 pushed into my PayPal account by a customer who owed me money. Wow, that was unexpected, but I knew I was on her mind the whole time in a nice way. "I have to pay Bart. He's been so kind and patient. I just can't sleep at night." See how that works? You don't have to be mean or get nasty legally, just follow some of these basic tactics to help make sure you get paid. Remember, we'll always need the money, today or tomorrow.

10. ❑ Always, Thank Your Customers!

Saying, "Thank You!" goes along way with building strong relationships with your clients and customers. Imagine how surprised they'll be if they go to their mailbox and instead of finding an invoice, they find a thank you card from you that says:

It's a very rare today that people stop and take the time to say, "Thank you!" Well, not you! You're going to take the time to say, "Thank you!" now, aren't you?

Each month, set aside some time to write a few thank you cards to some of your favorite clients. Especially those that bring you the most business. You definitely want them thinking of you again and again ... Your future income and payments depend on it! You can easily buy a 10-pack (or other quantity) of thank you cards at the grocery store or drug store. So, no excuses that you can't find them. Simple is best. It's the thought that counts. Gratitude goes a long way. While we're at it, consider sending some of my world famous chocolate chip cookies to clients you really want to thank. Imagine the look on their face and the tone in their voice when they call you to say, "Thank YOU, and I have more work for you ..."

Did you know? Doing this is a tax deduction activity for your business? Ask your accountant if the purchase of those cards can be classified as a "selling expense" or other expense. It's customer-related for certain. If allowed, take the tax deduction and say, "Thank you!" to your customers every chance you get.

INTERVIEW PREP
CHECKLIST

1.0 PREPARE FOR THE PERFECT INTERVIEW

1.1 ❑ Since most radio interviews are conducted by telephone, choose a quiet place in your home/office where you can speak freely and without interruptions. Lock the door if necessary and let others know that you are behind closed doors for an important call. Sit in your car or in your garage if needed. You get the idea.

1.2 ❑ Prepare interview questions, stories and talking points to cover the period of time that you expect to be interviewed. Interviews typically last 30-60-90 minutes.

1.3 ❑ Be prepared to answers any and all questions regarding your topic and know it well. Your responses should be concise yet fully informational because you only have a very short period of time to make your case.

1.4 ❑ If possible, obtain a toll-free number unless your website is the best way to contact you. People often remember names versus numbers so if you get a toll-free number, get one that spells something such as your name, your product or service in the number, for example, 1-888-GETMYBOOK. Go to TollFreeNumbers.com to check it out.

1.5. ❑ Is your website domain name easy to say, spell, remember? If you don't have a website

I f one of your goals as an expert in your field or showcase your book, product, service, website, etc., to build your brand and reputation, getting interviews is a clever public relations strategy. With more than 5,000+ high-level radio talk shows, 15,000+ online amateur talk shows, and 1,000+ TV news and talk shows, interviews have proven to reach enormous audiences.

Getting started, you need to identify your niche, find what media that customers in your niche consume, and get to know who the radio, TV, and podcast reporters are, which is why it's important to nail this checklist. Here are some steps:

yet, at least secure a domain name before your competition gets the same idea.

1.6. ❑ If you're being interviewed on a large radio or TV station, direct listeners and viewers to a website that first captures their eMail addresses. Then have an opt-in form ready to redirect them to where your book (or product) is sold. Capture the customers' names/eMail addresses and then push for a sale! Make a special offer such as a discount for buying more than one of your books. Instruct them to "Go to www.MyDomain.com to claim your FREE _____ when you buy my book at any retail store. Make sure you're on my list to qualify. If you don't enter to win, you won't qualify for the FREE gift."

1.7. ❑ Aim to be cordial, entertaining, informative, and respectful. Make sure that what you have to say is newsworthy and of genuine interest to your target market and don't be tempted to wander off topic.

2.0 HOW TO GET A RADIO INTERVIEW

2.1 ❑ Go to **www.Radio-Locator.com** to look up radio stations throughout the USA. This is helpful when looking for local radio stations as well. Ideally, it's best if you can secure a radio interview at the station. Be sure that you get pictures with them before you leave so you can post them on your website or press room.

2.2 ❑ You can search online for interview opportunities by using the keywords "be a radio guest" via Google. Search for online radio shows that cater to your business or topic. Also, go to **www.BlogTalkRadio.com** and other online radio station websites to locate specific stations that cater to your needs. I can recommend **www.LATalkRadio.com**. Their radio hosts are always looking for great guests. The number of opportunities you have for getting interviewed are virtually endless!

2.3 ❑ Learn the producer's name and/or others that work at the station or company you're trying to get an interview with. Look for links on their websites that might read, "Become A Guest" or similar. You could also call the station and ask, "Do you interview guest experts on your show?" Most will respond with a YES answer. Convincing them that you are a viable guest expert for theirs shows is the fun part. This is your chance to show your creativity and enthusiasm. Here are more tips.

2.4 ❑ If you can't give the station representative an overview of what you'd like to talk about, send a preview of the topic you wish to be interviewed for such as a new book, company, service, product, etc. This information could also be posted on your website or in your press room. A page on your website could be dedicated to convincing radio stations hosts and producers to book you for interviews. It has all the information they need in one place to make a quick decision. What you want to hear from them is, "Wow, this looks impressive. Yes, let's schedule a date/time to bring you into the station. Do you have your calendar handy?"

2.5 ❑ Provide the potential interview host/ producer with endorsements for your book from customers, clients, celebrities, experts, industry gurus, and anyone who is a fan of your work.

2.6 ❑ Provide endorsements from other talk show hosts that have interviewed you in the past and/ or links to their websites (and yours) where this information is posted. The more you have to offer, the more in demand you become. Start small, such as local stations, and continually build your reputation!

2.7 ❑ Depending on the method you use to send your material, include press releases, copies of your recent eZine/newsletter, flyer, postcard, one-sheet, articles published online/offline showcasing your profession and accomplishments. Ideally, this should be on a one-page on your website where you can refer interviewers to a specific link with all the information they require.

2.8 ❑ Don't forget to follow up 2-3 days after you send in your proposal for an interview and then follow up again if you don't get a response back within 10 days. Follow up with a phone call and/or eMail (or both) if you must leave a message. Another way to get their attention is to send a postcard with your book cover (for example) as a reminder that you are still interested in their station and speaking to their audience of listeners.

2.9 ❑ If you can't get in touch with the producer or show host, talk to and/or befriend a representative of the station. Send a gift (for me it's my world famous chocolate chip cookies), an autographed copy of your book, sample products you produce, etc. If you don't get the kind of response you're looking for immediately, don't give up. Keep the station updated on what's happening in your world, notifications of other interviews, a new product, etc.

3.0 WHAT TO DO BEFORE THE INTERVIEW

3.1 ❑ Listen to previously recorded/archived shows to get a feel for how a particular host interacts with guests. Also, pick up on talking points other guests or listeners or callers have made. You can bring them up in your interview if appropriate to make a stronger impact on the host and their audience. "I recall one of your previous guests talked about _____. That's an interesting point because _____. " Become the guest expert that get's invited back again and again!

3.2. ❑ Be sure that the station you are targeting has the best numbers to contact you and vice versa. Use caller I.D. to watch for their calls. Typically, a producer or staff member will contact you and connect you with the host of the show. Get that person's name and be sure that you thank (name) for patching you through.

3.3. ❑ What time of the day is the radio show? How long is the show? Be aware of varying time zones when soliciting numerous stations.

3.4. ❑ How long will your interview be? Practice interviewing for that length of time. Some interviews might be 15 minutes; 30 minutes or longer. Will you be prepared to speak for two hours? When participating in on a radio interview, it's live, obviously, and your big chance to make yourself known. Never go unprepared.

3.5. ❑ Get the host's direct eMail address at the station so you can send let the person know how much you are looking forward to the interview. Include any press material or sample of your work if possible. You'll want to send them a thank you note after the interview as well.

3.6. ❑ Research the host on the radio station's website. The more you know about your host for the show, the more comfortable you'll be speaking to him/her. Be aware of current events in their area/town/state if needed to present a power-packed, informative interview.

3.7 ❑ Does the host accept call-ins? This would be very good to know in advance so you're not caught off guard. You might want to prepare yourself with sample scenarios, case studies and more to respond to questions beyond what the host is prepared to answer about you.

3.8 ❑ Ask the producer what information you can freely give to your fans such as your website, toll free number or other number, eMail address, etc. Confirmation on the small things goes a long way when it comes to building rapport with the gatekeeper of the show you're going to be a guest on.

3.9 ❑ Suggest to the host that you will give away something (i.e., product, book, audio program) to 1-3 lucky winners before, during, and/or at the end of the show. Be sure to get the winner's full name, eMail address, mailing address and phone number. Then, personally autograph what you're sending and include a note that explains, "Congratulations on winning _____ on as announced on the _____ radio show last week." You can include a mini-catalog or one-sheet of your other products/services when you mail out the prizes. Include several business cards distribution. This is a great opportunity to network.

3.10 ❑ Ask the radio host if you could provide the show with a pre-recorded mini-commercial to promote your upcoming interview. You can record this on your computer, then save it to an MP3 and eMail it to the show as an attachment for their use. For example, you might record something like, "Hi, this is Bart Smith, author of *LAWS OF THE BEDROOM*. If you'd like to learn more about (topic), tune in to the (name radio show and station, date plus date and time). Join in on the conversation!"

Ask the producer of the show if this is feasible. They might have the perfect script prepared for you.

3.11 ❑ Does the TV or radio station have any relationships with bookstores or other entities suitable for your product? If you are promoting a new book, your local bookstores might be interested in a book signing at their locations knowing that you are scheduled for a TV or radio interview. Your interview could promote more business by driving more customers to their. Remember to video record and/or take photos of your book signing events.

3.12 ❑ Is there anything any topic that might be off limits (by you or the station) for your interview? Don't be caught unaware and say something you'll regret or will ruin your chances of future interview gigs.

4.0 RECORDING INTERVIEWS

4.1 ❑ If your interview is recorded, ask for a copy. Ask for permission to use it to promote your business online and offline. If your interview is recorded and the station is unwilling or unable (for any reason) to give you a copy, direct your audience to the station's website. If you obtain a recorded copy of the interview, post it on your website.

4.2 ❑ Post all your recorded interviews in your press room afterwards so future hosts and producers can go to that page and listen to how you interview. Your interview could potentially inspire other stations to pick you up. If all else fails, recreate the interview using another interviewer utilizing the same questions and content discussed on the show. This is a great way to bring home the powerful message you delivered on the show that you can now use with full copyright privileges.

4.3 ❑ Does the host of the show where you'll be interviewed blog? Consider asking them to blog about your upcoming interview. This will give you the chance to create a back link to your website and share valuable information with your readership. Be your own reporter. After the interview, discuss the outcome of the show on your blog. By having reciprocal links with the show, you both stand to gain in traffic and appeal. It's a powerful link activity.

5.0 MEDIA INTERVIEWS TECHNIQUES

5.1 ❑ Not all interviewers are experts on the topics they cover, which is why they rely on experts for facts and commentary. Depending on the media you choose to interview with, learn the names of the producer, host, former guests, previous show titles, staff members and more. No two interviews will ever be the same so your goal in an interview is to get your message across.

5.2 ❑ Know the radio station call letters (i.e., KFIZ, KQV, WDAY, KWAM, WOC, WBBZ, etc.) as needed.

5.3 ❑ Know the frequency of the stations (i.e., Newstalk 1290, 1065 AM, 95.5 FM, etc.).

5.4 ❑ Know contact numbers such as main office, direct or emergency contact telephone number in case you get bumped off of a call. This happened to me once. I was on an interview with a radio station and I was accidentally dropped. Luckily, I had the station's phone number handy and

called back immediately. I didn't want to rely on them to call me back. As there were several other guest experts on the call, I took matters into my own hands and was immediately reconnected within a couple of minutes.

5.5 ❑ Who is hosting the show and do they have any co-hosts? Be certain that you can pronounce their names properly. If you're uncertain, ask and don't wing it. Be certain you have the correct spelling for written communications. You might write the name on piece of paper and glance at it periodically to ensure you don't make any mistakes. This goes for any other information you might need to refer to. Consider creating a one-sheet with all you need to know ready at your fingertips.

5.6 ❑ While conducting a radio interview, feel free to take notes about a topic/question you want to respond to. When you and your host have finished with your talking points, look at your notes for any last detail you wanted to bring up. Make every effort to keep the interview smooth and free-flowing to avoid sounding confused or unorganized.

5.7 ❑ PREPARE for the interview days in advance of the interview. This is a case where practice makes perfect. Research the station and demographics of the show. Know who their listeners are such as gender, age group, etc. and tailor your interview toward that audience; good for you and good for the show.

5.8 ❑ Secure the date of the interview and put in on your online/offline calendars and schedule time to practice and prepare for your interview.

6.0 WHAT TO SEND PRIOR TO THE INTERVIEW

6.1 ❑ After you ask which method of communication the host and/or producer prefers such as telephone, eMail and/or regular postal mail prior to the interview taking place, send a letter to confirm that you know when the interview will take place, the time, and the subject nature of the interview and how much you're looking forward to it. Include benefits for

---

their listening audience and propose a plan to promote your interview on their show.

6.2 ❏ Provide a biography including your accomplishments. Send a short biography that the host can read on the air and a more detailed one so the host can learn more about you. Even though the show can access this information on your site, send either an electronic copy or a hard copy so you know they have it.

6.3 ❏ Include your website and specific page links to where you archive information for your press room and/or media purposes. Provide specific page links to your biography, samplings of previous interviews, press releases, etc. Make it easy to find, for example, http://YourSite.com/press room or /press kit … etc.

6.4 ❏ Send an eMail the day before the interview to acknowledge that you are enthusiastically anticipating the opportunity to interview the show. This can reassure them that you're on top of things and you haven't forgotten about the interview that was booked possibly a month ago. Include a link to your website where you are currently promoting the upcoming interview and the respective RV/radio station. If you record this information on your website, the station might want to listen in.

6.5 ❏ Send multiple (autographed) copies of your book, not just one. Ask if they'd like a couple to be sent. The wholesale cost of your book multiplied by 2-5 books is nothing compared to the value of exposure and notoriety you're going to get when you get interviewed on their show. Most hosts will read them or either skip through them before, or even during the show! Also expect the host not to know too much about your book. Don't make

them look bad in front of their listeners, but help them do their job well!

6.6 ❏ Send 10-20 suggested questions to the host, with suggested answers, which you'd like to be asked. Some hosts will ask the questions you provide them verbatim. Others will creatively tweak your questions, or come up with their own. Don't be shocked or offended, but prepared if they don't ask any of your questions but come up with their own. The answers help the host craft even more questions or topics for discussion.

6.7 ❏ Send the host/producer one-sheet with your full name, contact information and a brief description of your book/product/service and how the audience can obtain what you offer. I suggest you print the 8 ½ x 11 sheet using 16 font size for easy reading so the host can refer to it while speaking live.

6.8 ❏ Have the answers to questions and page numbers (if referencing your new book). Don't be caught off guard not knowing your topic or how to answer a question. If possible, ask for a set of questions that the host will be asking so you can prepare in advance of the interview so it goes smoothly.

6.9 ❏ If you are invited to the studio or station where the interview will be conducted, take extra copies of your book or samples of your product. Dress appropriately for the occasion, and be prepared to ask for photographs with the host, producer and staff. If your interview is scheduled for live television, ask for tips on what to wear and what colors work best for TV viewers. Take pictures with your cell phone of the name of the studio inside/outside of the building for display on your website. If don't get a recording of the show, you at least have photos to share with your audience!

6.10 ❑ Mention the station's call letters during the show whenever you get the chance. It helps the host remind listeners of the show's brand. You might say, "Thank you, (Host Name), for having me on your show here on NewsTalk 1290." Mention the host by name throughout the interview. It's all about exposure and branding and reciprocal promotions help you both particularly when you have such a broad reach of listeners unique to radio's listening audience.

6.11 ❑ If your book is not ready for release, especially by the time of your interview, direct everyone to a name squeeze page where you collect their names and eMail addresses. Start building your list before the book is available. Picture offering 1-10 winners a chance to win a FREE copy of your book or product! The cost for shipping a few FREE books/products pales to 500 people who sign up to buy having viewed or heard you on a TV/radio station interview.

7.0 PLUGGING YOUR OWN BOOK, PRODUCT, SERVICE, AND/OR WEBSITE

If you sense that the host is not promoting your book/product enough, then take advantage of the opportunity to plug it yourself, professionally, but with gusto. How often?

a) ❑ Once in the BEGINNING

b) ❑ Once in the MIDDLE

c) ❑ Several times THROUGHOUT (especially if it's a 45+ minute interview)

d) ❑ Once at the END

8.0 WHAT TO DO AFTER THE INTERVIEW

8.1 ❑ Be prepared to send post cards designed with your book cover on one side and an area on the other side to write a thank you message to everyone that helped you through the interview process. This goes for any product or service you may be promoting.

8.2 ❑ If you haven't already done this, be sure to contact the station to ask if you can eMail or fax one sheet containing all your contact information related to how listeners can reach you and/or buy your book/product/service. Since the receptionist is usually the only person a viewer or listener can reach, it's best to leave the information with the receptionist first and then ask to pass it along to other staff who might interact with listeners who call in. This one sheet should contain your full name, company name, telephone number, website, eMail address, book title (if selling a book) or product/service details. A one page website works for this.

8.3 ❑ If you had a good experience at the radio/TV station, recommend others to contact them to inquire about interviewing opportunities. Suggest they use your name as a referral. "My friend/associate was just interviewed by you, and I was wondering how I might get interviewed. My expertise is on _____." When sending your thank you letter, you could include names and contact information for those that you recommend. This is another way to network with people.

8.4 ❑ Within the following 24-48 hours, ask for a testimonial while the information is fresh. Also ask the host or producer for approval to post any testimonial or endorsement on your website or to use it in any marketing promotion: "(Your Name) was a superb guest on my show, (ENTER TITLE). I would definitely interview them again and I recommend others do the same." For your next interview, check out the **www.InterviewGuestsDirectory.com** for a wealth of interview possibilities via talk shows, radio, TV, podcasts, articles, blogs and more.

INTERVIEW TACTICS

HOW TO SURVIVE The Media Without Getting Clobbered

THE INSIDER'S GUIDE TIPS FOR GIVING A KILLER INTERVIEW

I mprove your interview skills by reading a book (I helped design and print) on how to deliver killer interviews by my good friend, Gayl Murphy. Gayl has been a Hollywood Correspondent for the past 30 years and has conducted over 15,000 interviews. Her motto? **"You gotta tell it, to sell it!"** Check out her book and FREE REPORT on interviewing at:

"YOU GOTTA TELL IT TO SELL IT" ★ GAYL MURPHY

INTERVIEW TACTICS

www.InterviewTactics.com

HOW TO SURVIVE The MEDIA Without Getting Clobbered!

THE INSIDER'S GUIDE TO GIVING A KILLER INTERVIEW

GAYL MURPHY, HOLLYWOOD CORRESPONDENT

Featuring The "14 LOST CHAPTERS" of Interview Tactics!

www.InterviewTactics.com

JOINT VENTURE
CHECKLIST

The (JV) Joint Venture process is a great way to build your lists of prospects, clients and affiliates; sell more product/services; make money; even build expert/celebrity status merely by associating yourself with those who are (already) experts and celebrities in their own niche industry and develop lasting business relationships!

When it comes to joint ventures and partnerships, here are a few things to remember! The following checklist should help you to identify some of the main factors to remember when it comes to looking for, evaluating and finding the right partner(s) for your joint venture project!

1. ❑ Determine WHY should you enter a JV?

2. ❑ HOW LONG will your JV run?

3. ❑ WHO is an ideal joint JV?

4. ❑ Specifically, WHAT would you like to create/sell with a joint JV?

5. ❑ WHOSE client/customer list will you use to promote a product/service/offer?

6. ❑ How will you DISTRIBUTE PROFITS from your JV promotional efforts?

7. ❑ How will you TRACK EXPENDITURES and INCOME from your JV project?

8. ❑ What should you LOOK FOR in a quality JV partner? Check this out in detail.

9. ❑ What can a potential JV partner EXPECT from you YOU?

10. ❑ What kind of SERVICES do you need to support your JV opportunity?

11. ❑ What are some of the PROS and CONS for joint venturing with others?

12. ❑ WHERE do you find potential JV affiliates?

13. ❑ How do you APPROACH a potential JV partner; getting started?

14. ❑ What are the STEPS AFTER a JV project is finalized? What do?

Visit MyTrainingCenter.com for more information regarding each one of these JV checklist items above. You'll be glad you did!

KINDLE PUBLISHING

CHECKLIST

amazonkindle

Publishing your work through Kindle is a great way to promote what you do, expand your brand, make money and much more. Traditional publishing royalties average about 15-20% while publishing on Kindle can generate as much as a 70% royalty.

Do you have any articles or books you can publish on Kindle? This is my quick checklist on the WHY you should publish with Kindle, WHAT kinds of things you can publish, and HOW to do it. Let's get started!

WHY PUBLISH ON KINDLE?

For your information, as of January 2015:

- ☑ Amazon.com estimates 245 MILLION active users.
- ☑ About 25% of U.S. adults are e-book users.
- ☑ Three in every ten U.S. adults read ebooks.
- ☑ eBook recommendations from friends and colleagues are often delivered online via social networks. Are you on the social networks? Is your eBook mentioned there? It should be.
- ☑ The Kindle stores has nearly 800,000 books for

sale. The average brick and mortar stores carry about 150,000 books.

- ☑ There are more than 30 Million Kindle eReaders currently in use.
- ☑ Estimates show Amazon might be earning between $265 million to $530 million per year from eBook sales alone.
- ☑ Amazon net sales for 2014: $88.99 billion.

Kindle offers a couple of lucrative promotions for publishers such as Countdown Deals (time-bound promotional discounting for your book while earning royalties) or scheduled Free Book Promotion where readers worldwide can get your book FREE for a limited time.

WHAT PUBLISHES ON KINDLE?

Here are some ideas that you could be working on so you, too, can publish on Kindle:

1. ❏ Collections of articles you've written, etc. (This checklist book is a good example.)
2. ❏ Your books, home-study courses, etc.
3. ❏ HOW TO or WHAT TO training materials, etc.
4. ❏ Transcriptions of speeches, interviews, videos, etc.

---

5. ❑ Short stories, fiction, novels, special reports, etc.

HOW TO PUBLISH ON KINDLE

1. ❑ **Create a Kindle account at KDP.Amazon.com** to upload your eBooks for sale or FREE. Royalties are paid via this account.

2. ❑ **Design front and back covers.** The back cover can be placed inside the eBook on the last page. The front cover must be less than 50MB, 72 dots per inch (dpi), RGB color mode (not CMYK), a minimum of 625 pixels on the shortest side and 1000 pixels on the longest side. For best quality, the front cover should be 2500 pixels on the longest side. Back cover images need not meet these specifications.

3. ❑ **Write your eBook using Microsoft Word.** Use Times Roman text, font size 12. Don't use strange fonts or excessive headers. Keep it simple. Save your Word (.doc) file as "Web Page-filtered" or "HTML-filtered" if prompted.

4. ❑ **Every section, chapter, and image** needs to be on its own page (CTRL+ENTER command).

5. ❑ **If you use images in your eBook document**, they should each be on a page. DO NOT submit PG, GIF, PNG or BMP image formats or images greater than 5MB each.

6. ❑ **The first page is your title page.** Sub-title and author's name are optional.

7. ❑ **The second page is your copyright statement** and should link to your website.

8. ❑ **The third page could contain a table of contents** or other message from you such as a link/offer to opt-in to your eMail list.

9. ❑ **DO NOT use tables.** They WILL NOT convert. Be cautious using tabs. If you must use tables of data in your text, create screenshots before transporting them into your eBook file.

10. ❑ **The last page(s) could include** your biography, special offers, upsells, other books you've written, products/services for sale, etc.

11. ❑ **You CAN link words, images, and phrases to websites** you want to direct readers to. Highlight the word or phrase, click CTRL+K and enter the full URL starting with http://.

12. ❑ **Bookmark your table of contents** to link to a specific chapter, page or section.

13. ❑ **Once you've proofed your document, upload it to your Kindle account.** Add a new title for this new submission and follow the prompts to submit your eBook.

14. ❑ **Save your new title as a draft so you can stop and finish it later.** On the second page of your eBook, note the selling price and the royalty rates you expect to earn.

15. ❑ **You can make changes** and re-upload your manuscript or cover or both anytime even after publication. For more on eBook publishing, go to www.MyTrainingCenter.com.

OTHER E-BOOK PUBLISHERS

Once you've published your content on Kindle, submit your Word .doc to other eBook publishers such as SmashWords.com. Here's why.

☑ **SmashWords distributes globally (**Apple iBooks (51 countries), Barnes & Noble, Kobo, OverDrive (20,000+ public libraries), Flipkart Oyster, Scribd, Baker & Taylor, Page Foundry, etc.

☑ **You earn 60% of list price** from major eBook retailers and **85% net from Smashwords.com.**

☑ **The will push preorder books** to Apple, Barnes & Noble and Kobo! Accumulated sales during this period can influence your book's posting on bestseller lists.

☑ **FREE ISBNs** or use your own. **FREE ebook conversion** to multiple formats from Word/.doc.

☑ **FREE unlimited anytime-updates** to books and metadata ... and much more.

You can publish your eBook on all of the online publishing sites for added revenue and why not?

LANDING PAGE
CHECKLIST

A landing page, also known as a name squeeze page or online sales letter serves several purposes. If you choose to build a landing page, for whatever reason, here are a few quick checklist items you might want to review before jumping into a project.

1.0 ☐ What kind of landing page do you need to build and why?

1.1 ☐ Name Squeeze Page: This collects the name and eMail address of potential customers only provided you're just building a list. Maybe you have a book or website coming soon and you just need to build your list of clients/customers or prospects. Then a name squeeze page is probably right for you.

1.2 ☐ Event Registration Page: This is designed to promote an event, such as a webinar, tele-seminar, etc. Landing pages often serve as registration pages for events, whether free or paid attendance.

1.3 ☐ Product/Service Sales Letter: This is great for selling a product/service. Another use for landing pages is to concentrate on selling one product/service. With no distractions, you can focus the prospects attention to reading your sales letter and making a decision on the spot to either buy or opt-in to your list for some freebies. Hopefully, you can sell the person later after a few frequent eMail blasts to him/her explaining the benefits of your product/service.

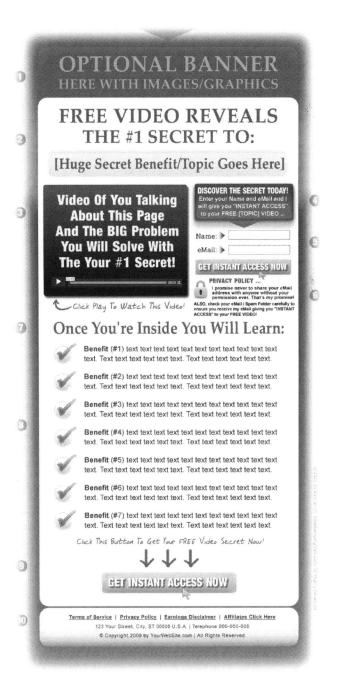

1.4 ❏ Video Message: Perhaps you have a message to get out that would be better served via video. Make a landing page that has that video only. Of course, you'll want other items on the page such as call-to-action buttons, opt-in form, etc.

2.0 ❏ Will it have a separate domain name or just a landing page on your website?

2.1 ❏ Independent Domain Name: If you're selling something or advocating a "coming soon" website announcement, register a domain name for the sole purpose of building a specific landing page.

2.2 ❏ Landing Page from Website: If you're just promoting an event or asking your list to register for something, why not build a landing page from your website? It would simply be a standard page added to your website.

3.0 ❏ Whatever you post on your landing page, it should address a need, solve a problem, and/or provide information.

3.1 ❏ Text: Typically, a landing page has text, banners, headers, bullets, lists of benefits, calls-to-action, a compelling story or two, buttons, etc. that instruct the visitor to your website and/or landing page with direction on what to do and how to use the page.

3.2 ❏ Images: Some say that images detract from content while text brings the visitor to your site closer to making a buying decision. My suggestion is to limit the number of images. One is perfect as long as it represents what you are attempting to sell.

3.2 ❏ Audio: Text is good, but an audio message to better. Research tells us that almost every visitor in the online world would prefer to listen and versus read. If you are questioning whether you have the skill for this, there are services that charge reasonable fees for their work. Don't be left out of this highly popular market.

3.3 ❏ Video: Video is always a plus for whatever you want to promote, sell or to explain the benefits to prospects that are considering your opt-in list. "A picture is worth a thousand words." tells a story; conveys information without having to read and gives the visitor the bonus of listening as well.

3.4 ❏ Testimonials: If you are attempting to sell, promote, influence a group of the integrity and quality of your goods or services, there's no better endorsement than testimonials from others that have experience with what you offer and are more than satisfied. Include testimonials on your landing page taking advantage of written, audio and/or video formats.

3.5 ❏ Case Studies: These studies are a great way to add value to your product/services. Who doesn't like to hear a good story, especially one with a happy ending where the customer is breathes life into what you're selling/promoting. Proven case studies can be very convincing.

3.6 ❏ Opt-in Form: This is mandatory in my book. It's good business to have some kind of name/ eMail opt-in form to capture leads in the event you're visiting prospects isn't ready to buy. And, then, if you're promoting an event, and you expect people to register, you'll need an opt-in form for that reason alone.

3.7 ❏ Terms & Policy Links: If you're selling something or need to provide links to terms pages such as Terms Of Use, Privacy Policy, Earnings Disclaimer, and/or Affiliate Commission Disclosure, then you might include this link in with your web design. I also recommend that you have a Contact Us or Affiliate Program link on your landing page.

4.0 ❏ How will you build it? Your options will depend on how you answer this question: How did you build your website?

4.1 ❏ HTML Website: If your website is built solely on html coding, then you can simply build a single page to serve as your landing page using HTML. It's not highly recommended, but it can be done. Why not? It might not be responsive, unless you build it to be responsive using Dreamweaver or use special coding software. Most people don't have strictly HTML websites anymore. If you do, you may wish to have your site updated so you can take advantage of all the bells and whistles available with other software.

4.2 ❏ Wordpress Site: The majority of websites are built using WordPress so we'll focus on building landing pages via WordPress.

4.3 ❏ Themes: Some WordPress themes are specifically designed for build landing pages. Some themes even come with a page template that removes the header and footer on the specific page you're working on. That's also good. If your theme doesn't do either one, you'll want to register a domain name for your landing page or consider buying a theme that is landing page design specific. Check out the links below to find these types of themes:

A. Landing Page Templates at ThemeForest.net | http://themeforest.net/category/marketing/landing-pages

B. WordPress Landing Page Templates at ThemeForest.net | http://goo.gl/KcJO5k

4.4 ❏ LeadPages.com: For a monthly fee (or annually) you can build beautiful landing pages that either stand alone on your server or you can insert them into your WordPress website with their custom WordPress plugin.

4.5 ❏ OptimizePress.com: For a one-time fee of roughly $97, you can purchase this WordPress plugin to build all types of landing pages for any purpose within your WordPress website.

4.6 ❏ InstaBuilder.com: For a small one-time fee of roughly $47, you can purchase this WordPress plugin to help you build landing pages within your WordPress website as well.

4.7 ❏ http://mytrainingcenter.com/learn/landing-page-plugins-for-wordpress/

When choosing which option is best for you, simply compare costs, features, layout designs and ease-of-use, when it comes to (1) going with a theme-based landing page template, (2) a WordPress plugin or (3) self-hosting landing page service elsewhere and not from your WordPress website.

When looking at FREE WordPress landing page plugins, I will caution you. Look at the ratings for each plugin and read the reviews for each of them. You might learn more about a particular plugin from someone else's experience. Read both positive and negative reviews. If you see a plugin that has a 50/50 positive/negative review, think twice about using it. Even an 80/20 might not be worth the risk of your time and trouble.

5.0 ❏ Who will build it and how can you make changes?

5.1 ❏ YOU: If you select an easy-to-use theme or plugin. You can probably build your landing page. It would benefit you to learn how to build landing pages and then you could easily make changes as

---

needed.

5.2 ❏ Hire Someone: If you decide to hire someone to build your landing page, be aware of the high turnover among technical designers and that their fees never go down. Sometimes, they ride off into the sunset never to leave forwarding contact information. So what are you to do? Get a good referral or check out www.Fiverr.com to find the best landing page designer for your dollars.

6.0 ❏ There are several ways to build a landing page. Here are the basics:

6.1 ❏ Promote your landing page to your own list of prospects, customers and affiliates.

6.2 ❏ Have others promote it to their lists. This can be done in two unique ways:

A. Create your own affiliate program and have them promote it.

B. Rely on affiliate networks, such as JVZoo.com and ClickBank.com and their built-in affiliate network of people who can promote your product to others with their marketing techniques.

6.3 ❏ Pay to advertise your landing page across websites and on search engines to help drive traffic to it.

6.4 ❏ Optimize the landing page for the search engines. Use search engines to pick up natural, organic traffic from people searching for what you offer such as products/services via your name squeeze page. There are even more ways to generate traffic. It depends on the purpose for your landing page.

LINKEDIN.COM
CHECKLIST

Linkedin.com is mentioned first, because it stands to be where over 300 million professionals are. Depending on your niche, LinkedIn just might be a hotbed of potential coaching clients for you. That said, here are five great LinkedIn tips for you.

CHECKLIST

❑ **Take the time to complete your LinkedIn profile page,** if it's not done already. We all have new accomplishments, experiences, credentials that we can update. Go and do if you need to.

❑ **Turn your company/profile page into a lead generation page.** Don't bore them with who you are, but what you have done for others with a pain/problem/passion they might be experiencing too. This can be done in the header image (think of the flyer and/or business card designs you learned about in this chapter), as well as in the company description area. Specifically, focus on the first 2 lines/sentences. Grab their attention and the rest will tell them what you can do for them.

❑ **Join a group for coaches**, where you might share coaching experiences among group members for growth purposes as a coach.

❑ **Form a group for your clients and coaching niche**. Invite LinkedIn members to join, ask/answer questions, and engage in discussions that lead folks to your self-assessments, quizzes and questionnaires. Ah, the sound of coaching sessions and clients are on the horizon!

❑ **Join groups that cater to your coaching niche,** and where you can be seen/heard as an expert answering questions.

❑ **Build up your network of connections.** Focus on having a quality network, while expanding your connections beyond.

❑ **Endorse and get endorsed!** List all your skills so people can endorse you. Endorse them, so that the madness goes back and forth until it looks as if LinkedIn has practically endorsed you!

Many of **MY CHECKLISTS** have video tutorials that teach you more at www.**MyTrainingCenter**.com.   **139**

❑ **Post a link to an article, webinar or training you just gave** not just on your page, but within the groups you circulate in pronto. Do this once/twice a week and watch the results fly your way.

MEMBER HOME PAGE
CHECKLIST

If you have a membership website, here's a checklist of items, links and options you might want to put on your home page so your members can get the most out of your site.

1.0 ☐ Create a video welcome message and/or video tour on your home page. Take members on a navigational tour so they know where and how to find valuable information and what they're looking for.

2.0 ☐ Tutorial/content spotlights can showcase some of your new training content that you want members to check out as soon as they log in.

3.0 ☐ Provide link(s) to access the other/regular member protected content they paid to access.

4.0 ☐ Make it easy for members to edit their Member Profiles.

5.0 ☐ Link to modify/update their payment information if that's an option with the membership software you used to build your membership website.

6.0 ☐ Provide a link to cancel a membership.

7.0 ☐ A link to join your Affiliate Program so they can promote your membership website will be profitable for both of you.

8.0 ☐ Include testimonials from other paid members

MEMBER TRAINING AREAS

- Online Training Courses
- Checklists For Everything
- Expert Training Guides
- Resource Links
- eStore / Get CD-Roms
- Live Training Programs
- Mentorship Opportunities
- Affiliate Program
- Site Map

MEMBER SUPPORT AREAS

- Member's Area Tour
- Make The Most Out Of Your Membership
- News, Updates & Events
- Help & Support
- My Account Profile
- About MyTrainingCenter
- Ask Bart A Question
- Feedback/Comments
- Contact Me

Personal Message From The Founder

Personal Message From The Founder

Once again, I would just like to take a moment and thank you for becoming a valuable Member of MyTrainingCenter.com. There is a lot to learn behind these walls.

As one might guess, I literally have spent years accumulating the experience, knowledge, expertise, written materials for lessons, on-going preparation and refinement for each audio and video tutorial you will be viewing inside the Center this month and in many months and years ahead!

This has been a life-long journey for me, as you can tell; and well, I just hope you'll join me as we continue to walk down the road of continued education and improving our computer, business, personal and professional skills to earn the kind of living we deserve for ourselves and those we care about, and for some, those who depend on us!

NEW CLASS ANNOUNCEMENTS: MyTrainingCenter.com is in the beginning stages of growth and expansion, which means during this time, some classes and their video counterparts, might not be available yet. But, throughout these early stages of growth, they will be released as they complete their final review. If you have any questions about any tutorial, please feel free to contact me, I would be glad to hear from you.

On a final note, I trust you will take the time to really go through the entire web site of MyTrainingCenter.com. Perhaps not in one sitting, that might be impossible. But, do take as long as you want. Again, there is so much to learn. I'm sure you will be amazed at what's inside, and still what's to come!

'Til we meet or speak to each other one on one at a live event, do enjoy your Membership. MyTrainingCenter.com, this web site and all its content was built for you...

attesting how great your membership website is.

9.0 ❏ Have a member spotlight to demonstrate how some members are benefiting from your membership website.

10. ❏ Link to Help & Support or a FAQ (frequently asked questions) page.

11. ❏ Link to your Contact Us page so members can get their questions answered.

MEMBER WEBSITE
CHECKLIST

Creating, designing and marketing your own membership website is easy provided you have my checklist to go by. For example, what software will you use to design your membership website? How will you design it? How will you get paid by subscribing members? All of these questions and more are answered in my Membership Site Checklist.

1.0 ❏ What is the purpose for building this particular membership website? You can always build more than one, but for your first one, what will it be about?

First, decide why you want to build a membership website. You could have a website for just about anything, but it's best to specify reasons why because there are different membership websites for different products, books, themes, services, needs and purposes.

❏ Product-related (protected content) membership website ...
❏ Training-related membership website ...
❏ Book/eBook protected membership site ...
❏ Audio content protected membership site ...
❏ Video content protected membership site ...
❏ Customer/client support membership site ...
❏ _____ membership site ...

2.0 ❏ Who will design your membership site?

❏ I will design my membership website ...
❏ I will hire someone to build my membership website and manage it entirely ...
❏ I will hire someone to build my membership website, but will learn to maintain it myself ...

3.0 ❏ What software will you use to build your membership website?

❏ MemberMouse.com (WordPress Plugin)
❏ S2Member.com (WordPress Plugin)
❏ MemberPress.com Size (WordPress Plugin)
❏ Other Software: _____

4.0 ❏ What type of membership levels will you create and what will they be able to access?

❏ Silver, Gold, Platinum, etc.
❏ Member Cap/Limit Per Month ...
❏ Other: _____

5.0 ❏ Membership Duration: How long will each membership package run?

❏ 1-Day, 3-Day, 7-Day Sample Memberships

- ❏ 30-Day, 60-Day, 90-Day Memberships
- ❏ 6-Month, 1-Year Memberships
- ❏ Lifetime Membership

5.1 ❏ Pricing Structure

- ❏ **One-time payments** are good for assessing a specified period of time and eliminates member cancellations and it's hassle-free.

- ❏ **Recurring payments** to maintain continued cover a specified period of time, but generates monthly income for you. Subscribers have the option to cancel their or manage their own memberships.

5.2 ❏ Payment Processing/Collection (i.e., How will you charge members and collect their payments?)

- ❏ Authorize.net
- ❏ ClickBank.com
- ❏ PayPal.com
- ❏ Stripe.com

6.0 ❏ How will you design your member site?

Membership websites invariably follow similarities in design theme, straight forward, very clean, easy login/ logout, etc. One of the major differences you'll find in membership sites regarding design is how much time and money the owner and designer invest in the site. Have you reviewed sample membership websites? Join a few and look at them closely. If you like what you see, consider adapting those ideas and fuse them into your site. There are some great looking, high functioning sites on the Internet. Consider studying other member sites and their:

- ❏ Guest-level (public access) web pages.
- ❏ Member home page design and layout.
- ❏ Member-level (private/member) pages.
- ❏ Membership cancellation page/procedures.
- ❏ Navigation between public and member pages.
- ❏ Login/Logout pages.

7.0 How will you promote your membership website when it's all done?

- ❏ Affiliate program ...
- ❏ Pay per click ads ...

- ❏ Podcasting ...
- ❏ Video infomercials ...
- ❏ Interviews ...
- ❏ Webinars ...
- ❏ Tele-Seminars ...
- ❏ Write/promote books/eBooks ...
- ❏ Free and viral marketing tactics...
- ❏ Other marketing tactics ...

8.0 ❏ What will you do to update your membership website to continually add value for members to stay and new ones to join!

- ❏ New articles ...
- ❏ New downloadable files ...
- ❏ New training programs ...
- ❏ New audio recordings ...
- ❏ New video recordings ...
- ❏ Other? _____ ...

9.0 ❏ What are all the ways you could monetize your membership website to make money?

- ❏ Sell membership access, of course ...
- ❏ Sell products ...
- ❏ Sell consulting/coaching services ...
- ❏ Sell virtual classes/continuity programs ...
- ❏ Sell seminars and workshops ...
- ❏ Sell other people's products and services ...
- ❏ Sell access to other membership websites ...

10.0 ❏ What will your next membership website be about?

Now that you've built your first membership website, where do you go from here? You might build another website for another product/service or with the acquired talent and skills, you could build a site for someone else. My next membership website will be about: _____

_____

Future membership website ideas are:

_____

_____

MY NETWORKING CHECKLIST

When it comes to networking with others, especially in person, here are a number of things to bear in mind, take with you, prepare for, say/not say, and take advantage of any opportunity network.

1. ❑ **Target Market** ... Know who you're networking with. Don't network just to get out of the house/office and socialize. Research the event in advance so your chances of securing a lead, client or sale are increased.

2. ❑ **Goals** ... What are your GOALS for the networking event? You should clearly know what your objectives are so you don't waste time or money. What do you hope to walk away with after event? When you know what your goals are, prepare and plan to get the most out of the networking activity.

3. ❑ **Resources** ... In order to be effective at networking, you must have a number of resources that you and other can SHARE to make money, alliances / acquaintances and more! With your tools and resources in place, you'll network much more effectively.

4. ❑ **Preparation** ... Research and rehearse your networking style. Research the companies that you'll meet with and then practice your opening remarks for what you can bring to the event. Plan ahead and find out the appropriate attire for this event.

5. ❑ **Be prepared to sell.** You might have an opportunity to sell product while networking. Rather that refer prospects to your website and risk the chance of losing a sale, always be prepared to sell. Create an easy to complete order form that people can generate on the spot. Have a mobile credit card processor handy (such as SquareUp.com or PayPal.com) so you can quickly ring up the sale.

Many of **MY CHECKLISTS** have video tutorials that teach you more at www.**MyTrainingCenter.com**.

6. ❑ Bring your tablet, laptop, or phone to show people your website or showcase what you sell or service to impress prospects and buyers.

7. ❑ Presence ... How you LOOK, walk, stand, speak, and hold your hands, posture, etc. can all work in your favor. A person will make an assessment about you within the first 30-seconds of meeting you so first impressions do all the difference when networking with people for the very first time. What they say about you after you're gone means more to your success than what they say in your presence. You want to make a killer presentation.

8. ❑ Conversation ... Network with the idea that you're not going to do all the talking, but rather you want to listen to what others are saying and what you can learn. In this way, you can hone in on those that appear to be good prospects and/or need for your products/services. Don't waste time trying to sell to someone who doesn't express any interest.

A networking event is not the place for hard sells.

9. ❑ Actions ... What you DO BEFORE, DURING and AFTER the networking event is very important and noticeable by others. How should you behave? What about etiquette, manners, gestures and mannerisms? Pay attention, observe, listen and learn.

10. ❑ Future Growth ... After the networking event has ended, how will you NURTURE your prospects to further grow your business in the months ahead? Here are a few keep in touch strategies to help you so you can follow-up and reach out to prospects on a regular basis.

- Prioritize your business cards!
- Organize your business cards!
- Follow-up immediately!
- When following up, you have choices!
- Stay In Touch – Always!
- Out Of Sight – Out Of Mind!

My Networking Tactics is also available in AUDIO format. Learn more about my personal networking tactics as you listen to me read the book to you in audio format. Learn how you can gain access to the audio earn more at:

www.MyNetworkingTactics.com

OPT-IN WEB FORM
CHECKLIST

CLAIM YOUR FREE
GIFT & GET MY EZINE
FILLED WITH TIPS
STRAIGHT TO YOUR INBOX!

ENTER NAME

ENTER EMAIL

CLAIM YOUR FREEBIES

WE RESPECT YOUR PRIVACY

Opt-in forms generally placed on a website to capture the name and eMail of prospects and potential customers. Give viewers a reason to opt-in to whatever you're promoting or selling. Make the benefits for opting in crystal clear. Most services have easy to use opt-in form templates and offer FREE 30-day trials. Your opt-in form should be highly visible and near the top of the page on your website. When creating and using opt-in forms, here are some more valuable tips to get your started:

1. ❏ **Why do you need an opt-in form?**

   ❏ People can subscribe to Newsletter
   ❏ People can sign-up for FREE e-Course
   ❏ Build lists to solicit business
   ❏ Solicit affiliates via pre-application
   ❏ Surveys and questionnaires

2. ❏ **What software will you use to build your opt-in form?**

   ❏ Aweber.com
   ❏ GetResponse.com
   ❏ MailChimp.com
   ❏ Other: _____

3. ❏ **What autoresponder will you link it to?**

   ❏ Every opt-in form could/should be assigned to its own autoresponder.
   ❏ Newsletter autoresponder
   ❏ Free e-Course autoresponder
   ❏ Announcement autoresponder
   ❏ Affiliate Pre-Application autoresponder
   ❏ Survey/questionnaire autoresponder

4. ❏ **Where will you put your opt-in form?**

   ❏ Header of your website.
   ❏ Hooter of your website
   ❏ Hidebar
   ❏ Above every post/article
   ❏ Below every post/article
   ❏ In a popup window

5. ❏ **Did you test the opt-in form?**

   ❏ Do this before your website goes live.
   ❏ Proof any autoresponder type letters going out.
   ❏ Fix any problems and test again.

Do you want more (benefit)?

Mauris mattis auctor cursus. Phasellus tellus tellus, imperdiet ut imperdiet eu, iaculis a sem.

| Name | eMail Address | **LEARN HOW** |

Sign up now to get the **latest news and special reviews** about **(topic)** from YourWebsite.com!

| eMail Address | **SIGN UP** |

DO YOU SUFFER FROM B.S. ???

Receive **5 FREE EXCERPTS** from **B.S. THE BOOK** and start living a **B.S.-FREE LIFE** with greater confidence, energy, attitude and more!

| NAME |
| EMAIL ADDRESS |

GET YOUR FREE EXCERPTS

OUTSOURCING
CHECKLIST

One of the best ways to grow your business is by **delegating** specific action items that are taking time away from coaching, speaking, writing, etc. You must know what your time is worth and how effectively you are using it. For example: Maybe your time is work $150 per hour and you could pay someone $15-35 do the same task so you can focus on other activities. do the math!

The MAGIC WORD IS = *DELEGATE*

Hire a virtual assistant to help you with administrative items while you concentrate on the big picture!

Here's a list of simple tasks that an assistant could help you with:

- ❑ Ad Placement / Management
- ❑ Administrative Support
- ❑ Affiliate Program Manager / Support
- ❑ Article Writing & Submissions
- ❑ Blog Writing / Comment Management
- ❑ Bookkeeping
- ❑ Book / eBook Layout / Cover Design
- ❑ Calendar/Scheduling
- ❑ Client Support
- ❑ Graphic Design
- ❑ Landing Page Creation
- ❑ Live Chat / Helpdesk Support
- ❑ Mail & eMail Services
- ❑ Making/Returning Phone Calls
- ❑ Marketing Support
- ❑ Mobile Phone App Creation
- ❑ Order Fulfillment
- ❑ Public Relations / Press Release Writing
- ❑ Research
- ❑ Seminar/Workshop Support
- ❑ Social Media Updates & Support
- ❑ Tele-Seminar Support
- ❑ Transcription
- ❑ Video Recording / Editing / Promotion
- ❑ Webinar Support
- ❑ Website Maintenance
- ❑ Writing & Editing

… among other duties!

Where can you find a virtual assistant? Go online.

Perform a search for "virtual assistant services" or conduct a search for online administrative help. Be sure that you give a good overview of the job and your expectations. Here are a few more tips and some interview questions to ask a potential "virtual" assistant prior to hiring one:

❶ Ask the applicant about skill training, accomplishments, and other abilities. Ask he/she handles stress?

❷ Ask for samples of work and links to other sites where work has been done.

❸ Ask how long has the person been a designer, virtual assistant, freelancer, etc.?

❹ Ask to speak with former clients for level of satisfaction and look for testimonials on their website.

❺ Ask the prospective assistants about their knowledge of a specific areas of business or your field of work. You might test the person with a virtual assignment to see how resourceful the person is. Consider hiring for a probationary period of time (30 days). This often works well for both parties.

Once you find a virtual assistant to help you with your business, be cautious about giving passwords and showing confidential information until the person demonstrates a level of trust. Without trust, communication, teamwork and performance invariably suffer. Share as much as you can about your business, your goals, and other information as appropriate for the job. Set the example with transparency, trust, respect and appreciation.

Where can you **find the help you need** so you can spend more time selling and making money and less time performing tasks you could delegate?

99Designs.com	99DollarSocial.com
AllDevJobs.com	AllGraphicDesign.com
Aquent.com	Authenticjobs.com
BidHire.com	Bixee.com
CodeGuru.com	ComputerAssistant.com
DesignCrowd.com	Dice.com
Donanza.com	Elance.com
eJobs4Pros.com	Fiverr.com

FlexJobs.com	Freelance.com
FreelanceAuction.com	FreelanceDesigners.com
LogoMyWay.com	FreelanceSuccess.com
FreelanceSwitch.com	FreelanceWebMarket.com
FreelanceWriting.com	FreelanceWritingGigs.com
Freelanced.com	Freelancer.com
FreelancingJob.com	FreshWebJobs.com
GetACoder.com	GetAFreelancer.com
GoFreelanceWork.com	Guru.com
Joomlancers.com	JournalismJobs.com
JustAnswer.com	LimeExchange.com
LogoArena.com	NoAgenciesPlease.com
Odesk.com	OnlineWritingJobs.com
Patch.com	PeoplePerHour.com
Pro-Freelance.com	Project4Hire.com
RatRaceRebellion.com	Rent-ACoder.com
RentaCoder.com	SEOClerks.com
ScriptLance.com	SmashingJobs.com
SoloGig.com	Tutor.com
WitMart.com	WordPressFreelance.com
Workaholics4Hire.com	iFreelance.com

For VIRTUAL ASSISTANT companies, try these:

247virtualassistants.com	AToZTasks.com
AdTriboo.com	AskSunday.com
AssistantMatch.com	ContemporaryVA.com
DailyPA.co.uk	EAHELP.com
EZYVa.com	FancyHands.com
GetFriday.com	GetVirtualServices.com
GlobeTask.com	HireYourVirtualAssistant.com
iMySecy.com	IVAA.org
Job-Drop.com	LongerDays.com
MyNDCconsulting.com	NSVirtualServices.ca
Outsourcing2Vietnam.com	PAEveryday.com
Perssist.com	Prialto.com
ProcedureRock.com	RemSource.com
RentASmile.com	TaskArmy.com
TaskBullet.com	TaskRabbit.com
TasksEveryday.com	TimeEtc.com
Uassist.ME	VANetworking.com
VAStaffer.com	VASumo.com
VMGBPO.com	VirtuWorx.com
VirtuWorx.com	VirtualAssistUSA.com
VirtualAssistantAssistant.com	VirtualEmployee.com
VirtualAssistantForums.com	VirtuallyHere.net
VirtualAssistantSolutions.me	VirtualStaffFinder.com
VirtualAssistantville.com	Worldwide101.com
YourDailyTasks.com	Zirtual.com

PERSONAL GROWTH
CHECKLIST

When it comes to personal growth and development, I authored a book called B.S. The Book: Your How-To Guide On Cutting Through: Personal B.S. Why? I wrote about FOUR very critical areas of LIFE and PERSONAL B.S. to share my own experiences with the idea that I might possibly save you some time and money:

HEALTH & FITNESS B.S.

- ❑ What to eat ...
- ❑ What to drink ...
- ❑ Workout tips and exercise routines ...
- ❑ Self-care tips ...

SELF-HELP FROM B.S.

- ❑ Personal affirmations ("Bart Builders")
- ❑ How to deal with depression, anger, doubt, hopelessness, hard decisions, trust issues, etc.

FAITH & MORE B.S.

- ❑ How to handle stress, find balance, piece, wisdom from the ages, understanding who God is, and more.

RELATIONSHIP B.S.

- ❑ How to deal with the B.S. from enemies, in-laws, step-relationships, friends, family and others that impose on your happiness, rain on your parade, drain your time/energy, etc.

I took some of the HOTTEST B.S. topics that not only have affected my life, but the lives of people I care about and discuss stress, pain, setbacks, heartache, strife, poor health, depression, anxiety,

A B.S. TIMES Best Seller

B.S.
THE BOOK
Because The World Is So Full Of It!

Your How-To Guide On Cutting Through:
PERSONAL B.S.
Get Healthy, Lose Weight & Overcome Personal B.S. With My Personal Self-Help / B.S.-Busting Tips
BART SMITH
www.BreakThroughBS.com

relationship issues, you name it! B.S. is virtually everywhere!

B.S. THE BOOK is full of personal, spot-on, proven advice and time-tested mental strategies, as well as worthy tips on a wide range of life-enhancing topics. The recommendations are designed to empower you with extreme levels of "lethal confidence" and an "unshakable positive attitude!"

"Ignorance is NOT bliss!"

On the contrary, ignorance is 100% B.S. Not knowing what to do, how to do it and other truths, you only postpone the inevitable, good or bad. "B.S. The Book" is designed to provide you with specific, highly-targeted, time-tested, useful information on a wide range of life-influencing topics including health, relationships, starting a business, making money, saving money, computers and the Internet, how to find a date, find love, make love, and deal with the enemy that is at the root of your B.S. and more!

With more than 700+ personal "Bart Builder" testimonials, you can take any situation or B.S. that stands in your way of living a vigorous and rewarding life and make it happen.

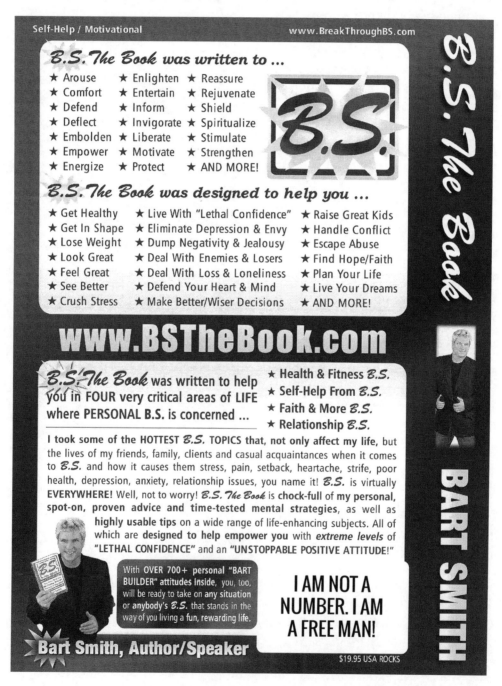

PHOTOGRAPHY
CHECKLIST

Y ou don't need to be a professional photographer to add photographs to your website, blog, products, etc., With some of these tips, you'll learn how to produce and place digital images and turn images into links to another page. With my checklist, you will learn about design, angles, light and composition to successfully upload photos to the Internet.

1. ❑ What are the pros and cons for hiring a professional or doing it yourself?

❑ **YOU?** — If you're shooting a simple setup for your website, you can probably shoot it. Direct the camera, turn the camera LCD viewing screen towards you, zoom in or out using a remote and viola! If you like what you see, start shooting. Make note of where you were positioned in front of the camera and place a marker on the floor for retakes.

❑ **FRIEND / FAMILY MEMBER?** — If you need help, ask someone with some skill to photograph and even record what you need provided it's a simple shoot. Examples of previous footage could help the person under your goals. Consider compensating the person for time and effort such as lunch/gift certificate/tickets.

❑ **HIRE A PROFESSIONAL?** — Everyone today takes photos, but few are considered masters at their craft. If your shoot requires expertise, hire a pro. Besides having top of the line equipment, a professional has the talent, artistry, and the ability to produce really creative images. If you have only one chance to get it right, hire a pro. Check a local directory or online for a proven professional. Sometimes you can hire film/photography students for less.

2. ❑ What basic photographic equipment will be needed to take good images?

❑ Tripod (Minimum 72" high!) ...
❑ Digital camera (or cell phone) ...
❑ Lighting ...
❑ Green screen background ...
❑ Black background ...
❑ White background ...

3. ❑ What to wear to a photo shoot?

❑ Wear something that you feel comfortable in. You want to display the best version of yourself.

❑ Unless you are required to wear a uniform, costume or other professional attire, wear

MY CHECKLISTS

something that doesn't distract from your face.

❑ If you're going for a casual look, baggy or too-tight clothing only accentuates the negatives. Solid colors are best (not bright ones). Unless a photographer tells you otherwise, take other outfits to a shoot.

4. ❑ How do you prepare for a photo shoot?

❑ Grooming is everything when you're trying to make a good impression.

❑ **Get plenty of rest (1-2 WEEKS) prior** to a photo shoot. The camera is not forgiving. You want your eyes to speak for you in a positive way, not a tired one.

❑ **If you're worried about your looks or your weight**, start now to slim down prior to a photo session. Even losing a few pounds can make you feel better about yourself and crash dieting is not the answer; moderate exercise and a healthy diet. The camera never lies!

❑ **Equipment** ... Test your equipment to ensure that everything works before you shoot. Checking the day before an event could be disastrous when you need a part or battery. Plan ahead so you are prepared, confident, and enthusiastic about your photo shoot.

5. ❑ What kind of photo will you need?

❑ Heads hot
❑ Full body Shot
❑ Facial gestures
❑ High resolution
❑ Half body shot
❑ Action shot
❑ Landscape / portrait
❑ Props

6. ❑ Location: Where will you be shooting your pictures?

❑ Studio, home, office
❑ At your desk, on phone, with a client
❑ Speaking engagement
❑ Conference room

❑ Networking
❑ Book signing
❑ Other locations/ideas

7. ❑ Editing Images

You have taken a boatload of photos, so what's next? How do you upload them from your camera to your computer? How do you crop and edit photos?

❑ Transfer your images from the camera (cell phone) and store them on your computer for editing and other needs.

❑ Use free graphic design and image editing software like Artweaver or Inkscape to edit your images.

❑ Crop (resize, shrink), add rounded corners or a drop shadow to your images.

❑ Feather the edges of your photographs for that really cool faded edge look.

❑ Create a collage or group several photos together to form one image.

❑ Insert your photo into banners, website header or buttons, which you might need to create for your website, shopping cart, or affiliate program.

❑ Insert a new photograph of you into a web page or a post on your blog.

❑ Prepare your (hi-res) image to be inserted into your book's "About The Author" page.

8. ❑ How often should you take pictures of yourself?

❑ Every 1-3 months ...
❑ Every six months ...
❑ New product/service launches ...
❑ Annually ...

PINTEREST MKGT
CHECKLIST

With more than 50,000,000+ users, Pinterest.com is a FREE web and mobile application company that allows you to upload, save, sort, and manage images (also known as pins) as well as other media content (i.e., videos) through collections known as pinboards. The company is a "catalog of ideas" versus a social network and acts like a personalized media platform where users can browse for content that others have pinned on their boards. It's a very popular way to share in visual, text, image and video formats. Get started today and pin away!

❑ **Research what your competition (or ideal client) is pinning**. Look for influencers within your niche. Pinterest has nearly one billion "Place Pins," which means you should be pinning!

❑ **Setup your Pinterest account, choose a great vanity URL for your account**, create categories and start posting! Read their terms and posting conditions closely so you don't violate any rules or copyright laws.

❑ **Study other boards.** What can you learn from them? Pinterest pins are 100 times more spreadable than a tweet even more effective than Facebook.

❑ **Add your own watermark to your images** to preserve your images' pin-tegrity (i.e., integrity). Pinterest is red hot and with a business account, you get more tools exclusive to businesses.

❑ **Take advantage of Pinterest Analytics.** Learn which strategies and content work for you so you can constantly improve your marketing efforts.

❑ **Pin across a range of boards such as group boards with large followings.** Pin on several boards to get even more pins. Pin popular pins and repin them. Follow them, repin influencers, comment on popular pins, rinse and repeat. Pinterest is fun and easy to use .

❑ **Pinterest has so many ways to say, "Thank you!"** Get creative when you show appreciation and acknowledge visitors that pin and repin on your board.

❑ **Tall images are more interesting** and eye-catching than small, tiny ones. Be absolutely certain that any photos you use are rightfully yours prior to posting anything. Images with smooth texture are repinned a massive 17 times versus images with rough texture.

MY CHECKLISTS

❑ **Include your website address on images** that you pin so others know the source (i.e., www.YourSite.com).

❑ **Pin on a schedule and during optimum times.** If you post mega pins on your board or others all at once, you could be labeled as a **spinner**; similar to a **spammer**. Gradually, add content. Saturday is considered a good day to pin, because that's the day most pins get repinned. Optimally, the target number of pins per day should be 10-15.

❑ **What can you pin on your board?**

  • Book cover images, table of contents, etc.
  • Coaching packages; one image per package or one per group
  • Coaching products/services
  • Facts and stats about your business niche, etc.
  • Favorite resources, links, lists, etc.
  • Business cards, posters, postcards, flyers, etc.
  • Images without faces get more pins and repins
  • Images of video snapshots
  • Images with prices: Add "Prices subject to change. See website for current pricing."
  • Images with text, tall images, affirmations, etc.
  • Images that represent your clients' desired dream outcomes and lifestyles.
  • Images that drive referral traffic. Get creative!
  • Infographics. (Check out ShareAsImage.com, PikToChart.com, Visual.ly.com, and, of course, Venngage.com)
  • Inspirations for clients and others!
  • Logos, designs, etc.
  • PowerPoint slides.
  • Seminar, webinar or presentation slides.
  • Tips, what-to-do, how-to-do, checklists, etc.
  • Videos. (See Pinterest.com/videos/)

❑ **Include a call-to-action** in your pins to drive more traffic to your product/service/website.

❑ **Cross promote pins on other social networks** such as Twitter, Facebook, YouTube, etc.

❑ **Red gets pinned more than blue.** While blue is a favorite color for most, red gets more repins and that's what you want - more repins!

❑ **Words that resonate on Pinterest** with pinsters include DIY, cup, recipe, idea, ideas, home, style, love, great, etc.

❑ **Want more repins?** Pins with descriptive detail, text, 300+ characters, etc., get more pins.

❑ **Encourage visitors to share your images and repin them on other boards**. Give them permission when asked!

❑ **Save your image file names with intent.** For example: your-name-coach-at-yoursite-com.jpg. The image file name is often used as the description for the image being pinned. The file name should be clear and easily accessed.

❑ **Don't use shortened URLs on Pinterest.** Use only full URLs. Why? Pinterest flags such shortened URLs as spam. Not good for you.

❑ **Include PIN-IT buttons on all your images.** This can be done with a WordPress plugin: WordPress.org/plugins/pinterest-pin-it-button/

❑ **Be aware of the images getting repinned from your site** at Pinterest.com/source/yoursite.com.

❑ **Add categories, keywords and #hashtags** to get your pins found faster when people search.

❑ **Tools to get the maximum from Pinterest:**

  ■ Buffer.com   ■ Instagram.com
  ■ Loop88.com   ■ LoveList.com
  ■ Page2Images.com   ■ PinAlerts.com
  ■ PinGroupie.com   ■ Pinerly.com
  ■ Pinpuff.com   ■ Pinstamatic.com
  ■ Pinterest App   ■ Pinvolve.com
  ■ Pixlr.com   ■ Quozio.com
  ■ TailWindApp.com   ■ Viraltag.com
  ■ MadeWitHover.com   ■ Viralwoot.com

PODCASTING
CHECKLIST

Yου too can start a radio show to share your message or expertise to millions of listeners, worldwide! Whether you do this for FREE or to make money, this checklist is for you! Here's what you can accomplish with a podcast:

❏ Communicate your message globally!
❏ Find new prospects/clients/customers.
❏ Acquire affiliates.
❏ Build brand exposure.
❏ Position yourself as an expert!
❏ MAKE MONEY and much more!

WHAT IS PODCASTING?

Podcasting is simply a method of using the Internet to "broadcast" or distribute recorded audio files in MP3 format that you create on your computer, in a studio, over the telephone or live where your audio recording, such as an interview, is transmitted worldwide. Podcasting is a powerful way to syndicate your own audio and/or video on the Internet.

Podcasts could be considered "pre-recorded shows" that you record, produce, then upload for the others to subscribe to, download and listen either for FREE or for a fee. Many people liken podcasting to radio on demand. Podcasting, however, offers more variety, content and flexibility for your listening audience.

What Are Some CREATIVE WAYS To Use Podcasting? Podcasts can be used for a number of different things and as the industry continues to evolve, I'm sure broadcasters and webmasters will find additional ways to use podcasts in the future.

❏ **Talk Shows** — Start you own Internet radio show and discuss topics that interest you and your listeners! Podcasting allows you to get the word out in a creative way to potentially millions of listeners!

❏ **Information Publishing** — Get creative! Do you write? Record what you write and podcast for the masses. Get unlimited exposure for your writings, books, reports, articles in audio-format via podcasting! If you wrote it, you can podcast it!

❏ **Training Tutorials** — Make your own educational training programs and deliver informational training on all kinds of subjects to others across the globe via podcasting.

MY CHECKLISTS

❏ **Interviews, Reviews & Commentaries** ... Conduct your own programs where you review the latest movies, books, software, consumer products, music, etc.

❏ **News Broadcast** ... Is there something going on in your community/industry others would benefit from? Read your own news report on topics of interest.

❏ **Entertainment** ... Are you a comedian? Do you write stories? Fiction? Poetry? Do you enjoy reading stories to others? Start you own podcast show and/or start entertaining people!

❏ **Music** ... Do you sing? Play an instrument? Are you in a band? Promote your musical talent online through podcasting and acquire a whole new set of fans! Publish interviews about you and concerts of your work that you might have record live!

MAKING MONEY BY PODCASTING

There are several ways to make money through podcasting. Here are some of the more popular ways:

❏ **Promote Your Products** ... In between "segments" of your podcast, tell people about the products you offer. Did you write a book? Record an audio program? Create a home-study course? If you're currently without a product, check out the special report on product Ideas at MyTrainingCenter.com. To get started creating podcasts quicker, learn how to interview experts (in any field of expertise) that you could introduce or reinvent on a podcast show!

❏ **Promote Your Consulting Services** ... Are you a consultant? Do you provide services to others? Then mention them in your podcast. When people hear what you do, they're more inclined to contact you for help!

❏ **Promote Your Affiliate Relationships** ... Become an affiliate for other people's products and promote them with a podcast. Ask others sign up for your affiliate program and mention your products in their podcasts. Why not interview each other and promote each other's products on the same call?

❏ **Promote Your Seminars, Webinars & Tele-Seminars** ... Perhaps you have a regular tele-seminar series you host to promote your live in-person seminars and workshops. Mention your tele-seminars or live seminars in your podcast. You could even provide a "sample audio" clip from one of your tele-seminars or live performances so people can hear you in advance. This goes the same for speaking. If you're a professional speaker, (a) mention you're a speaker and would like to be booked for speaking engagements, and (b) provide a sample clip or more showcasing you speaking at different events. Don't forget to include the raving applause!

❏ **Sell "Advertising Slots"** ... Promote other people's products on your podcasts. You could sell advertising "air time" on your podcast or link to potential affiliates through a domain name that you own and forwards to your affiliate link; another way to make money through podcasting.

❏ **Sell "Sponsorships"** ... Where blatant commercialism isn't always welcome, why not ask a company or entity to "sponsor" your FREE content. Allow the sponsor to advertise FREE of charge on your podcast. Some will even pay you to promote their business.

TYPES OF PODCAST SOFTWARE

❏ I prefer **Sony's Sound Forge "Audio Studio"** for all of my recording and editing because I like the interface for both recording and editing audio.

❏ Some people prefer **Audacity**, a FREE audio

recording, editing and mixing program. Its features don't work for me audio compared to SoundForge's interface.

❑ Some people use **Skype** and **Pamela** to record their Skype calls because it's easy to use; requires little to no training. Skype is also a great way to chat with people and take their questions live during a podcast show.

❑ If I have to MIX a podcasting audio recording with music or special effects, I will use **Audacity** for mixing, or another audio program specifically made for mixing audio on multiple tracks, such as **MixPad**.

EQUIPMENT NEEDS FOR PODCASTING

❑ The **AT2020 USB Cardioid Condenser USB** is all I need for my own podcast recordings.

❑ **SKYPE** is what I use for recording. All you need is a USB headset with microphone.

❑ Some people use an external **MP3 recorder**, such as **TASCAM's DR-05,** with a lavaliere microphone plugged into it to record their podcast remotely. Then, they'll transfer the audio from the external MP3 recording device to the computer for editing, mixing and posting online.

HOW TO CREATE YOUR OWN PODCAST

1.0 ❑ What is your passion or expertise?

What do you feel motivated to talk about? There are over 1,000 different topics of interest people want to learn more about and here is a list of some of them.

❑ Arts
❑ Entertainment
❑ Autobiographies
❑ Biographies & Memoirs

❑ Business
❑ Careers
❑ Child Development
❑ Children & Young Adults
❑ Classics
❑ Comedy
❑ Computer Technology
❑ Drama
❑ Education
❑ Fantasy
❑ Fiction
❑ Geriatrics
❑ Health & Fitness
❑ History
❑ Home & Garden
❑ How-To
❑ Information Technology
❑ Internet & World Wide Web
❑ Investing
❑ Language
❑ Magazines & Print Media
❑ Management
❑ Marketing
❑ Mystery
❑ News & Current Events
❑ Non-Fiction
❑ Photography
❑ Poetry
❑ Press Release
❑ Radio
❑ Relationships
❑ Religion & Spirituality
❑ Science
❑ Science Fiction
❑ Self-Help
❑ Social Issues
❑ Speeches & Lectures
❑ Sports
❑ Technology
❑ Television
❑ Travel

2.0 ❑ What is the ideal length of a podcast show?

The standard length of time for a podcast show runs 5-30 minutes long. Notably, the average listening time is 10 minutes long; so, keep that in mind.

I've seen some podcast shows that consisted of a series of 10-minute segments (or shows). They were nice and clean; short, to the point, brief and very entertaining and enlightening to listen to.

I've also seen a series of podcast shows which last between 25-30 minutes for each show. These shows typically involved an interview with a guest expert or perhaps calls into the studio from listeners, etc.

3.0 ❑ How many podcast shows do you need to produce?

Once you start podcasting, you won't want to stop. Typically, people who listen to podcast shows expect more than one episode! That's right! So, be prepared to record, produce and publish more than one "episode!" Weekly podcast shows are very popular. As long as you keep and maintain some form of consistency in publishing your shows: daily, weekly, biweekly, etc.

4.0 ❑ What FORMAT should you use?

Whatever format you choose, stick to it for consistency. Typical podcast shows closely resemble radio talk shows; they have a host, one topic per show, an optional guest, people calling in, etc. While other podcast shows simply consist of the host pre-recording an episode by him or herself with or without guests, and people calling in, etc.

FORMAT EXAMPLES

❑ Duration: 10-30 Minute Shows
❑ Recording Quality: Studio quality; live in-person with guest/co-host; recordings on the phone, etc.
❑ Advertisements: Advertise your book, consulting services, seminars/workshops, etc.
❑ Other Advertisements: Plug advertisement spots

for other people's products/services.

RECORDING TIPS

❑ Create/rehearse/record a standard introduction to introduce you and your show (voice + music) ...
❑ Record your show separately, then mix other elements (i.e., music, people/interviews, etc.) ...
❑ Be careful about background noises; they come through ...
❑ Be careful with your voice, be clear, don't slur, stutter or pause ...

TOPICS/CONTENT

❑ Cover everything surrounding your topic/expertise to create numerous shows ...
❑ Give away "tips", sell "details" ... Encourage your listener to visit your website to learn more ...
❑ Create a series of podcast shows with topics you already know about, research, etc.
❑ Create content by interviewing experts in fields that serve your listeners ...
❑ Record telephone interviews and produce a podcast that includes that interview ...
❑ Run an "ask campaign" to gather questions from clients and answer them in your next podcast ...
❑ Are you writing or did you write a book? Use content within the book for your podcast ...
❑ Do you teach, train or coach? Use some of that content for your podcast ...
❑ Do you have a hobby, interest or passion? Use some of that content for your podcast ...

Sample Welcome & Introductory Dialogue/Talk For Talk-

SHOW STYLES

❑ Add a disclaimer if necessary at the beginning of your podcast (e.g., medical, legal, over 18, etc.)
❑ Mention your website in your intro ... Tell people

who you are/credentials, etc.

- ❏ Tell people what's on "this" podcast and what's on the "next" podcast.
- ❏ "Hello and welcome to the debut podcast of (your podcast show name) ..."
- ❏ "Welcome to today's / this week's podcast from (YourDomain.com), my name is (your name, title) ..."
- ❏ "Welcome to '(your podcast name) Radio' ..."
- ❏ "Welcome to the show ..."
- ❏ "Welcome to episode #__, hey, this is (your name) ..."
- ❏ We'll also be ... bringing you a tip of the week ... taking your calls ...
- ❏ "... for more information about our guests you can ..."
- ❏ "We're talking about (topic). Send us your questions/ comments at (email). Or visit us online at ..."
- ❏ "Welcome from sunny / snowy / rainy / foggy (wherever you are/location) ..."
- ❏ "Hello everyone, today is (date) and you're listening to the (your podcast show name) ..."
- ❏ "... with our partners (announce paid advertisers, partners, associates, etc.), we bring you ..."
- ❏ "You can also listen to us on the web at our website, www.YourDomain.com."
- ❏ Start off with a question and answer it ...
- ❏ "Have you ever wanted to learn more about / how to ..."
- ❏ "Today we're going to address your question / concern / the topic of ..."
- ❏ "Hey, everyone, welcome back to (name of your podcast) ..."
- ❏ "So, if you're listening, I'm open to getting your eMails at MyPodcast@YourDomain.com ..."
- ❏ "If you have any questions for us? You can eMail us at Question@YourDomain.com ..."
- ❏ "What's on the next show ..."

CONVERSATION/DIALOGUE SAMPLES

- ❏ "with me in the studio is ..." (state/restate your guests name, listeners need to be reminded) ...
- ❏ "with me on the phone is ..." (state/restate your guests name, listeners need to be reminded) ...
- ❏ "we're talking about _____" (restate what you are talking about if you come back from break) ...

MORE NOTES

Until you get your podcast going, ask to be a guest on other podcast shows for the experience. It can help get you into the mode of producing your own shows and gives you the opportunity to promote your upcoming event and announce your podcast show date.

PODCAST DIALOGUE WORKSHEET

When you're ready to start producing your first podcast, use this simple format to organize and make decisions regarding your ideas, music, verbal content, ads, etc.

"Enter Your First Podcast Title Here"

10-MINUTE PODCAST SHOW (POST/EPISODE #1)
SCRIPT FORMAT SAMPLE

INTRO MUSIC (5-10 SECONDS)

MUSIC ... All you need is some easy listening OR somewhat upbeat music to introduce your show. Once you find it, use it again so people will associate with it every time you introduce your show. Listeners will learn to expect it!

STANDARD INTRO (10-30 SECONDS)

- ❏ "Hello and welcome to the debut podcast for (YOUR PODCAST NAME) ..."
- ❏ "Hi, and welcome to (YOUR PODCAST NAME) ..."
- ❏ "My name is (YOUR NAME / TITLE) ..."
- ❏ "Be sure to check us out online at our website at (YOUR Website) ..."

❏ "And, if you like what you hear, let us know. Contact us at our (eMail address) and/or (telephone number) with your questions."

CONTENT (5-25 MINUTES)

"Today, we're talking about _____." (Introduce your topic; your guest/expert on the call or in the studio; invite people to call you; engage small talk to get started; etc.)

(Music Fade In/Out Quickly)

COMMERCIAL (10-180 SECONDS)

After you've entertained/educated your listeners for 5-10 minutes, plug one of your products, services, seminars, an affiliate/sponsor/advertisers product/ offers. Length of time: 10-60 seconds. You could have multiple ads at 10-15 seconds each or two ads at 30 seconds each, etc. It's your show!

MUSIC / TRANSITION (5-10 SECONDS)

(Music Fade In/Out Quickly)

CONTENT (5-25 MINUTES)

Welcome back to the show everyone. Let's continue with our topic (name)." … "Thank you for joining us, we're back and we're discussing … (topic) … My next question for my guest is …", etc.

STANDARD EXIT (10-30 SECONDS)

"Well, our time is up. I hope you've enjoyed the show … Next time we'll be discussing … Be sure to check out our website at www.YourDomain.com. Be sure to send us your questions (provide eMail address) … Until next time, take good care of yourself and thanks for listening."

EXIT MUSIC (5-10 SECONDS)

(Music Fade In/Out Quickly)

5.0 ❏ **Give Your Podcast a NAME, TITLE, DESCRIPTION, ALBUM ART, etc.**

6.0 ❏ **Podcast URL Name** … An example of a valid name is my-name-my-topic. Spaces and punctuation other than hyphens (or underscores) are not permitted. The name may be up 64 characters in length. FOR EXAMPLE: your-name-your-topic-website-com

7.0 ❏ **Podcast Title** … Create a main title for your podcast. This is the title that describes the overall theme of your podcast and not the individual shows you will post on-going. FOR EXAMPLE:

MyTrainingCenter.com (Computer, Business and Marketing Tips)

8.0 ❏ **Podcast Description** … Create the main description for your podcast. This should explain the overall theme of your podcast and not the individual shows you'll post on-going. FOR EXAMPLE:

Learn computer, business, marketing, website design, graphic design, eCommerce, audio recording, self-publishing tips, tricks, techniques and tactics to accelerate your career, on the job experience, or in your business so you can make more money.

9.0 ❏ **Album Art** … You have the option to provide "album art" for your podcast that will be seen and associated with your podcast's main theme. Album art can range in size from 170x170 to 300x300 pixels square at 72 dpi in either JPEG/GIF format. You're encouraged to use a photograph of yourself to help listeners "identify" with whom they're listening to! You never see the host on a radio show, but if you had a picture of the person, you might feel as if you were making a "connection."! Help your listeners visualize you speaking to them live with a photograph of you. Even a creative logo can make a connection!

> Your podcast show artwork can include images of you, your product, stock photography, etc.

10.0 ❑ **Mobile Podcast Post Title & Description** ... Enter a default podcast title and description for posts via the telephone. That's right! Some people listen to podcasts on their cell phones. Create a clever description for that niche medium. It's okay to use the same title and description you created above.

11.0 ❑ **Genre** ... Choose the category you might like to assign to your podcast. Some websites will ask you to select up to three (3) different categories, while others may insist you to choose sub-categories as well.

12.0 ❑ **Website URL Information** ... Decide which website URL you will attach to your podcast and which podcast listeners can click on to get to your site!

Website URL #1: Instead of using your usual domain name, create an Ad Tracker to "track" the numbers of click-through from your podcast to your website. Wouldn't you like to know how many people actually click on your podcast link to get to your site? Use an "ad tracker" to do that. FOR EXAMPLE: http://www.MyMarketingCart.com/app/adtrack.asp?AdID=237492

Website URL Tip #2: Instead of sending people that listen to your podcast to your main web page, send them to a "name squeeze page!" This helps you build your list of prospects because it collects names and eMail addresses prior to visiting your website. Offer a FREE gift, eCourse, subscription to your eZine, etc. Either way, get them on your list! This is a potential customer that has clicked on your link because they are interested in your product/service.

13.0 ❑ **Copyright** ... It's always a good idea to copyright your audio recordings. When you create your own podcasts, there's a field where you can enter your copyright information. FOR EXAMPLE:

Copyright 2015 by Bart Smith, TheMarketingMan.com.

14.0 ❑ **Managing Editor eMail** ... You may provide an optional eMail address to allow subscribers to communicate with you about the content. Please note that this eMail address WILL be made public as part of the RSS Feed. FOR EXAMPLE

podcast@YourDomain.com
... or ...
feedback@YourDomain.com
... or ...
YourName@YourDomain.com

15.0 ❑ **Promoting Your Own Podcast** ... While there are several ways to promote your podcast, the fastest way is to utilize the online services of a podcasting service company called Libsyn.com (Liberated Syndication) that will help create, store and publish your podcast with just a few simple mouse clicks. Liberated Syndication (libsyn) pioneered the system to host and publish podcasts in 2004 and they have become the largest leading podcast network with over 1.6 billion downloads, 10,000+ podcasts delivered to more than 18 million monthly audience members in 2011. Their iTunes expertise in podcasting and Smartphone apps is the basis for their world class tools, service and support.

15.1 ❑ Sign Up For Podcast Publishing Services , such as, Libsyn.com

15.2 ❑ Follow Libsyn's prompts to create your first podcasting title for your podcast show. (http://support.libsyn.com/faqs/)

15.3 ❑ Use Libsyn to host your podcast and submit it to iTunes.

15.4 ❑ Promote your podcast through other sites by posting your podcast feed to their podcast directory.

15.5 ❑ Create a podcasting information "cheat sheet" that lists the different parameters for your podcast's RSS feed. You'll use this information again when you submit and promote your podcasts on other podcasting websites.

15.6 ❑ Visit MyTrainingCenter.com for a list of websites that will promote your podcasts. With your podcasting information cheat sheet, submit it to all the sites that accept podcast submissions.

15.7 ❑ Create a folder in your eMail program and a filtering system to label any and all incoming eMail notices from the podcasting websites that you submit your podcasts to. Most will eMail a confirmation link to verify you are who you say you are and that your podcast submission was created by a human being and not a Spambot.

15.8 ❑ Submit your first podcast to an actual website that accepts podcast submissions.

15.9 ❑ Check your eMail for a second response (i.e., podcast submission approved).

15.10 ❑ Search the internet via any search engine (i.e., Google.com, Yahoo.com, etc.) within 7-10 days once you submit your first podcast. Do you see your name in lights? In other words,, do you see your podcast coming up in the search results? Hopefully, you just added increased exposure to you and your website on the websites of many. If you don't readily see your podcast online yet, be patient. It will appear.

16.0 Promote Your Podcast From A Website ... You can do this with a simple WordPress plugin called www.SimplePodcastPress.com. This plugin publishes your podcast show directly on your website so people can listen to it immediately.

17.0 ❑ Other Ways To Promote Podcasts

❑ Post a video on YouTube with the audio of your podcast.

❑ Transcribe your podcast and post it on your site as an article.

❑ Post podcast images on Pinterest such as your show's outline, you and a guest, and do this for all your shows:. Other venues include:

❑ Link to Twitter, Facebook, LinkedIn, and other social media websites.

❑ Promote other podcast shows to your list and ask others to promote it to their lists.

❑ Sign up for an Amazon "Author Central" account.

❑ Interview others and ask them to post the interview/show on their websites.

❑ Include your podcast show within your Google+ profile.

18.0 ❑ Check Your Podcasting Statistics ... Periodically, check your podcast download statistics (i.e., total playtime, average playtime, how many people downloaded it, etc.). With this information, you can approach advertisers/ sponsors to pay you to advertise on their podcast shows.

19.0 ❑ Making Money by Podcasting ... Can you take your niche or topic you are knowledgeable about, put some real effort into a podcast for a period (i.e., 6-12 months), build a loyal following/audience, and then have sponsors requesting to get in front of your listeners? ABSOLUTELY, YES, if your podcast show is downloading more than a 1,000-10,000 times in a given period of time, you can earn residual income. Podcast advertising as a marketing tool can be very effective. Charge a fee to advertisers and sponsors to announce or endorse their products/services on your podcast.

PRESS ROOM
CHECKLIST

The purpose of a Press Room is to post any and all items concerning you and your business in a central place where the media and others will find what they need to do their jobs! The easier you make it for them to view interview questions, biography, photographs, press releases, write-ups and articles, the easier it will be for them to say, "When can we interview you!"

A great Press Room must have at least some of the following sections so the media can pick and choose the information that answers their questions and meets their publishing needs.

1. ❑ About You: This section either addresses you and your business or links to the About Us page on your website. When the media visits your Press Room and require more information about you, your company, product, refer them to your online Press Room.

Getting FREE publicity and using the media to get the word out about your business/service/profession, is one of the most under used methods of marketing you could spend time on.

Remember this quote when dealing with the media ... "Help them do their job!" What does it mean? It means, don't make members of the media and other people struggle to get information about you so they can conduct a good interview with you or write about you in their papers.

2. ❑ Articles, Stories, News Releases: You should provide links to articles and more in your press room. Articles give members of the media ideas for their own shows, especially if the work is inspiring.

3. ❑ Awards and Recognition: Have you received any awards or recognition for what you do? Post these achievements in your Press Room.

4. ❑ Biography: Make it easy for the media to learn more about you in your Press Room. Make

---

your biography available via PDF so it's printable from your website and can be read on air or noted in a TV introduction.

5. ❑ Highlights & Special Announcements: Do you announce new products, services, etc. to your lists? Post these in your Press Room for media attention. The media thirsts for information so keep it updated and interesting.

6. ❑ Facts & Figures: Are there any particular facts or figures the media or visitors to your website could know about your company success, earnings, stock market performances, etc.? Post this data under Facts & Figures or Fact Sheets.

7. ❑ Images / Photo Gallery: This is a must-have section in your Press Room. When the media or others ask for more about you, refer them to your Press Room where they can download web-ready or high resolution images of you, your products, book covers, etc. Provide 72 dpi (for web use) and 300 dpi (for print use) image quality in your image gallery

8. ❑ Interview (Your Name) This is another must-have section of your Press Room. When members of the media peruse your Press Room and see a section called, "Interview Bart Smith," they might just be inclined to pick up the phone and call you, immediately. In this section, you can list other ways to contact you, in addition to a list of questions they might ask you about you, your business, etc.

9. ❑ Interview Questions & Talking Points: Make it easy for the media and others to interview you. Create a list of ideal questions or "talking points" and make them available on your website. You can either list these questions on their own

page, and/or provide a download link to a PDF that can be printed for easy reference.

10. ❑ Investor Relations: Are you looking for investment capital to fund your growing business? Mention it in your Press Room. Sometimes a simple statement that you're looking for investors will generate interest. You might also list documents or references to where your stock information (if any) can be found for serious investors.

11. ❑ Latest News: What's the latest development in your business? Do you have a new product? Did you attend (or plan to) a seminar or networking event? Share the latest and greatest happenings in your world from your Press Room.

12. ❑ Media Contact Information: This section is a must-have area, too, should the anyone wish to contact your relating to your website, publicity, public relations, media, interviews, etc.. Have a separate phone number for media only calls and provide customers, affiliates and prospects with another number.

13. ❑ Networking & Sightings: Will you be attending a networking event, seminar, workshop or other public showing? List it inside your Press Room under a section called, "Sites & Appearances" for a couple of reasons:

(1) It lets people know where you'll be so they can attend the same event with hopes of meeting you. (2) Get lots of photos for your Press Room (and not "selfies"). You give the media and others options when you post more than one photo on your site. Multiple photos can stimulate more interest. Don't sell your short when it comes to using photos to promote what your business.

---

14. ❏ News & Media Coverage: Are you getting attention by the public eye? Post the buzz about you on your website. Use other company logos and corporate sponsors if appropriate in your Press Room. Sign up for Google Alerts, which communicates via email with updates when your name, product, company are mentioned on the Web.

15. ❏ Newsletter Sign-up: If you have an online newsletter or eZine, invite the media and others to subscribe to it so they're always updated. Sign up for MyMarketingCart.com for eMail broadcasting, eZine delivery plus opt-in boxes to collect names and eMail addresses. Offer previous issues in your Press Room. Reading your eZine articles might initiate an idea or a phone call to you.

16. ❏ Podcast Shows: Do you have your own online radio or podcast show? You can post a link to those recordings and/or how to listen to future podcast shows. If you don't know what a podcast show is, check out my tutorial at MyTrainingCenter.com called, "Create Your Own Podcast Show."

17. ❏ Press Kit: This is the online version of a regular press kit. Members of the media interested in interviewing you or having you on a show will request a press kit. Depending on the nature of your business, your press kit might include: press releases, photos, a copy of your book/article, a list of interview questions, a DVD of a speaking engagement, business cards and anything the media might request of you. With the Internet, videos can be viewed online, interview questions downloaded, images copied/saved/printed and more.

18. ❏ Press Releases: Press releases are newsworthy, one-page announcements about you, your book, a new joint venture, or other events written for distribution by the media. Press releases are not advertisements. They are crafted to "inform". Ideally, you should post at least one new press release in your Press Room weekly.

19. ❏ Product Information, Reviews or Synopsis: Again, make it easy to get information about you and your products/services with quick links to your Press Room. When someone's surfing your Press Room and learns what you offer, with one click you could be selling or motivating someone to contact you, directly.

20. ❏ TV/Radio Interviews: Were you recorded on a TV or radio show? Post it in your Press Room. If a prospective interviewer knows you've been a guest on other stations, you establish credibility with other interviewers.

21. ❏ Rave Reviews: What are others saying about you? Provide a quick link to testimonials and praise in your Press Room. There's a good chance your audience might be interested in hiring you as a guest speaker or participant in a number of different programs.

22. ❏ Reports: Do you have financial information (annual or financial reports) that can be uploaded to your website and Press Room? In disclosing this type of data, people respect your transparency and authenticity and are prompted to know more about you and work with you.

23. ❏ Social Networking Profiles: Are you registered with Facebook, LinkedIn, Twitter, Pinterest, Instagram, Google+? List all of your social networking sites in your Press Room. People that want to learn more about you, can check your social networking pages and connect with you there.

24. ❏ Speaking & Seminar Coverage: Do you

conduct tele-seminars, webinars or teaching/training events? Provide a link to your calendar in your Press Room. People that have heard you speak may be interested in your other engagements. Be sure to include photos. Some might be interested in hiring you for their next event.

25. ❑ **Video Presentations & Coverage**: Do you have videos on your website or take advantage of YouTube.com for video sharing? YouTube.com has more than 1 billion users! This is premium real estate for communicating your brand, business, and more. Create a section in your Press Room to show videos or provide a link to a web page where they can be viewed.

PRODUCT CREATION
CHECKLIST

EBOOK SPECIAL REPORTS AUDIO BOOK CD DVD MP3 HOME-STUDY COURSE

Creating products that you can sell to potential customers globally is easy when you have a checklist to follow! Below you'll find my checklist for creating a product, preparing it for market including a checklist for marketing and fulfillment. If you have an idea for a product, you'll want to take a list of this list to ensure you cover all the important elements from creation, launch and success.

1. PRODUCTS YOU CAN SELL

❑ Sell "Information" Products
❑ Sell "Your" Own Knowledge
❑ Sell "Other People's" Knowledge

2. CREATING PRODUCTS

❑ Research, Research, Research
❑ Search Engine Research
❑ Forums & Blogs
❑ Ask About wants/needs
❑ Survey, Test & Poll
❑ "Create a better mousetrap!"
❑ Specialize (Per Product)

3. INNOVATIVE IDEAS

❑ Tap into your own expertise, experience and training.

❑ Create a name/title for your product.

❑ Register the domain name for your idea.

❑ Determine the "format" your information products will be created in. There are several ways to create and package what you sell. Here are a few more tips:

❑ Write about your knowledge from experience, expertise, research, study, etc.

❑ Record audio products live or from printed material ...

❑ Video record your knowledge live from seminars, etc.

❑ Transcribe all your audio/video recordings into

MY CHECKLISTS

print/digital format ...

❑ Print your knowledge via books, reports, newsletters, eZines ...

❑ Digitize your knowledge in the form of eBooks, membership sites, etc.

❑ Bundle your knowledge with other products you (or others) created ...

❑ Create seminars, workshops, webinars, and tele-seminars with your knowledge ...

❑ Product Packaging ... Depending on the form your information product takes such as books, eBooks, videos, audio products, etc., you'll need to plan for packaging and artwork designs.

❑ Hire a professional if you need that expertise to create your information products.

4. PRODUCT PRICING

❑ Physical products = You should charge 10 times the cost it took to make the product, for example, if a book costs $3.98 to print (per book), you could potentially charge $39.80. Price according to page count, content and demand and do check to see what other like books are selling for. You'll want to be competitive.

❑ Digital products = perceived value, which is 10-100 x the cost to make them.

❑ For online products, marketers suggest the list prices end with a "7" ... $27, $47, $97, $147, $197, etc. In the offline world, typically products end with a "9" ... $29.95, $19.95,

$14.95, $12.95, etc. The power of "9" is everywhere.

❑ Of the information product you are selling "makes money for the customer," you might charge 10% of what the customer will make. For example, if he/she is slated to make $2,000+ from your $197 product, sell the product for $997. You get the picture.

❑ Products should be reasonably price, but don't undervalue your price just to make sales. Psychological studies on pricing tell us that one of the obvious drawbacks is that people won't "value" your product as much as the same product that you might sell at a higher price. Value sells!

❑ People will pay more for information (no matter the cost) provided it helps them solve a problem. So, don't be afraid to charge more for a product that is in high demand. Many information product sellers say they sell more when they raise their price!

❑ ADD more value to your product to increase the price. Are you looking for bargain buyers or value seekers? Know your market and test different levels of pricing to determine how to price your product/service. Don't take pricing for granted, but do keep it simple. Many customers struggle when told that they can pay $1095, $1,095 or $1095.00 for a product thinking the last two prices are higher.

5. ❑ ACCEPTING PAYMENTS

❑ PayPal.com
❑ Authorize.net (Merchant Account)
❑ Stripe.com
❑ ClickBank.com
❑ JVZoo.com
❑ E-Junkie.com

PRODUCT CREATION

6. DESIGNING "PRODUCT-FOCUSED" SITES

❏ Name Squeeze Page & Autoresponder

❏ Check List For Websites That Sell

❏ Shopping Cart

❏ Affiliate Program

❏ Restate Benefits On Order Form Page

7. SHOPPING CARTS

Depending on the shopping cart you might have or are considering, make sure you have these built-in features. You can obtain plugins to enhance your existing shopping if needed.

❏ **"Opt-In" List Builder** — An "opt-in" box is a small form visible on your website, usually located in the top right corner that asks for the name and eMail address from visitors to your website in exchange for receiving a FREE gift. The people who "opt-in" agree to receive information from you via eMail. The purpose of an opt-in box is to build a list and generate leads, which will generate sales!

❏ **Autoresponder** — An autoresponder is a computer program that automatically answers eMail sent to it such as a pre-written eMail message or a series of eMail messages. Autoresponders are often used as e-mail marketing tools, to immediately provide information to their prospective customers and then follow-up with them at preset time intervals.

❏ **Ad Trackers** — An "ad tracker" is a marketing tool (website link) that tracks the numbers of click-through to a specific URL, website, order form, sales web page, etc. These are helpful for tracking how many people are clicking through to your site and have some interest in your product/service. You don't want to lose

this valuable information.

❏ **Shopping Cart** — If you want to sell physical products such as eBooks/eReports, audio/video products, downloadable products, seminar/tele-seminar registrations and more from your website, the several shopping cart solutions might help you.

❏ **eBook & Digital Delivery** — Did you write an eBook? Would you like to sell the digital version of your book? With the right shopping cart system, it will deliver your digital content for you in a variety of different formats: PDF eBooks, EXE eBooks, WEB-BASED "HTML" eBooks, DOC eBooks, XLS eBooks, and eBook Pro eBooks.

❏ **Social Media** is the number one activity among Americans. If you are not marketing on it, you're missing out on a large portion of the consumer market.

❏ **Fulfillment support** and export tools that can help you efficiently fulfill orders. Check to see how your shopping cart helps you handle fulfillment. Do they link with any fulfillment houses, or can you download and print data from Excel spreadsheets, labels and envelopes, and more?

❏ **Affiliate Program** — How do you start your affiliate program? Remember, the quickest way to wealth is in building your own sales force (affiliates). The more people promoting and selling your product/service, the more money you can potentially make!

8. AFFILIATE PROGRAMS

❏ Setup your own affiliate program using a variety of different affiliate program software plugins that work best for you and your product.

❑ Assign which products you want to pay commissions on. Some products will have different commission payouts.

❑ Create/upload marketing tools, banners and letters for your affiliates.

9. FULFILLMENT COMPANY

❑ Digital product fulfillment, delivery, software companies ...

❑ Companies for physical fulfillment ...

10. MARKETING TACTICS TO DRIVE TRAFFIC TO YOUR WEBSITE

❑ Offline marketing tactics ...

❑ Online marketing tactics ...

❑ Social Media marketing tactics ...

❑ Tele-seminar marketing tactics ...

❑ Interview marketing tactics ...

❑ _____ marketing tactics ...

11. SPIN-OFF PRODUCTS/SERVICES

Now that you've realized success at selling your first information product, why not create another one and grow your income? Use these procedures for your next product.

PRODUCT LAUNCH
CHECKLIST

Are you ready to unveil your latest product/website/service to the world and motivated to make a million dollars? Do you know how to make a million dollars with a product launch? Well, let's do the math. For starters, 1,000 sales multiplied by a $997 product or 10,000 sales at $100 (in a 24-hour window). Those are two ways and several have done just that. You can do it, too, or at least make a nice profit with your launch depending on your product, the willingness of the market to buy what you sell, timing, staging and HELP!

This is my quick checklist for launching any product, service, website, etc. while making the kind of impact most dream about!

FOR STARTERS: Don't expect to open your doors to a heavy flood of traffic just because you've work tirelessly to produce a product or service or website for the past many months, even years. Why? You have to plan your launch wisely and meticulously based on what you're selling, your target (niche) market, pricing, and so much more.

SECONDLY: Stage your debut by doing the following:

1. ❑ **Test, Measure & Confirm** — Make sure what you've created and are launching into marketplace that is well tested, measured and results confirmed so when you're ready to debut, you're confident that what it is you have to sell was already vetted by a controlled test group of friends, select clients/ customers, affiliates, etc. Ask them to try a FREE sample of your product/ service for their genuine feedback. Also ask for their approval to use their testimonials when you launch. Be sure you get their permission in writing prior to launch.

2. ❑ **Testimonials, Reviews, Case Studies & Endorsements** — Collect as many of these as possible. Create a controlled test group to review, test and use your product/service. What were their findings? How did the product/service/website help them? Conduct your survey over a 90-period well in advance of your launch. Make sure they're current and convincing reviews. By using testimonials and reviews from satisfied customers whether it is in text, audio or video format, you can transform your sales presentation into an unbiased, popular recommendation for your product. It's this information

---

you'll want to incorporate into your website and other communications.

3. ❑ Affiliate Preparation — Reach out to a few of your top affiliate producers months in advance and let them know they've been specifically chosen to be the first to promote your product/service prior to any other affiliates get a chance to promote it to their lists. Super affiliates tend to have list subscribers on other affiliates' lists. By giving these top affiliates a chance to get in early on the action and score (potentially) big, they'll work harder to earn that coveted spot. They have incentive to take out their own pay-per-click ads and conduct mini webinars/seminars on your behalf.

4. ❑ Lock Down — Keep the ordering process on LOCK DOWN until you're ready for blast off and launching your product/service. You might post a video (3-5 minutes) of you announcing your product launch and what people can expect. People who are really interested will listen to the end if what you're selling has value for them. Using a countdown timer can build enthusiasm and suspense, which people generally like, and it will hold their attention up the point when you're ready to debut.

5. ❑ Countdown / Timer — As mentioned, post a countdown timer on your website that lets people know when they can buy what it is you have to sell.

6. ❑ Inventory Preparation — What are you selling? Do you have enough product in stock? How many of "X" did you have printed, produced, made, and developed? Is your fulfillment house ready to fulfill ... how many orders in a single day? How long did you promise to send out or deliver on their order? 2-4 weeks? Is this a digital product or online service? Maybe there's no problem with fulfillment, then. In that case,

sell away when the time comes. You still might need customer support on hand and help ready for any online inquiries, questions and requests. So spend some time putting together that part of your business model for this launch.

7. ❑ Promotion — When you're ready to launch, but you're not yet (going to launch), schedule back to back interviews, tele-seminars and webinars all week/month long with top affiliates and their lists, with other promoters, publishers and owners of high-trafficked websites, blogs and forums; minimum 3-5 per week for 2-4 weeks in a row. This goes for making special announcements via social media, in the press, sending out press releases, broadcasting your message via video and audio all over the Internet as well. Don't forget offline, if you can reach local news outlets, if you think they'll find your story, product, website, service newsworthy, why not!

8. ❑ Affiliate Training & Preparation — Hopefully, you already gave them all the marketing tools, banners and materials they needed to promote your product/service the day of the launch. Hopefully, you took time during 4-8 weeks prior to the launch date to spend time with them going over sales and marketing strategies, tips for making sales, important selling points about your product/service so they had time to devise and implement their own marketing plans.

9. ❑ Affiliate Bonuses — You can award your affiliates different bonuses based on how much they sell. Come up with at least three prizes. You can offer cash, electronics, entertainment products, computer products, cell phone products, valuable services, cars, gift certificates, etc. Whoever sells the most within a certain time frame immediately after launch wins "X" or "Y" or "Z." Track all sales by the minute! Who made the first affiliate sale? Who made the second? Third? All orders are tracked by time and date.

Use this to dish out the awards. You could give out smaller cash bonuses for sales made within the first 10 minutes, first hour, the total number of sales made by an affiliate within 24 hours, 48 hours, etc.

10. ❑ Days/Weeks Prior To The Launch — Talk about what you're working on and when it will be released in your newsletter and on your website for a minimum of 30 days prior to the launch taking place. Get people stirred up about it!

11. ❑ Limited Number / Quantity Available — Ever been out shopping on Black Friday, right after Thanksgiving? How many TV monitors are sitting on the shelf? 30 at a cost of $997? How many people are lined up outside to buy them? 90? You get the idea. People will RUSH to buy something if they know more people want it and there is a limited quantity.

12. ❑ Website / Sales Letter — Build (and write) the perfect website sales letter to sell what it is you're selling. Start with the header. Make it problem-solving, to-the-point and in LARGE BOLD RED LETTERS against a WHITE background. Then, proceed to tell a quick story about the problem so many people have that you're about to solve with your product/service. Tell how your product solves their problem in bullet/list format. Tell how you've helped people solve their problem and what they said about you helping them.

Address the most frequently asked questions prospects might have about buying what you're selling. Talk about your guarantee. How there's no risk to buying what you have to sell. Mention the bonuses people will be getting before they even see the buy-now button. Put a dollar value on those bonuses so people can compare what they're paying with what they're getting. Provide an obvious, easy to read/find, big, fat golden buy button with a call-to-action message in the button, such as, "ORDER THIS NOW", "ADD TO CART", etc. Include logos of all the credit cards and payment processing companies you allow payment through. Underneath the buy-now button area, include a personal note from you, along with your photograph, and 2-3 sentences of why folks should get what you're selling and you thanking them. Include 1-2 P.S. with any final "take away" remarks about either time limitations and/or bonuses are limited to only those who purchase today.

With every day (or hour) that passes, the bonuses go down in value, per se. Include a few pictures of your product, and order buttons throughout the sales letter. Show people what they're buying and make it easy for them to click and buy from you. Include your terms of use, privacy policy, applicable earnings disclaimer, affiliate links and contact link at the bottom of your letter. Lastly, copyright the whole page. It's your artwork for selling what you created. Copyright it and date it by the year.

13. ❑ The Week Of The Launch Date — Go over everything related to the launch: website (☑), payment processing in place (☑), thank you page and other pages working (☑), images showing up on the website (☑), product inventory in and systems ready to fulfill (☑), affiliates are anxious and ready (☑), website sales copy has been proofed 10 times (☑), order button links properly through the shopping cart to collect orders (☑), etc.

14. ❑ On The Eve of Launch Date — Send a wishful eMail to all your super affiliates letting them know you're rooting for them tomorrow. Ask if there are any last minute questions. Then, get your rest. Try not to stay up all night working on last minute items. You should have prepared for that so you could get some good rest.

---

15. ❏ **On Launch Morning** — Have a great breakfast, take a walk/jog/workout, etc. Get ready and excited. Today's the day! Check in with them. Is everyone ready? Reconnect with all your affiliates with a simple eMail out to them. "Today's the big day. Here's to a great day of sales! I wish you hundreds of them! - Your Name"

16. ❏ **What Time Should Your Launch Be?** — That depends on what you're selling of course, and who (and where) you're selling it to. But, consider launching your product at 12:00 P.M./ noon Pacific time. For example, by this time, everyone is awake, they've had their breakfast, perhaps lunch (EST). Affiliates have the whole rest of the day (and night) to make all the sales they can up until midnight when either you change the price or take away certain elaborate bonuses, etc. Customers have that same time frame to make their decision to buy or think about it, then come back to the site and buy.

If 12:00 noon isn't good for you, that's okay. I just chose this time just to show you why it's important to pick a time that's good for everyone based on their geographical location, alertness, free from the morning activities, availability before/after lunch (which can always be moved around; driving kids to school cannot), and their energy level for selling all day long. Hey, by midnight, just imagine how many sales you'll have made! Ten to twelve hours of rush sales is a lot. Then, people can still buy at night. Run a 24 hour sale; NOON TO NOON; easy to remember.

One reason not to have your launch too early is so you could have a couple pre-calls/webinars/ tele-calls about the launch event that morning before the actual launch time, which is happening "today, folks" and "in a few hours!" Get people excited. Pump affiliates and prospects up. Make them wait. Can you stream some video of you talking on your headset via Skype to a whole group of people? Make customers and affiliates trigger happy to click that send or buy button. Also, this gives prospects time to arrange any finances if necessary so they can purchase what it is you're selling.

17. ❏ **Days/Hours Prior To The Launch** — Reach out to any of your super/top affiliates. Check in with them if need be. It's still a good idea to get them excited! Everyone at this point deserves any number of revving, pep talks to get them excited about launching. Do one more pass through checking every little thing in your launch project event.

18. ❏ **Debut the Launch** —This is when your website (sales letter) is made public and people are reading your website copy over to see what's in it for them. Of course, you've connected any number of traffic tracking programs/plugins to track where traffic is coming from, how long do visitors stay, where do they go if they leave, how many have actually clicked the order button and not ordered, etc. This is all valuable information.

19. ❏ **During the Launch** —While the launch is happening, conduct a marathon tele-call where that could be streamed online through your website so customers can listen in to the latest news and events occurring while people are buying and affiliates are selling. You could say things like, "Tom J. out of Minnesota just purchased (your product/service name). Thank you, Tom." Or, "I just spoke with Mary out of Washington state. She's going to be using the product/service to _____. She's really excited to start using it."
Seriously, think about it. You've got to conduct your launch like it's some kind of home grown QVC show on TV selling x-product during a win-

dow of time and at a great price, but get it while supplies last. This tele-marathon doesn't have to be for long, but at least run it 1-2 hours past your launch time. Take a break for dinner. Then, get back on the phone (or live on the web) to give updates to affiliates and prospects. You might have a separate call just for affiliates and one for your prospects/customers.

Affiliate calls should be pre-scheduled and occur at specific times so affiliates can call in with questions, hear good news, gather reports on who's winning the affiliate contest. Prospects can hear your live streaming communication from your website during certain times of the day. By nightfall, you've undoubtedly made a number of sales and received personal feedback from customers who are excited to receive/use your product/service. Share their excitement with prospects that remain on the fence, and sales with affiliates.

20. ❑ Refunds & Returns — Sad, but true. Prepare for 30% (+/-) returns and/or negative reviews. This is only said because you have a large number of people buying in a hurry, for example. There isn't always time to make a proper buying decision when you're rushed. Many customers buy a product/service knowing they could get their money back within 30 days if they weren't at all satisfied. Maybe they just wanted to see what the product/service was all about. They forked over the cash and to their honest discovery, they learned it wasn't for them, but wanted to be part of a limited timed offer and see what commotion is about. Now they're returning the product because it's really not for them. That's okay. You weren't shooting for 100% sales, but 60%.
So, just prepare for it. Think nothing of it. You'll win tremendous favor with everyone if you quickly honor those refund requests.

When you do get refund requests, state on your site that you handle them by sending them a check or pushing the money to them via PayPal. Have them fill out a refund form on your website to make it all formal, in addition to following other guidelines you may set for refunds and returns. The only form can also work as a survey to gather information about why they returned the product/service.

You can then give them at least these 2 choices on how they'd like their money back (i.e., via check or PayPal). I say these two options as you DO NOT WANT TO REFUND PEOPLE'S MONEY THROUGH YOUR MERCHANT ACCOUNT, if you used one. Merchant companies frown against too many refunds within a certain period. If you refunded $25,000, they might think that suspicious and temporarily close your account. This is actually another great time to mention merchant accounts.

If you plan a large launch with dozens/hundreds of affiliates and pose to make at least $50,000 in gross sales, you're better off handling all those sales transactions through a company like PayPal.com. They have no limits to the amount of money you can charge or refund to customers. Smaller merchant account providers, such as banks, aren't used to professional marketers, like you and me, making a lot of money fast and within 24 hours like this. For these launches, consider using a payment processer who has no problem with receiving these large amounts. One thing you could do is simply call your merchant account company and tell them what you're up to, but for the most part even that's a bad idea. They may like you. They just don't like the hassle of client refunds hitting all those credit cards on their watch. It makes them look badly to their funding bank or financial backer up the food chain, if you know what I mean. Having said that, if you can still make a lot of money

---

despite the potential for high returns/refunds, then you're okay! Live with the returns and the sizeable profit you made within 24 hours and prepare for your next launch!

21. ❑ AFTER THE LAUNCH —Your work isn't over yet! Here's the time to thank all those affiliates who helped you get rich quick! Send them a personal thank you eMail and even a phone call. Make a private affiliate web page announcing the winners and their prizes. This works as an incentive to motivate those affiliates who didn't make the grade to work even harder during your next launch, which, they hope you have again. These are fun. Fulfill your orders, if you need to, or they were already fulfilled digitally.

About 24-48 hours following the launch, take time to reflect. What did you learn? What went well? What didn't? What would you do next time? Make notes and prepare for an even more impressive and successful launch NEXT TIME! Congratulations on this one, I know you did a great job!

PRODUCT WEB PAGE
CHECKLIST

Depending on the product or service you sell, you'll need a product web page. These pages should feature images and video plus a description, price, and option to buy. The way you present the information will depend on your success at turning prospects into paying customers.

Product pages are fairly easy to create and once you build one, save it as a template for building subsequent product pages Here's a checklist for creating web pages for products, physical and digital, as well as services.

Refer to the illustration on the following page, top to bottom, while you follow the checklist.

1. ❑ Every page, especially product pages, should have a **VIEW CART** and/or **CHECKOUT** link in the top right hand corner so customers can see what they're buying at a glance or checkout and pay for their purchase(s) quickly.

2. ❑ Product pages should have a good sized **image of the product** with an optional **image gallery** below to show other products.

3. ❑ A **product presentation video or trailer** is a GREAT selling tactic to explain what you're selling! Include video on every product page.

4. ❑ **Provide a short description**, along with a **buy button** and **price**. You might display options such as S, M, LG, XLG if selling clothing.

5. ❑ **Offer more detailed descriptions**, rave **reviews or testimonials**, and other sections related to the product you're selling. What do you want customers to know? Tell them!

6. ❑ **Related products** at the bottom of the page can showcase other products related to the one customers view.

7. ❑ Optionally, you can have a **left or right sidebar** showcasing other products, categories, specials, discounts, or other information.

These pages can be built automatically via a shopping cart system such as Woo Commerce or manually with the help of a WordPress page builder plugin such as Visual Composer.

COMPANY LOGO BLOG PRODUCTS SERVICES ABOUT CONTACT

Product Name Title

PRODUCT IMAGE

PRODUCT VIDEO PRESENTATION OR TRAILER

▶

PRODUCT IMAGE GALLERY

Mauris mattis auctor cursus. Phasellus tellus tellus, imperdiet ut imperdiet eu, iaculis a sem.

ADD TO CART

$29.95 + S/H

Category: Books

Product Description	Rave Reviews	Optional Tab

Mauris mattis auctor cursus. Phasellus tellus tellus, imperdiet ut imperdiet eu, iaculis a sem. Donec vehicula luctus nunc in laoreet. Aliquam erat volutpat. Suspendisse vulputate porttitor condimentum. Proin viverra orci a leo suscipit placerat. Sed feugiat posuere semper. Cras vitae mi erat, posuere mollis arcu. Phasellus venenatis, lacus in malesuada pellentesque, nisl ipsum faucibus velit, et eleifend velit nulla a mi. Praesent pharetra semper purus, a vehicula massa interdum in.

RELATED PRODUCTS   < >

SEARCH ENGINE OPTIMIZATION CHECKLIST

Search engine optimization doesn't have to be a mystery or a chore especially when it can help your website achieve higher, organic rankings on the search engines. SEO assesses what each page is about, and how it can be useful for users. What it can do is provide a business branding, traffic, a higher ROI, credibility, and insight into customer behavior. Without it, a website could be virtually invisible. Follow this checklist to understand how SEO paves the way for the customer to get to you without any detours. Here are a few basics.

1. ❑ **Keyword Research** — It doesn't take long to get the hang of doing your own keyword research. Spend a minimum of 30 minutes a week looking up keywords you can use in your current and future copy. Track how visitors come to you and the keywords they enter into the search engines to find you. Insert those words into your copy to improve your search engine ranking positions.

2. ❑ Your website title and content should have relevant keywords unique to your specific business, service and industry.

3. ❑ Every page should have 3-5 unique keywords such as:

   <meta name="Keywords" content="training, videos, video tutorials, online learning, computer training videos, bart smith">

4. ❑ Every page should have unique descriptions such as:

   <meta name="Description" content="Learn computer software at your own pace with Bart Smith, Founder of MyTrainingCenter. com.">

5. ❑ ALT tags and image titles for all your images. An ALT tag is a simple bit of HTML code in the event an image on your web-

---

site does not appear and contributes to the SEO's overall performance.

6. ❑ Backlinks (links on other sites that link back to you) on high-trafficked websites are highly effective. The more the better. I have 250+ product review websites linking back to BartsCookies.com. All of my back links help to boost my site to the #1 spot on Google and other search engines.

7. ❑ Use a FREE Search Engine Submission Service. These automated submission services allow you to enter some information about your website, and submit your site's URL to up to 100 or more search engines with just a few clicks of the mouse.

8. ❑ Submit your website to various directories like Dmoz.org. While directories are just one tool in the toolbox, the benefits of Dmoz.org is that they have actual editors who oversee every application to ensure accuracy, which is in contrast to the vast majority of online directories, that are automated, easy to manipulate

9. ❑ Generate a sitemap.xml file website right. This can be done with a simple WordPress plugin.

10. ❑ Check for broken links, missing images, and 404 pages to avoid damaging your website's usability, rankings, and potential revenue.

11. ❑ Use keyword density checkers to populate pages with the right amount of keywords. Keywords used on a website generally have higher density and are depicted in a larger fonts. It is impor-

tant for your main keywords to have the correct keyword density to rank well in Search Engines.

12. ❑ Use keyword generation tools to generate the right number of keywords you need for a page is critical. No amount of brainstorming will produce the keyword suggestions that you'll need for your website.

13. ❑ Get your website mentioned in the news and get reviews for increased search engine rankings. A couple of tips have already been mentioned (backlinks, exclusive content) which ensures that you will be discovered.

14. ❑ Use paid and FREE submission services to get your websites submitted to the search engines.

SELF-PUBLISHING
CHECKLIST

Self-publishing can be a fun and profitable business in large part due to the many "technological" and online advancements that have been made in the past five years where it concerns printing, publishing, distribution, demand for ("how-to") information ... you name it! Well, in this Self-Publishing Checklist report, you will learn what personal checklists I run through whenever I want to write, self-publish, self-promote and profit from the book ideas I get.

1.0 BOOK IDEA

1.1 ❑ It all starts with an idea! What do you feel driven to write about? A personal experience? Your expertise? No matter, take your idea and run with it!

1.2 ❑ Research The Market: What's NOT out there? Write about it! What (kinds of topics) are people looking for? Research them, and write about them.

1.3 ❑ Write From Your Experience: Did you personal go through an experience, which you feel others might benefit from? Write about!

1.4 ❑ Write A Better Book: Did someone write a book, which you think you could write a better one? Go for it! Spin the idea to your liking, fancy and point of view.

1.5 ❑ Other Reason? _____: What other reasons do you have for writing a book? Write down your ideas and publish them in book-format!

2.0 BOOK TITLE & SUB-TITLE

Let the fun part begin! Coming up with a title for your book is a real joy! Why? Because it's the most creative, puzzle-solving, brain-tinkering time when writing a book.

2.1 ❑ **Study Other Titles:** One of the best ways to come up with your own title is to study other titles out there on the market. Why? For starters, you don't want to come up with a title that's already in print. You also don't want to come up with a title that's close to someone else's title.

Further, you want your title to be unique and original. You can come up with your own unique/original title when you know what else is out there on the market in the form of titles.

For example, imagine you're in a bookstore looking at titles already in print and you're looking for ideas for your book. "... That's not bad ... I don't like that one ... That's boring ... Not too bad ... I got it! (Wow, after looking at all these titles ...) I think I'll call it _____."

Run your title by a few people you TRUST. You can call it an inner circle of friends/associates you know won't take your idea and yet will be honest with their feedback.

Remember, titles sell books alone! So, ask people this question, if you saw a book that was titled, "YOUR TITLE", would you buy it? Listen for all the people who'd say, "Yeah!" You have your title!

2.2 ❑ Creating Titles: Titles should be just a few words and uniquely crafted while subtitles should describe what your book is about without the reader having to turn to the book or TABLE OF CONTENTS for more information.

Keep titles short, sweet and to the point; no more than five words in length. If your title seems to be a bit more descriptive than five words, break it up and toss the extra words into a sub-title and keep the main title short.

2.3 ❑ Register Domain Name For Your Book Title: Once you come up with the title for your product, check to see if the domain name is available, and if it is, buy it! Do this for every information product you want to create! Even if you don't have time to create the product now, buy the domain name and lock it away for your use later.

3.0 ❑ BOOK COVER

They say, "People DO judge a book by its cover!" Truth

is, no one even reads the book before they make a "buying decision" based on the cover! Don't believe me? Check out these words from a famous few:

"Packaging is everything." "Your cover page is one of the most important pages in your publication." "Never underestimate the power of the cover page, even an electronic one."

3.1 ❑ Study Other Covers: One of the best ways to get ideas for your book cover is to look at 20-100 other books on similar (and not-so-similar) topics.

3.2 ❑ Design A Unique Cover: Your book cover should be easy to read from across the room or desktop. Use bold-type lettering and avoid using ALL CAPS unless your title is five words or less. Use light-colored lettering over dark backgrounds or dark lettering over light backgrounds. Your subtitle should usually have a different font or typeface than your main title.

If you feel like designing the front cover of your book, before you start writing it, go for it. I do that all the time. The cover burns an impression on my brain, keeps me reminded of the book, until I find the time to write it. Plus having all that extra time to go over the design helps too. I remember, at the last minute, before print, I changed on major thing to the cover. I'm glad I designed it months ago and had the time to sit on it for awhile.

3.3 ❑ Hire A Professional Book Designer: If you don't feel you can create your own book cover, not to worry. You can hire a professional book cover designer to design one for you. Go to www.Fiverr. com and search for a couple different designers. Compare their work, and take the plunge. You shouldn't have to spend more than $500, roughly, for both the front and back cover. BUT, keep in mind, if you ever change the page count, you'll have to go back to that graphic designer to adjust the spine width. If you can have them turn the files over to you upon completion and payment, that'd be great. If that designer drops out of site, you have your original artwork to give the next designer.

4.0 WRITING THE BOOK

Remember, there's no right or wrong way to write a book. There's just your way! Now, when writing the actual book, here's how it will break down:

4.2 ❑ **Front Pages:** These are individual pages that make up the "front part" of your book. These pages usually include the copyright page, dedication page, acknowledgment page, preface, introduction and the table of contents.

4.2 ❑ **Body Pages:** The "body pages" consist of your chapter pages.

4.3 ❑ **Back Pages:** These pages typically consist of individual pages in the back of the book that might be used to promote or upsell the reader to one or more of your other books, products, or services.

4.4 ❑ **Book Design & Layout Software**: Depending on the software program you might use to write your book (i.e., Microsoft Word, Adobe InDesign, etc.) I would suggest you save your work in two separate files. That is, the FRONT PAGES and the BODY PAGES.

Then, name them respectively:

By naming your book files like you see below, you can easily tell: 1) What book title you're working on, 2) whether the file contains FRONT or BODY+BACK page matter, 3) the 13-digit ISBN#, and 4) the last date you worked on this particular document.

Trust me, all this information is necessary for naming book files. They're also built in separate files because of the page numbering system works. You can usually only choose one format, either regular or roman numerals. (i.e., 1, 2, 3, 4 or i, ii, iii, iv, etc.) When each file is done, you simply print them individually, then merge them into one PDF for the printer to print your book.

4.5 ❑ **Table of Contents:** Believe it or not, while you might come up with a simple "outline" to start writing for your book, the Table of Contents actually might write itself when the book is done. You don't know specifically what might be found in Chapter 4, but you know when that chapter is done, specifically what to list under Chapter 4 in the Table of Contents (after the book is done).

So, when writing your book, just jot down a simple outline of what you'd like to write about, then start writing. No doubt, by the end of your writing, you'll

Here's how I name my book files in my computer ...

FRONT PAGES:

01_BOOK-TITLE_FRONT-PAGES_978-00000000000_091515**.doc**   (Microsoft Word)
01_BOOK-TITLE_FRONT-PAGES_978-00000000000_091515**.indd**   (Adobe InDesign)

BODY+BACK PAGES:

02_BOOK-TITLE_BODY-PAGES_978-00000000000_091515**.doc**   (Microsoft Word)
02_BOOK-TITLE_BODY-PAGES_978-00000000000_091515**.indd**   (Adobe InDesign)

be adjusting the Table Of Contents a few more times to make sure it's just right. Besides, you won't know the page numbers until you're done writing the book anyway.

5.0 COPYRIGHT / ISBN / BAR CODE

5.1 ❑ Copyright Protection: If you don't PROTECT IT, no one will RESPECT IT! If you write, film, dream, sing, paint, act, draw, publish ... PROTECT YOURSELF and YOUR CREATION, and register your work with the US Copyright Office. The fee is roughly $40 per item you wish to copyright. If it comes out of you, copyright it in this manner! You own the right to your work and creation so long as you take the steps to PROTECT IT via COPYRIGHT!

5.2 ❑ ISBN#: Are you writing a book (or series of books), recording audio programs, producing videos and DVD's of your work for sale? Well, then you'll need your own set of ISBN#'s so you can sell them in stores around the world!

If you're publishing your book through a printer, like CreateSpace.com, they can issue you free ISBN#'s, but they are noted as the publisher. Not a bad thing, per se. They are printing and distributing the book. If you don't want that, then you can buy your own ISBN#'s from ISBN.org. They cost roughly $128 for just one; $295 for 10; and 575 for 100. So, you do get a break the more you buy. Each version of a book, print or digital, requires its own ISBN. Be sure to purchase enough for your needs.

5.3 ❑ Bar Codes: If you wish to sell your books and other products to regular chain stores and/or wholesale outlets, then you might have to get a bar code for each product you wish to sell. Bar codes help identify the ISBN, which in turn helps to identify the product's price, publisher, title, author, edition, etc. You can get them made online for free, if you search for "bar code generator." CreatSpace.com will generate the bar code for you if you elect them to issue you ISBN #.

6.0 EDITORS

Your work, whether it's an article, a newsletter, an eBook, a report, an audio seminar, an audio-visual presentation, ... needs to experience editing. That's right, editing!

Editing is the process of closely examining a piece of literary, audio, or audio-visual work for the purpose of identifying errors, inconsistencies, and opportunities for improvement. Editing is not to be confused with proofing which is similar to editing, but in which the examination is much narrower in scope.

6.1 ❑ Hire (1-3) Editors: As you finish the first draft of your (book) manuscript, you will need to hire an editor to look at it so they can "clean it up" and help find mistakes in your writing (i.e., grammar, punctuation, spelling mistakes, typos, etc.)

6.2 ❑ Enter Your Corrections/Suggestions/ Changes: After the editor returns your manuscript back with a number of edits in RED PEN markings, you'll need to enter those edits and make those corrections in your manuscript. This can be a lengthy process, taking up to a week or two to enter the changes your editor makes and suggests, depending on how many pages your manuscript contains.

6.3 ❑ Hire (1-3) Editors (AGAIN): After you enter your changes, and add a few more sentences/paragraphs/ sections to your book (which you might do in the process), it's wise to hire a second editor to review the latest version of your manuscript. Since the first editor might be a little too familiar with the manuscript they proofed, it's a good idea to get a "new pair" of eyes to look at it for the same purpose (i.e., grammar, punctuation, spelling mistakes, typos, etc.).

6.4 ❑ Enter Last Minute Corrections/Suggestions/

Changes: After the second editor returns your manuscript with a number of new (and hopefully fewer) edits in RED PEN markings, you'll need to enter their edits and make the corrections they suggested in your manuscript.

Note, every editor is different in their style, what they look for, how they work, how fast they work, etc. Depending on the changes/corrections the editor sends back to you, entering their corrections/suggestions can be a lengthy process, taking up to a week or two to enter the changes your editor makes and suggests, depending on how many pages your manuscript contains.

7.0 PRINTER / DISTRIBUTOR / FULFILLMENT

Now that your manuscript and book covers are finished, it's time to see a proof of your work before you invest hundreds, perhaps thousands of dollars printing books and spending time working with book distributors to list your book with bookstores all around the world.

7.1 ❑ DO NOT (WASTE YOUR TIME) Looking For A "Traditional Publisher!": Let's get this out of the way, right now. Since you're just starting out, and let's assume you've never printed or published a book before in your life. Here's a reality check ... Publishing companies really won't spend time on any author who (at this point in time) doesn't already have some kind of following, fan-base, track record, etc. Why? Follow the money ... that's all they want. MONEY!

Publishing companies are not in business to make YOU famous. They're in the business of printing books and making money from the sale of books in volume by well-known, experienced and seasoned authors. Period! Let's repeat that ... they're in the business of PRINTING BOOKS! Which means, only if you're well-known, have a track record, are already successful speaking, on the road, on the air, people know you ...

will they even think of talking to you about a "book deal!"

Knowing this all-to-important fact, let's move on to the fact that, you're better off printing your own book first, using your own money, spending your own time marketing it and gaining publicity and popularity on your own terms and efforts ... You're better off doing all of that so that when a publishing company does come around, who do you think has more negotiating power? You do! Absolutely! The publishing company (who makes their money printing books) needs you and not the other way around.

So, knowing these two little facts that publishing companies are book printers in disguise and really won't talk to any new author until that author has a track record of some kind and can move books in (high) volume, let's walk down the simple, controllable and predictable path of ... SELF-PUBLISHING! If you have any questions or concerns about the plusses and benefits of self-publishing over traditional publishing, check out this quick chart outlining the pros and cons:

Submit Your Book Files To A Printer! Depending on the printer you choose to print your first book, you'll need to find out (from them) how you can submit your manuscript and cover files to them so they can print a "proof!" A "proof" is simply a "sample copy" of your manuscript with a color print of the front/back/spine covers of your book for you to "proof" with your own eyes. While you're at it, ask for a cost for a proof! Some printers give you one for free. Each thereafter might cost your $30 per book! OUCH!

❑ How many book proofs should you print in the beginning? ONE! Unless you have a couple people looking over your first proof printing with you. So, it's normal to order 3-5 your first round. Why such a small number? Because in your very first printing, there WILL BE mistakes in them. Guaranteed! So, spending just a few dollars for a proof is nothing. I have friends who printed 1,000 books their first time around. WRONG! They have boxes of unsold books in their garage filled with mistakes. Don't YOU make that mistake.

❏ All you need first time around is a few books to pass out to those who will help you proof it. Make your corrections, then order another round of proofs for you and your proofers/editors prior to distribution..

7.2 ❏ Submit Your Book Files To A Distributor/ Publisher: Once you're satisfied your book reads right, looks good, and is ready for sale, submit it to the printer one more time. At that time, you can list your book with the big bookstore databases, Amazon. com and others.

7.3 ❏ Submit Your Book "Audio" Files To A Distributor/Publisher: Once you submit your book to the printer, it's time to record your book and make an audio product out of it, which you can sell for a very nice profit. When you're done recording your book, you'll then submit the audio files (and cover art) to companies who can duplicate, print, package and ship (or deliver the MP3 downloadable files) of your audio products from sales you make through Amazon.com, your website, and online audio selling retailers.

7.4 ❏ Fulfillment Company: Write this down and repeat it 100x until you believe it true to your heart ... "I do NOT want to do my own fulfillment!" That's right. Plain and simple. YOUR job is twofold, (1) write and (2) market!

Authors who keep writing new books, make more money than those who stop after book one. Authors who market their own books make more money (on average) than those who don't. So, what's left? Enjoying life!

Let a third-party company handle your fulfillment duties. Sure, you might hire an assistant to overlook the duties performed by the fulfillment company, but if you ever make it to television and sell 10,000 books from one appearance on a nation-wide TV show, you do not want to be sitting in your garage 'til all hours of the morning, packing and shipping those book orders.

Printing your book through CreateSpace.com can help you get into Amazon.com. Both outlets help you by doing the printing and shipping at their end when orders come through.

8.0 OTHER PRODUCTS

Now that you're mastering the art of self-publishing, it's time for you to consider creating a host of other products related to your book, which will help you bring in more income for you as you promote and sell your book!

8.1 ❏ Record Your Book: Yes, we just discussed this in the previous Checklist, but it should not be overlooked. Audio is a big money maker, and with iPods and podcasting and MP3 players abound, you can imagine how some people might prefer listening to your book, rather than reading it! So, record your book for pure profit! You'll be glad you did! Oh, and so will your bank account!

8.2 ❏ Create a Workshop/Presentation Out Of Your Book: One of the best ways to promote your book is to speak! One of the best ways to prepare a presentation outline is to steal (content) from your own book! Pick a juicy chapter, create a 30-45 minute speech around the content of that chapter, and start pitching that "speech" to different clubs, groups, businesses, chamber groups, associations, etc. who will invite you to come and speak! Check out these reports on speaking to help get your speaking energy flowing.

8.3 ❏ Create an eBook From Your Book: People might want to get your book fast and won't wait for the mail to ship them one! So, why not create an eBook out of your book. It's easy to do and it's very profitable since there aren't any shipping or printing costs. Take your original Word document, or convert your Adobe InDesign document into Word and format it to submit to Kindle. Once you've done that successfully, submit the same Word document to SmashWords.com for free and get it distributed to all the other eBook retailers around the world. They might take up to 20%, the submission is free and so are their ISBN#'s; last I checked.

8.4 ❑ Create a Home Study Course From Your Book: If you wrote a non-fiction book, you certainly need to create a "home study course" to be sold next to your book and at a higher price point.

Let's say your book sells for $19.95, the audio book version for $49.95; the home study course could sell for as much as $79.95 or even $145.95 ... It's up to you and the value of your content. What does it provide the end-consumer? Does it help them lose weight? Make money? Fall in love? What?

Home study courses can be printed and packaged in 3-ring binders, on 8 1/2" by 11" size paper. They might include audio MP3/CD recordings, DVD/online videos and/or books.

9.0 MARKETING PLAN

With a few dozen books in your possession, your book listed with the big bookstore chains, your book recorded into an audio to sell as an audio product, speeches (written from content in your book) ready to go, it's time you start marketing and exposing your book and all its glory to the world!

9.1 ❑ Build a Website around your book if you don't have one already.

9.2 ❑ Install a Shopping Cart on your website. Add the book as a product to your shopping cart so you can sell it from your website. Create a product page for your book to be sold.

9.3 ❑ Use a merchant account or payment processing option to collect payments for book sales (i.e., PayPal.com, Stripe.com, etc.)

9.4 ❑ Affiliate programs are advisable when selling any product, especially the print version of your book earning a commission for every sale. If you do, don't give them more than 30% commission if there's enough profit in the sale of your book for you and for them.)

9.5 ❑ Hire a publicist to book you with the media, radio and TV shows and interview appearances. For this professional, budget $500-$5,000 per month.

9.6 ❑ Conduct podcast/radio interviews to get the word out about your book. Get interviewed!

9.7 ❑ Launch a Pay-Per-Click advertising campaign on various websites, social networks, and search engines; very affordable. Drive traffic to your book page to start the flow of prospects coming your way and talking about your book ... oh, and buying it!

9.8 ❑ Book store signings are fun and generally people will buy at brick and mortars even when your book is available on Amazon.com, and other bookstore websites.

9.9 ❑ Start having tele-seminars to share your expertise and experience. Seize opportunities for speaking engagements.

9.10 ❑ For more book marketing ideas, check out my special report called: 121 WAYS TO PROMOTE & MARKET YOUR BOOK

http://mytrainingcenter.com/121-ways-to-promote-market-your-book/

10.0 BOOK LAUNCH PARTY

With marketing going strong, books selling, interviews

---

scheduled, why not celebrate with book party? You certainly have good reason to celebrate. Besides, you might sell more books, get some good press coverage, and connect with people that want to hear from you. The five main ingredients for planning a party are audience, location, date /time, budget and venue or theme for your event. Check out some of the details for organizing a book launch party in my book launch checklist!

"BOOKS I WANT TO WRITE, THEIR TITLES & TOPICS"

EXERCISE: Below, write out any book title ideas you have for books you'd like to write. They don't have to be written today, but write down the titles for them and a brief description. Doing this starts the mind in action towards keeping you on track to write them one day. I have a list of about 20+ books I'd like to write. I have their titles and sub-titles written down. So far, I've got 12 written. Then, keep notes in a folder (or on your computer) per book. When the time comes, you already have content waiting to dump right into writing those books!

BOOK TITLE:

DESCRIPTION:

BOOK TITLE:

DESCRIPTION:

BOOK TITLE:

DESCRIPTION:

BOOK TITLE:

DESCRIPTION:

BOOK TITLE:

DESCRIPTION:

SELLING ONLINE
CHECKLIST

When you want to sell something online, look no further than this quick checklist to get started! Selling online is easy when you have the right product, know your target market, have the right pitch/sales letter, shopping cart, marketing tools, fulfillment services, and have excellent customer service in place to ensure success.

1. PRODUCT/SERVICE/CONTENT TO SELL

What you sell online will depend largely on who you are selling to, what need you fulfill, and what problems you can solve. Defining your target market is the hard part, but when you know who your ideal customer is, you can customize your marketing pitch and then everything else will fall into place. In today's market, it's important that you hone in on your target market and focus your marketing efforts and brand message on potential customers that are more inclined to buy from you versus anyone else. This method proves to be more affordable, efficient and effective for reaching potential buyers and generating revenue.

2. WEBSITE OR INTERNET SHOP

To sell online, you don't necessarily need a website. You could sell products on:

- ❑ eBay.com
- ❑ Facebook.com
- ❑ Amazon.com
- ❑ Your website
- ❑ Other websites (auction, retail, etc.)

3. SHOPPING CART

If you plan to sell directly from your website, you'll need a shopping cart to accept and process all of your customer orders. The best way to determine what kind of shopping cart to get is to factor in these considerations:

- ❑ Budget
- ❑ Web-hosted shopping cart
- ❑ Off-site/third-party-hosted shopping cart system
- ❑ eBuilt-in features versus plugins you have to install separately whether FREE or fee-paid plugins. If the plugin you want to use carries a small monthly fee, go for it! If your sales are low at the time, I would opt for the FREE shopping cart (such as WooCommerce. com provided you have a WordPress website). Link it up to PayPal for payments and then purchase one or two plugins to really enhance it. For now, save your money and upgrade later as your needs change.

4. ❑ FULFILLMENT SERVICES

How many products do you want to sell online? Dozens? Hundreds? More? How you answer this question will point you in the direction you need to go. Here are a few more:

❑ Do you have the proper space, supplies, inventory and TIME to do your own fulfillment or should you outsource it?

❑ Would it be more cost effective to do it yourself or hire someone to maintain quality control and fulfillment excellence?

❑ If you plan to sell product in large quantities or on a large scale, consider contracting with a fulfillment house to handle the daily issues and responsibilities. They are the logistics and shipping experts.

❑ If your sole ambitions are marketing and management, a company like Amazon is a go-to option for many because they can offer storage, pick/pack services, and provide enormous exposure. On the other hand, you might be tied to the ideal of customized packaging and have a personal relationship with your customer. Only you can decide what makes sense for your business. Again, weigh the pros and cons related to time, effort and what it will cost.

5. ❑ PAYMENT PROCESSING OPTIONS

If you're going to sell products online, you'll need a method (or two) for collecting receivables from your customers in the form of credit card, PayPal, etc. If you currently have a system that is working for you, stick with it otherwise check out a few other reliable options. It can be daunting task to find one that is a perfect fit for your business. At a minimum, compare rates, fees, processing time, incentives and whether it can be customized.

❑ PayPal.com   ❑ Stripe.com
❑ SquareUp.com   ❑ Authorize.net
❑ JVZoo.com   ❑ ClickBank.com
❑ E-Junkie.com   ❑ Cash/Check
❑ Bitcoin   ❑ 2Checkout.com

6. MARKETING PLAN

You know the old saying, "Build it and they will come?" Well, that doesn't work anymore in the online world and less frequently in the offline brick & mortars.

If people don't know you exist, how will they know where to find you? Once your web site is built, however, you can plan to spend equal amounts of time and money promoting it.

You would never expect a new restaurateur to open its doors before doing any marketing and promotion would you? You expect to see local television commercials, coupons on the back of grocery store receipts, and more. In this business, people are using integrated technology more than ever today from mobile ordering, digital menu boards, to table top e-ordering, coupons and more coupons because many of your customers will be tech-savvy buyers. How do you expect to market your product/service:

❑ Offline Tactics   ❑ Online Tactics
❑ Paid Advertising   ❑ Affiliate Marketing
❑ Social Media Marketing Tactics
❑ Webinars, Tele-seminars, Workshops, etc.
❑ Online/Offline Networking
❑ Other: _____

7. ❑ CUSTOMER SUPPORT SYSTEM

Before you hit the big time on the Internet and as your site/products grow in popularity, it will be important to set up a quantifiable customer service system to support customers and affiliates. Don't count on eMail to handle your customer support needs especially as your business continues to grow and expand. Here are some needs you should implement:

❑ Telephone number visible all over website.

❑ A CONTACT US form on website versus your eMail address.

❑ Support ticket system in place of a CONTACT form.

❑ FAQ page or HELP & SUPPORT page directing customers needing assistance.

❑ Video tutorials on how to use your product/ service.

❑ Refund policy highly visible to protect you and advise customers on refunds/returns.

❑ Purchasing terms and assurances so customers know what to expect and depend on.

SEMINAR/CLASS
CHECKLIST

I f you sell information products, write books and/or offer consulting/coaching services, at some point, you may be asked to be a guest speaker, make a presentation or you may decide to host your own seminar.

Seminars are a great way to introduce new products/services/ideas and more. Success is largely dependent on the venue and how it is produced. Whatever the seminar, the basics are (1) the seminar sets the speaker up as an expert, (2) it targets a select, well-defined group of people, (3) it can motivate the audience to take action, it establishes you as a qualified professional, and (4) it sets you up to sell. Use the checklist for an overview to plan your next event.

1.0 SEMINAR TOPICS & TITLES

1.1 ❑ Seminar Topic

Be sure that you have a good grasp of the topic you speak of particular if you plan a Q&A. Perhaps you'll train a group of people on a particular topic related to a book you authored or on a particular skill. What's the market calling for? What do people want to learn more about? Know the public's views and opinions on the topic you select such as writing, self-publishing, selling books, and making a living as an author.

1.2 ❑ Seminar Title

The title should be persuasive and make an impression on the prospective attendee. The title should be used in communications, learning materials, seminar handouts, etc. Your title should not only be unique, but suggest value, authenticity, even a sense of urgency or need for action in some cases. FOR EXAMPLE: "Write Your Book & Sell Millions!"

1.3 ❑ Seminar Website (Domain Name)

Check to see if the domain name you've chosen is available and then quickly register it for your seminar! Now you can build a website to promote and sell your seminar online.

2.0 SEMINAR DURATION, TIME, DATE & LOCATION

2.1 ❑ Duration

Some seminars last only a few hours while others span

---

several days with a few breaks and/or lunch. If you have multiple speakers over a longer period of time, a three-day seminar, for example, can be exhausting even when you have awesome content. Trust your instincts on people's attention span. Know your audience. You could potentially lose them if the topics aren't engaging, entertaining, and informative.

2.2 ❑ Time

When will your seminar start? This will depend on the group you address. Many business types prefer daytime seminars, but there are also many who cannot get away during normal work hours. Evenings aren't ideal for obvious reasons while mornings can offer a more focused and refreshed audience. (Serving coffee/tea/water at break time helps.) Be certain that attendees know what to expect so they can plan ahead. For example, will you serve lunch or will they be on their own? Suggest where they can grab a quick bite.

2.3 ❑ Dates

Plan ahead. Give attendants ample time to decide to register, pay the fee and schedule your dates on their calendars.

Don't send out an eMail invitation to a seminar for the upcoming weekend or even next week! Take time to promote it properly and ensure that you have all the materials and equipment that you will need, ideally 3-6 weeks in advance.

2.4 ❑ Location

Where will you hold your seminar? At a hotel, club house, office building, school, etc.? Consider holding your event at a location pertaining to your topic such as a history museum or restaurant. Planning ahead potentially save money in terms of reservations and fees. The location should be easily accessed, comfortable, provide ample/affordable/FREE parking, and close to restaurants. Start scheduling your event at least 3-6 months prior to the event. If possible, go

to the facility you are considering for your seminar. Does it meet all of your needs? Do you require catering services? Get a couple of referrals and compare rates and services.

3.0 PRICING & PAYMENT PROCESSING OPTIONS

Your goal should be to generate maximum total revenue for your event, but this will depend on several variables. Suppose you know that attendees will buy product you offer at your seminar. If you can count on high sales, you might want to leverage the fee for your seminar and charge a less amount or offer it at no cost. Depending on content covered, duration of the seminar plus setup/material/marketing costs, you should price your seminar to at least cover your costs. Make it affordable and ensure you produce a nice profit for your time spent in planning, preparing, delivering and cleaning up. The price should be high enough so those who attended are satisfied that the seminar was well worth their time and the information they received was valuable.

3.1 ❑ Pricing Examples

Here are some guidelines when pricing your seminar or other live event.

HOURS / RATE PER PERSON:
1-Hour Seminar $30 - $497
3-Hour Seminar $97 - $497
1 Day Seminar $97 - $997
2 Day Seminar $197 - $4,997
3 Day Seminar $497 - $9,997
1 Week Seminar $997 - $25,000+

You can frequently charge even higher rates when coaching/teaching/training people about business, marketing, how to make money, job training, unique skills, certification programs, etc.

3.2 ❑ "Early Bird" Registration Discount

You can offer "Early Bird" discount registrations

to people when they register early to attend your seminar. It motivates people to pay in advance and it helps to offset your costs prior to holding the seminar. If people wait to register at the door and pay the fee, you can charge more.

3.3 ❏ Offer People "Payment Options"

If you plan to speak, train, coach over several days, you might offer payment options so more people can afford to attend your event such as regularly scheduled monthly payments. Offer a small discount if people do pay the full price up front and charge a small % processing fee for people that opt to make payments to attend your seminar.

FOR EXAMPLE: if it you charged $497 (one-time pay) to attend your seminar, you might offer people the option to make 3 monthly payments of $175 ($525 includes the small fee). How many payments you should allow will depend on the length of your event.

3.4 ❏ Collecting Cash Payments

Depending on the amount you charge to attend your seminar event, most people will not pay with cash. Some will, if it's less than $100 and they can pay at the door, but most will write a check or use a credit card. I you accept cash payment, be sure you are prepared to make change if needed for this type of transaction.

3.5 ❏ Collecting Payments via Checks

If people want to pay by check, let them. Be sure to verify the address, get the telephone number and ask to see a driver's license to compare signatures. Ask for a business card for your records. The information on business cards is generally current when an addresses or phone on a check may not be.

3.6 ❏ Collecting Credit Card Payments

Some people will register for your seminar and pay by check and most will pay with a credit card. That's

our world! If people pay with a credit card, you'll need a merchant account to accept their credit card payments

What's more, if you accept payments via credit card in person, compare the account number on the credit card with the registration form the person completed. Always ask for addresses and phone numbers when accepting credit cards as this information is not on the card.

4.0 SEMINAR, LITERATURE & OTHER PREPARATION

When it comes to the content or topic of your seminar, this part will take some time to develop so close attention to detail and accuracy and even some scheduled rehearsal will ensure that your event is a complete success.

4.1 ❏ Presentation Outline

Whether you're speaking for the duration of the seminar or sharing the platform with another speaker, it will be important to outline your entire presentation on paper, print it out, and rehearse it frequently prior to the seminar. You might ask a few people to listen in and give you feedback on parts of your presentation.

4.2 ❏ Seminar Handouts

Prepare brochures and handouts, fill-in-the-blank forms, survey sheets, resource sheets, order forms well in advance of the seminar. You don't want to be rushed the week of or the night before getting these things copied at the local copy store to avoid feeling rushed, stressed and pressured to get every last detail finished.

4.3 ❏ Seminar Props

Make a list of all the props you will require for your seminar to enhance special points, show real-life examples, give demonstrations, etc. You don't want to forget anything related to this important event.

4.4 ❑ Speaking Attire

Wear clothing that is appropriate for the occasion. Make sure what you wear is clean, well-pressed and doesn't distract. Everything about your speech will affect how your audience perceives you and what you have to say including hair style, body language, grammar, mannerisms, etc. If you are a guest speaker, ask the event coordinator what the usual dress code is. Conventional wisdom says to make a good impression, take your dress code up a notch higher than your audience is dressed. The image you want to present is PROFESSIONAL even if you are speaking to a large group of comic book collectors.

4.5 ❑ Audio Recording (Your Seminar)

Would you like to record your seminar and turn that recording into an audio product that you can sell? Here are your options:

4.5.1 ❑ Record It Yourself

Hook up a microphone to a recording device, whether you're latptop, cell phone, mp3 digital recording device, tablette, etc., and start recording.

4.5.2 ❑ Hire Someone To Record It For You

How long is your presentation? One hour? Three hours? All day? The shorter your presentation, obviously the easier it is to record yourself. For long presentation, I recommend that you hire a professional or individual that has some experience so you aren't distracted and you can count on a quality recording.

4.5.3 ❑ Record Each Segment Separately

Timing is important when recording voices. For example, one should start recording prior to the speaker's first word and then stop recording after the speaker stops speaking. Each audio file should be named and numbered accordingly, preferably starting with 000- (three digits in the front of each recording so you know the sequence for each recording. That

might look something like this:

    001-Topic spoken on.mp3
    002-Topic spoken on.mp3
    003-Topic spoken on.mp3
    004-Topic spoken on.mp3
    005-Topic spoken on.mp3

Use three digits opposed to two digits. There's no accounting for mistakes and retakes.

4.5.4 ❑ What kind of equipment do you need to record?

❑ Lavaliere Microphone

❑ Wireless Headset Microphone

❑ Handheld (not the best if you want hands-free)

❑ Portable MP3 Recorder or Cellphone

❑ Laptop

❑ Tablette

❑ Cell Phone

4.5.5 ❑ What kind of recording software do you need?

❑ Sony's Sound Forge "Audio Studio"

❑ Audacity

❑ Other: _____ (Your Choice)

If you don't have recording software, equipment or the ability to record yourself, here some suggestions:

❑ Buy equipment and learn how to record your own seminar or have an expert record so you can focus on your presentation.

❑ Hire a professional to record it for you. Get quotes from customers if possible. Ask, "What do you charge? What's your process for recording seminars?" You might ask about the software and equipment he/she will use. Discuss editing and turnaround for producing a quality product. What format will the recording be delivered in? CD? MP3? WAV? Regarding their fees, offer a partial payment with the balance paid in full when you have the finished product and you're satisfied with it. If you are interested in learning how to record, you might ask the recorder to give you some tips for a fee, of course.

4.6 ❑ Video Recording (Your Seminar)

Would you like to record your seminar on video for a DVD product? All you need is a really need is at least one good video camera, a high quality microphone that ties into the video camera(s), tripod(s) and someone to monitor them. This is something you can't really do yourself, unless you have the type of equipment that actually follows you via motion detector. Otherwise, hire a pro.

Get quotes from video recording experts and ask questions. "How do you go about video recording the seminar event?" Check their availability for your scheduled event. Ask about their editing process and how quickly they can turn your video recording around. In what format will your video be delivering? DVD? MP4? WMV? MOV? Compare rates.

4.7 ❑ Rehearsal

Practice your seminar presentation outline, handouts, props and other aspects of your seminar ready and accounted for, do a dry run of your presentation to ensure that it flows and you consistently emphasize the major points of your message. Ideally, give your presentation to a selected fee (family/friends/business associates) who will give you constructive feedback.

If your presentation includes props, practice handling them and ensure they are accessible and in working order. If you are speaking on a stage or platform, be sure you know the dimensions and how much reach you have to navigate the space. TIP: Rehearse 5-15 minute sections of your presentation so you don't feel overwhelmed to perform. Those first five minutes will speak volumes to your audience about your comfort level with your materials, so, practice!

5.0 GUEST SPEAKERS [OPTIONAL]

Will you have a guest speaker at your seminar or will you be co-hosting the event? If you plan to share the stage with another speaker, here are a few tips:

5.1 ❑ Contact your guest speaker(s) long before the seminar is promoted, scheduled and booked. Check to see if they're interested and available to speak at your event. You'll want speakers to be sure they know what your expectations are. Once you've made initial contact, send a formal letter via regular mail to confirm their accepting your invite to speak at your event and then check in with the person, periodically, until the day of the event. You may even ask for a copy of the person's speech to certify that the content complements the theme for your event. This will also ensure the person's commitment and guarantees that he/she has all the information needed prior to the event.

5.2 ❑ Get a photograph and biography of guest speakers prior to the event. This may be available on the person's website otherwise ask for a digital copy of both that you can include in your seminar packet and handouts. If you have a seminar web page or another website, post any seminar literature that you publish to showcase your credentials as well as the guest speakers.

5.3 ❑ If you do not plan to pay a fee for your guest speaker, offer an opportunity to sell their product/ service at the event, particularly if the individual has travel expenses. Set aside a specific time to sell so neither of you is interrupted when giving your presentations. Don't be surprised if a potential guest speaker comes back to you with a request a speaking fee. If the fee is significant, it could potentially cut into your profits for hosting the event. Negotiate. Maybe there's a reciprocal service you can provide the guest speaker for his/her time.

5.4 ❑ Have each speaker you invite to speak at your seminar promote your seminar to their list. Increase the number in your list that has already given you permission to send them eMails on a regular basis. Secondly, ask your guest speaker to either provide you with his/her list or ask the person to send your eMail to them on your behalf. More tips will be mentioned later in this checklist under "Tele-Seminar Preview Calls!"

5.5 ❑ Have each speaker you invite to speak at your seminar sign an agreement stating you have the right to record their presentation and resell it with/ without compensation. As a courtesy, offer your guest speaker an audio or video recording of his/her presentation. Don't give the other speaker a recording of the entire seminar as that would be giving away YOUR potential profits. Do be certain that you have the guest speaker's permission to use his/her participation of the recorded event.

6.0 SELLING PRODUCT [BACK OF THE ROOM]

What's great about conducting your own seminar is that you can make money, not just from ticket/ registration sales, but also by selling product in the back of the room or more ideal location. You can sell your product(s) for 100% profit and sell your guest speaker's product(s) for a percent of sales depending on your agreement.

6.1 ❏ If you don't have a product, create one. Assuming you want to make money at your seminar in addition to ticket sales, create something that aligns with your theme or relates to what you are speaking about. At a minimum, sell a copy of the audio or video of your presentation.

6.2 ❏ If you don't have time to create product, sell a recorded seminar. You'll need to pre-sell your recording in advance of the event unless you record a polished dry run of it. Announce at the beginning of the event, that a recording will be available for sale and provided your content is especially note-worthy, buyers may be inspired to buy the recording versus taking copious notes. Give people a couple of options when selling any product/service and don't over-sell. You want to appear masterful and not like some hotshot. For those attending the seminar, offer a discount if they buy the product at the seminar otherwise, they'll pay more online, later.

6.3 ❏ Do you have invited guest speakers? Provide your invited guests speaker(s) with a separate table to showcase their products. Some events place speaker tables outside of the seminar room so inquiring customers don't disturb other speakers that are performing in the seminar room.

6.4 ❏ Negotiate a percent of sales deal (up to 50%) with your invited guest speaker(s) for the opportunity you've given them to speak and sell product/service at your seminar. Another way to do this is to sell table space. This is often done for a fee of $50-$100 and the guest speaker keeps all the profit from his/her sales. Positioning table sales can also be advantageous and for both. After all, you're providing the space, venue, marketing and handling registration and other administrative tasks! If you're doing all the work, it's fair to ask for a % of sales or a flat fee to set up their products for sale at your event.

7.0 STAFFING [SEMINAR SUPPORT]

Depending on the size of your event and the duration, you may or may not need assistance. Ideally, you should have one person that can ensure everything runs smoothly.

7.1 ❏ A proven formula states that for every 10 people in your audience, it's advisable to have one designated person to help out. This will depend, obviously, on whether you are selling product/services, refreshments are served, etc. Your time should be dedicated to making your presentation, answering questions about the topic, and networking. I would suggest that you have at least one person selling for you and more if you know that you'll be selling a lot of product.

7.2 ❏ Support staff can be volunteers, paid staff, or anyone willing to work for lunch/dinner/hotel such as a friend or family member. A flat rate such as $100 per day is recommended versus an hourly rate. You can also offer your products/services provided they have value for the person. Whatever you agree to put it in writing and commit to it.

7.3 ❏ Employ someone to manage the registration table, manage the room and product table, etc. If during break time, there are 30 people in the seminar room that are mingling, asking questions, buying product, trying to get your attention ... you need help! Again, it can be any trustworthy, respectful, capable individual.

7.4 ❏ Where can you find the help you need? Family, friends, clients, affiliates, students, and neighbors can work. Just be sure they are reliable and committed to your success. During long seminars, "helpers" may get tired, bored, even distracted. Keep your eye on them and let them know when they are doing a great job and show your appreciation for helping you make your seminar a success. DO compensate them for their time and effort, especially, if they volunteered. A dinner at a special restaurant, theatre tickets, and a gift certificate that the person will enjoy are just a few ways to say, "Thank you! I couldn't have done it without you!"

8.0 WEBSITE & SHOPPING CART [PROMOTION & PAYMENT COLLECTION]

If you want to promote your seminar effectively (and on the cheap), build a website that is informative and attracts attention! Showcase every topic/benefit you'll cover/teach/train at your seminar, introduce guest speakers (if any), and provide testimonials from satisfied customers regarding your teaching/credentials), and them provide the time/date/location of the seminar, cost to attend, along with numerous opportunities on your web page so people can register for the event and pay online!

When it comes to designing a "seminar website" to promote your event, there is a specific layout to follow. FOR EXAMPLE: Look over the following sample "seminar web page" layout design. See the large, bold headers? Insert your seminar title here.

Note how each section is clearly identified by its own header? This makes for easy reading. Can you see how the top of the web page talks about benefits and what one can learn? This gets readers' attention and keeps them interested. Also, notice that there are numerous registration buttons throughout the page making it easy to immediately register.

This is just a sample "seminar website!" You don't have to follow this layout exactly. I expect you to have some of your own ideas for how you want your seminar website to look. Get creative! Your seminar is intended to showcase one main idea and should not be loaded down with heavy content, but make the viewers' experience easy to use and get what they need.

9.0 MARKETING & SEMINAR PROMOTION TACTICS

You know the old saying, "Build it and they will come?" Seminar websites are usually one-page websites dedicated to one event. These sites are usually straightforward and require just a couple of clicks to sign up, register, buy, etc. They communicate a simple message and work smoothly and effortlessly. Once your seminar website is built, spend equal amounts of time and money (optional) marketing your site to niche groups and organizations, your community and much more depending on what you have to offer. You would never expect a new restaurant to open its doors without promoting themselves? How will you promote your seminar website and everything you have to offer?

9.1 ❑ Affiliate Program

The key to success with affiliate programs is taking what you know best, developing a website on it, honing in on your passion/talent/abilities/credentials, and attracting as much targeted traffic as you can and an excellent way to promote your seminar website is to get others to promote it to their lists of prospects/clients. Affiliates could host tele-seminars with you as their invited guest to discuss your area of expertise (on the call). They could also provide the link to your seminar website in their eZine, on their website and in every eMail they send! Does your shopping cart have a built in affiliate tracking system? If not, this is lost revenue. You could use a third-party system like iDevAffiliate.com or WPAffiliate.com to do this for you. Here are a few more ideas to promote your site.

9.2 ❑ eMail Your Own List

If you have a list of prospects, clients and affiliates, be sure to eMail them in advance of the scheduled time of your seminar. If the reader is not already an affiliate, encourage them to sign up for your program where everyone is a winner.

Regardless of your exact needs, you want an eMail broadcasting tool that is reliable, affordable and easy to use. You can probably use the software that you already have however if you're planning to send hundreds and more eMails from your server, your eMail could be flagged as spam. There are several straightforward, inexpensive, even FREE broadcast eMail services such as Google Groups and Yahoo

Groups. Before you make any decision regarding which tool, answer these questions: (1) How many eMails do you need to send and how frequently? (2) Will you be able to integrate eMail addresses? (3) Will you eMails be highly formatted or simple text? Knowing the answers to these questions should give you good direction in choosing the tool that will work best for you.

9.3 ❏ Tele-Seminar [Preview Calls]

One of the best ways to inform, generate interest and motivated others to register for your seminar is with a series of tele-seminar preview calls! If you are the only speaker at your event, you can host any number of these preview calls with your own lists and lists that others will share with you.

If you have guest speakers, they too can conduct their own tele-seminar preview calls with their list. Simply interview them or ask them interview you about a key topic that is of interest to both of your lists. The preview call is designed to motivate and inspire people to want to know more and they can get that level of detail when they sign up for your seminar.

9.4 ❏ Webinar [Preview Sessions]

Another great way to inform people about your event is to go through a number of PowerPoint slides (presentation format) of the topics you'll be covering in your seminar. Peak their interest via webinars and then sell them on your content by encouraging them to register for the live event. If you are the only speaker at the event, you could host several webinar preview sessions with your own lists and lists owned by others. If you have guest speakers, have them conduct the same time of webinars with their list and return the favor.

9.5 ❏ Speaking

If the seminar is in the not too distant future, take

advantage of every opportunity to speak before live audiences. At these times, mention your seminar and how you can give them $100 off (for example), if they sign up with you today! Or, refer them to your website and say, "Just mention that you heard it here _____ to qualify for the $100 discount off the registration price." Be sure to sign up the person that invited you to speak as an affiliate. Now, people have more incentive to mention your seminar in their eZines, eMail blasts, speaking engagements, etc.

9.6 ❏ Your Own eZine

If you have an eZine (online newsletter), be sure to announce your upcoming seminar in every issue. The more exposure you can get, the more success you'll have. It can take people several reminders to sign up for something so allowing them ample time to register (2-3 months or more) gives people plenty of time and opportunity.

9.7 ❏ Your Own Website/Blog

Why not blog about your upcoming event and the

Many of **MY CHECKLISTS** have video tutorials that teach you more at www.**MyTrainingCenter.com.**

things you'll be teaching including your guest trainers if any. Ask your guest speakers for content for your blog that you can post under a category called "Events." There are a number of FREE services that will host your blog. It requires minimal technical knowledge and posting entries is as simple as entering content onto a screen and pushing the "publish" button. Blogging has become a highly useful marketing tool.

9.8 ❏ Your Website Calendar

If you have a calendar on your website, you could post the event upcoming on online calendar so people can view it. If you have a WordPress website, you can find FREE and low-cost calendar plugins. I recommend you get one or embed a Google calendar if you have a Gmail account.

10.0 THE DAY BEFORE & THE DAY OF THE SEMINAR

On the day of your seminar, you want to feel fresh and on track for making a winning presentation. Avoid stress at all costs. Here are a few suggestions:

10.1 ❏ Pack & Prepare (The Night Before)

Don't make the mistake of forgetting something important for the seminar. Create a "to-do" checklist and pack your suitcase/auto (if needed) so you aren't running around on the morning of the event.

10.2 ❏ Get Plenty Of Sleep [The Night Before]

Try to get 8 hours of sleep in advance of your big day. You want to look and feel your best through the course of your seminar and don't forget to breathe! Breathe right by inhaling through your nose, holding it for 6 seconds, and breathing out through your mouth. Doing this for several minutes than lower blood pressure and create a sense of calm that will pay off.

10.3 ❏ Arrive At Least 1 Hour Early

Think about the things you need to do when you arrive at the seminar location. This will determine how early you should arrive. You'll need to check in with the site manager, unload your car, set up registration/product tables, oversee that the facility has set up everything as expected including the right room. Allow for any last minute emergencies in your window of prep time.

10.4 ❏ Registration/Product/Other Tables

If the facility hasn't already done so, set up the registration table so you (or assistant) can register people who walk in early! Be sure your product tables are ready for these early-birds preview items before the event begins. If there is ample time between breaks, you can sell product, but I don't recommend it, because handling and/or reading about your product can be distracting. Wait to sell after the presentation and be prepared to sell quickly because you don't want anyone to have to wait to buy when what's really on their minds is leaving the building, facing traffic, another engagement, and going home.

10.5 ❏ Distribute Any Seminar Literature

If you created any seminar handouts or other literature, place them on chairs or make them available on tables. Again, I discourage you from distributing handouts prior to your presentation because you don't want people to read along while you're speaking. You want all eyes on you. Now, if you are training or coaching and it's important for the audience to follow a printed booklet or worksheet, it's a challenge to maintain their attention when they're writing notes and flipping page to page.

10.6 ❏ Assigned Duties For Staff /Helpers

See that everyone associated with making your seminar a success fully understands their role and assigned tasks. Give them an opportunity to ask questions and feel satisfied that all assignments are clear prior to stepping on stage. Even if you've delegated someone to oversee your event, it's your responsibility that everything runs well.

Check in with your staff and assist where you're needed. Recognition and appreciation for jobs well done are empowering especially when people are working tirelessly and share your success.

10.7 ❑ Set Up Any Props

Ensure that any props you planned for your event are in the right place and in working order. How many times have you witnessed a speaker click a remote anticipating the DVR to work only to discover that it wasn't plugged in? You don't want any delays or mishaps. In certain cases, it's good to have a useful person in the wings while you deliver your presentation just in case.

10.8 ❑ Audio/Video Recording Set Up

If you're seminar is recorded, make sure the audio/video team is ready and don't anticipate any problems. The finished product they deliver needs to be an example of their best work. To ensure that it is, check in with them and compliment their work and efforts. Their day, no doubt, started early like yours and ended late like yours.

10.9 ❑ Lights, Camera, Action!

"It's show time!" Everyone to their station, it's time to begin!"

"Good morning and welcome to today's presentation of _____. I'm so glad you could join us. Before we begin, let's take a quick look at the seminar handout you found on your chair. It has a detailed itinerary for today's schedule and the next couple of day so you know what to expect. (You might read through it and emphasize any important points on the schedule.) Now, let's get started.

11.0   Follow-up, eClasses, Making Money & Your Next Seminar

With all of the activities, duties and responsibilities associated with setting up a seminar and conducting it, following up with your audience AFTER the seminar is equally important, if not MORE valuable than any other step in the process! Informative follow-up AFTER a seminar can be very lucrative and, yet, it is often overlooked, undervalued and rarely capitalized on. Here's why and here's what YOU should do after every seminar you conduct:

11.1 ❑ Survey Your Attendees

How else are you going to get valuable feedback, know what people thought about the seminar,

---

what they learned, what they didn't? Is it what they expected? What did they learn? What did they think about your speakers (if any)? What did they think about you and the content you presented? What would they suggest you add? Remove? Change? Improve? You want (and need) this information for your next seminar performance!

Now, you could send out a one-sheet survey form at the end of the event, but most people don't want to take the time to fill it out then and if they do, their answers will be scripted in haste and barely readable.

Instead, send out an eMail survey that asks no more than 10-20 simple questions and then give them space to add comments (optional). Sending the survey immediately following the seminar ensures that the feedback will be honest and on point. Let people know that you are eager for their replies to convince them that this is important to you and you value their time and input. You can create your own survey or go to SurveyMonkey.com that will help you create an online survey with ease.

Don't forget to include that your services are available for coaching and/or training in your field of expertise.

11.2 ❑ [Follow-up] eClasses

How many times have you been to a seminar and upon returning home said, "I am completely overwhelmed by everything that I learned, today! How can I remember all of it? And, there were so many good speakers!"

Here's your opportunity to be their hero. Whether there were multiple speakers at your seminar or not, you are the speaker that you want others to remember. Encourage your audience members to sign up for "eClasses" (If appropriate) that will follow up on the seminar material. Inspire them with more details and more content, etc. Let them

know that you'd like them to join your elite valued customer program where they will be privy to your tele-seminars, webinars, and eMail blasts on many interesting topics going forward.

Assure them that with your guidance and direction, they'll learn how to apply the rich nuggets they took away from your seminar(s).

11.3 ❑ Private Consulting

Perhaps, some of your audience members are ready to take the next step and hire you as their personal mentor or private coach. There is money to be made consulting and coaching clients to higher levels of success with your help. Let your customer base know that you are available to discuss private coaching opportunities in their field of interest.

11.4 ❑ Seminar Product Sales

Now that your seminar is recorded (audio and/or video), buyers of your products can appreciate them in the comfort of their homes or offices. This is especially worthy when you cover a lot of content, demonstrated tools, showcased examples, and more.

Make an announcement to your subscribers by eMail that the recorded version of the seminar they attended is now available for purchase and then offer a discount for the first 100 people that sign up for it now or a reduced price to those that buy within the next 24 hours or offer a FREE copy of your book, tools, guidelines, directions, etc.

11.5 ❑ Your Next Seminar

If your first seminar was a success, then you have paved the way to more rewarding seminars. Typically, large seminars are conducted once per quarter or biannually or they are seasonal events.

SHOPPING CART
CHECKLIST

CHOOSING THE RIGHT SHOPPING CART

Do you need a shopping cart for your website? There are plenty of options, but how do you narrow the scope on which is the best shopping cart? Here are some facts to help you with your decision …

1.0 TYPES OF SHOPPING CARTS

1.1 ❑ Shopping Cart Installed On Your Hosting Server

This type requires a lot of knowledge about databases, software installation, and setup. If something goes wrong, most of the responsibility falls on you, or someone you would have to hire. Support MIGHT be available, but not without a fee. OUCH! Customer data is stored in a database on your server. From a security standpoint, that's not wise.

1.2 ❑ Shopping Cart Plugins (*Such as WordPress, Joomla, or Drupal, etc.*)

This kind of shopping cart requires that you install a shopping cart plugin specifically designed to work with your website content management system, such as WordPress, Joomla or Drupal. Installation takes only a few minutes. Then you must customize the cart inside your website's dashboard, which takes about 30-60 minutes. This is required for any cart you choose. Customer data is stored in a database on your server. From a security standpoint, this is not recommended, per se, unless the credit card information is stored offsite, through your payment processing company like PayPal.com, Stripe.com, etc.

1.3 ❑ Third-Party/Off-Site Shopping Carts

No installation is required AND customer/order information is stored on their servers and not yours. That's a big plus, from a security standpoint. The downside for those starting out is that these shopping cart systems typically charge a monthly fee of $50-$350 per month.

Which system is best for you will depend on your comfort level with the technology, your budget and a desire for built-in shopping cart features, bells and whistles.

Most people opt for the third-party shopping cart solution or a plugin type shopping cart solution. Another determining factor is pricing, which I discuss in more detail in my checklist.

2.0 PRICING, FEES & COST

Shopping carts come in a variety of pricing options:

2.1 ❏ Some are FREE, except for a one-time fee for support and/or extra features/benefits/plugins to enhance the cart.

2.2 ❏ You pay a one-time fee for the shopping cart that is moderately priced fee at $50-$2,500.

2.3 ❏ You pay an on-going/monthly or annual fee. This can run from $50-$250 per month depending on the number of extra features you need, or $97 per year for some I've seen.

What's your budget? Can you afford a $50-$250 monthly fee for a shopping cart? Do you have enough sales coming in to justify that cost? You might opt for a lower-cost, perhaps free, shopping cart in the beginning. Let's look at basic functionality so you can better access your immediate needs.

You could start out with one cart, which is more affordable, then leap to a better one as sales come in. Up to you!

3.0 FUNCTIONALITY (BARE ESSENTIALS)

These are the bare essentials you should expect from any shopping cart:

3.1 ❑ Ability to add products to the cart is simple, easy and be able to quickly display products on your website. Generate simple product buy-me links, which can be placed on your website or blog (or in an eMail), and provide links for customers to "view cart" or "checkout" when they're ready to buy.

3.2 ❑ Calculates sales tax, country tax, and any other taxes.

3.5 ❑ Calculates shipping costs based on weight, item count, selection, and/or geographic location.

3.6 ❑ Offers coupons and discounts.

3.7 ❑ Prints customer order packing slips (without pricing on them) or invoices (with prices included) that are then inserted into the customer's order.

3.8 ❑ Accumulates customer information and allows you to eMail those customers directly when you need to within the shopping cart system without having to link up to a 3rd party eMail/autoresponder system.

3.9 ❑ Option to export customer's order information so you can use it offline for your use such as printing reports to fulfill product, printing postage labels, etc.

3.10 ❑ Provides sales reports that show sales by customer, product, day, week, month, year, sales tax collected, etc.

3.11 ❑ Gives you the ability to search/add/edit clients when the need arises.

If some of the last few features don't come with the shopping cart you're looking at using, but gives you the option to add them via a plugin with little to no extra cost, no problem. However, if these features don't come with your shopping cart and they cost to add them to the cart, think again. At least you know the minimum requirements for your needs.

There are additional features that can enhance your shopping cart under a single login account, but don't overdo it. Having to piece together all the different components of a full-blown, feature-rich shopping cart can be time-consuming and costly.

4.0 EXTRA FEATURES, BELLS & WHISTLES

What's a worthwhile enhancement to add to a shopping cart?

4.1 ❑ Digital Product Delivery

4.2 ❑ Email Broadcasting

4.3 ❑ eZine/Newsletter Broadcasting

4.4 ❑ Opt-In Form Creation

4.5 ❑ Autoresponders

4.6 ❑ Affiliate Program

4.7 ❑ Ad Tracking & A/B Testing Tools

4.8 ❑ Fulfillment Notification

4.9 ❑ Membership Site/Management Functions

If these features aren't built into your shopping cart, in most cases, you'll need to track down an app or plugin compatible with that shopping cart. You may need to use a third party service to accept some of these enhancements that will charge a monthly fee (or one-time purchase) based on usage.

5.0 PROS & CONS FOR BUILT-IN FEATURES VS. ADDITIONAL PLUGINS

5.1 ❑ BUILT-IN FEATURES:

- The PROS: You have one account and numerous features to help grow your business.

- The CONS: The cost ranges from $50-$250 per month.

5.2 ❑ ADDITIONAL PLUGINS:

- The PROS: These plugins can be added as needed.

- The CONS: Some are fee-based, one time fees, and generally affordable.

What kind of cart do you need and what features do you need with that shopping cart? If you're making enough sales to pay the monthly fee for the shopping cart that has virtually everything you need to run your business under one login, that's the one I recommend!

On the other hand, if you're just starting out, sales are guarded, go with free shopping cart plugins, and then add feature plugins as needed.

Once you start making sales, upgrade your shopping cart. Don't rush when it comes to changing shopping carts either. You don't want to upset the flow of orders. Study the new shopping cart system and plan how you'll make a smooth transition.

6.0 HAVE YOU DECIDED?

6.1 ❑ FREE SHOPPING CART

If this is the route you're taking, then you might choose WooCommerce if you have a WordPress website. Connect it to your PayPal or Stripe account for payment collection, and install any of the FREE or pay-for plugins related to what you need in addition to the shopping cart from the list Checklist #4 to upgrade your cart. Within 24 hours, you should be selling online from your website/blog. Save your money, and add more robust features later.

6.2 ❑ FEE-BASED, THIRD-PARTY HOSTED SHOPPING CART

If this type of shopping cart is for you, and if you know what features you're looking for, here are some shopping cart solutions to look at:

- Cart66.com

- Shopify.com

- UltraCart.com

- MyMarketingCart.com

- AmericCommerce.com

- CoreCommerce.com

- BigCommerce.com

- InfusionSoft.com

- Magento.com

... among others!

SHOPPING CART
CHECKLIST

ADDING A PRODUCT TO THE CART

ADD TO CART

BUY NOW

REGISTER NOW

ORDER NOW

When it comes to adding a product to the shopping cart, the process is about the same for all shopping carts. I recommend you review this checklist and "check off" each item when adding any product to your shopping cart:

1.0 ❏ Assign a product category and/or sub-category.

2.0 ❏ Select the type of product (digital, physi-cal, service, event/registration, membership level, etc.).

3.0 ❏ Add product title.

4.0 ❏ Add short and long product description.

5.0 ❏ Add product price.

6.0 ❏ Upload an image of the product.

7.0 ❏ Customize product recurring billing options to allow for more than one payment when customers purchase products.

8.0 ❏ Charge shipping and handling (yes/no).

9.0 ❏ Collect sales tax (yes/no).

10.0 ❏ Is this product on sale or offering any special discount pricing (yes/no).

11.0 ❏ Add additional tab information and content if your cart builds automatic product pages like WooCommerce does to make more sales. You might add reviews/testimonials, video trailers, etc.

12.0 ❏ Quantity discount if bought in bulk, set a minimum quantity purchase and/or set discount

%/$-off.

13.0 ❑ Set inventory limits. (Leave blank=unlimited, or insert a number like 20 units left. "Out Of Stock" message will appear when the count runs down to "0".)

14.0 ❑ Add product options/features (small, regular, large, and additional pricing for x-large, etc.).

15.0 ❑ Assign an autoresponder to this product.

16.0 ❑ Assign product to an affiliate program.

Have a default affiliate program or a specific one for one product.

17.0 ❑ Assign specific affiliate commissions for each product with either 1st and/or 2nd tier affiliate commissions.

18.0 ❑ Active / Inactive product allow you turn sales of products on/off.

What else do you need to know about adding a product to the cart? That will depend on the shopping cart and the features that come with it.

Here's an example of adding a product (i.e., book) to a shopping cart system:

Like many shopping cart systems, adding a product is easy. Simply enter a name for the product, short description, a price, sku# (optional), and when you're done, you should be provided a BUY-ME link to place on your website.

Add/Manage Product

Product Information	Subscription Plans	Product Image	Product Options	Links

Product Name: **B.S. The Book by Bart Smith (Print Version)**

Product Type: **Product** ▼

Short Description: **This is a self-help, non-fiction book designed to help rid your personal life of B.S.**

Status: **Active** ▼

Price: **$19.95**

SKU: **1038335**

Name	Link	Copy
B.S. The Book by Bart Smith (Print Version)	https://yourname.shoppingcartco.com/app/addProduct?productId=48&subscriptionPlanId=5	Copy

TELE-SEMINAR
CHECKLIST

One of the best ways to get your message out to the world, whether you are promoting a book or seminar or your expertise on a specific topic is a tele-seminar! Tele-seminars are "seminars" by "telephone" conducted from the comfort of your own home, office or other location. With tele-seminars, you can reach potentially thousands, even millions, of people via the phone! Before conducting your tele-seminar, take a look at the checklist to ensure that your tele-seminar is a success!

1.0 TELE-SEMINAR PURPOSE & TITLE

Determine the purpose or reason why you want to conduct a tele-seminar. Create A catchy title for it.

For Example: "10 Ways Win the Lottery With (Your Name)"

1.1 ❑ Affiliate Training Call

Is this tele-seminar meant to train your affiliates? Maintaining regular contact with your affiliates (weekly, biweekly or monthly) is critical to your success. Each call should be about training, motivation, insights to using your products/services, contest announcements, etc. The more your affiliates know and are engaged in selling for you, the more revenue for both of you.

1.2 ❑ Ask Campaign

What's your prospect/client thinking? What are their needs? What are their concerns? What are their suggestions for improvements? ASK THEM! You could run an "ask campaign" with your telephone where you create a web page that asks a simple question: "What is your biggest question about _____(Enter your area of expertise.)?" When you compile all the questions, choose the top ten and respond to them on your next tele-seminar. Record it! Ideally, post it on your website. Tele-seminars are a powerful training tool and means of sharing information.

1.3 ❑ Expert Interviews / Ask The Expert

Invite guest experts to participate on your tele-seminar. This is usually done at no additional cost to you as guest speakers get a lot of FREE exposure

MY CHECKLISTS

for their products/services.

1.4 ❑ Membership Calls

This is a mutual way to add value to your membership site as well as other membership sites. Record the calls, and archive them behind a membership-protected website. The more calls you conduct, record and archive, the more valuable it becomes to your members.

1.5 ❑ Preview Call

These calls preview and showcase items for purchase such as seminars, workshops, home study courses, etc. They can also alert prospective buyers in a niche market about a new product or service that's ready to launch and you selected these callers to view it first.

1.6 ❑ Virtual Book Tour

Did you write a book or design a product that the market has been waiting for? Reach a global market by offering a virtual tour of what you have to offer. How convenient! Just eMail your list (and/or other people's list) to announce the tour date of your tele-seminar. This is a great way to make sales. Think of the possibilities!

1.7 ❑ Other? _____

Tele-seminars are one of the most effective ways of promoting and selling products and services. They help you build closer relationships with customers and prospects and there is no limit to what you can do. Create a unique list or campaign in your eMail system along with a specific sign-up, confirmation eMail and autoresponder series.

2.0 ❑ Date, Time & Duration Of Tele-Seminar

WHAT are the best days to conduct a tele-semi-

nar? Surveys say Tuesday through Thursday. This may depend on whether your reach is national or global. You might conduct more than one tele-seminar unique to a geographic location. For example, Eastern Standard Time (EST) can work for most European contacts. Otherwise, query your target audience and then assess when they have the most disposable time before you set the schedule.

The duration of a tele-seminar will depend on how much content there is to cover. People appreciate being able to block out time on their busy schedules so if you anticipate several sessions, plan ahead to people can schedule that time. If you provide an itinerary in advance of the event, people that can't stay on the call for the full length of time can call in to listen regarding a specific topic. On average, most people tire after an hour call. A 90-minute tele-seminar is rare, but it's doable, based on how captivating your material is.

3.0 ❑ Create The Tele-Seminar Outline

Create the outline for your tele-seminar. Having an outline for your tele-seminar and what you're going to talk about will help you stay on track and pack the most information into every tele-seminar you give. On the next page, you can see just how 45-60 minute tele-seminar should be outlined. Feel free to customize what you see.

4.0 ❑ Prepare/Organize Your Materials

Are you going to provide handouts for callers that register for your tele-seminar to follow along?

MAP OUT Your Tele-Seminar BY THE MINUTE

Based on a **1-HOUR (60 Minute)** tele-seminar, you might map out your call in the following manner:

❶ FIRST 5 MINUTES: Before the call starts (on time), welcome people to the call; ask them to state their name and where they're from. This helps kill time before the actual call starts!

Then, when the call starts, introduce yourself, and the topic of the call and a few "rules of conduct" for the call (i.e., mute your phones, questions will be asked/answered near the end, etc.).

❷ NEXT 15-20 MINUTES: Start the tele-seminar. Depending on the way you conduct your call, you may or may not have a guest on the call. You may simply plan to cover your own material alone. Typically, the bulk of your call is spread out across sections 2, 3 and 4.

❸ NEXT 10 MINUTES: During this time zone, you might still be covering your own material on the call, or you could open the call up to take a few questions or invite a guest on to the call to start commenting on what you began discussing in time zone 2. Your choice, it's your call. Customize it any way you want.

❹ FIRST 15-20 MINUTES: Typically, by this time, you know you're call is coming to a close, so you might start to wrap up by stating your final points, or inviting your guest to talk finish up. Towards the end of this section, you might also choose to open up the call to some questions. Typically, the last 10-15 minutes can be spent answering questions.

❺ LAST 5 MINUTES: Finally, within the last 5-10 minutes of your call, you might pitch your product, service, seminar announcement, special offer, etc. By this time, you've served your audience well. You've provided them with a lot of valuable information, you've answered questions, so you know by now they're ready to hear what you have for sale! Then, after you've made your offer, thank everyone for being on the call and tell them you look forward to another one real soon!

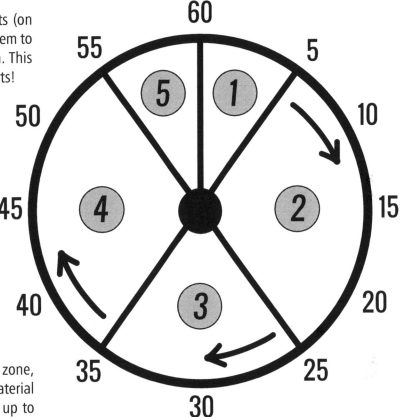

TELE-SEMINAR TUTORIALS

There is much more to learn when conducting and running your own tele-seminars. For more training, detailed steps, and video tutorials on running your tele-seminar, just go to:

MyTrainingCenter.com

For example, "fill-in-the-blank" handouts are a great way to keep your tele-seminar participants organized and on topic while they listen and learn the material you plan to cover.

Otherwise, if you don't offer some kind of outline or schedule for the call, you may lose some of your audience. Either they will be taking copious notes or they will end the call. You want your audience to engage and be an integral part of the call. If you have not planned to supply a handout, why not select some of the highlights from your presentation and generate an outline of your program for them.

4.1 ❑ Create Your Handout Materials

Determine what materials you'll need for your tele-seminar. Create them and then convert them to PDF format so your tele-seminar registrants can download it, print it, and use it on the call. Here's a special report I wrote on how to create fill-in-the-blank handouts. Go to:

http://mytrainingcenter.com/create-fill-in-the-blank-handouts-for-speaking-and-training/

4.2 ❑ Upload Your Handout Materials [So, They Can Be Downloaded]

Upload the materials you created (in PDF format) to your website server so your tele-seminar participants can download the document. Double check the site to ensure that your audience can download it properly.

Include the link to your site when material can be downloaded in your eMail message to confirmed registrants. This makes it easy for them to access what they need for the call.

4.3 ❑ Test-Download Your Handout Materials

Click on the "handout download link" you placed inside the eMail message your tele-seminar participants will receive after they enter their name and eMail address in the opt-in/registration form on your tele-seminar registration page. Does the link work? Does it open a web page with the PDF in it so you can print it?

5.0 ORDER TELE-SEMINAR CONFERENCE CALL LINE & PIN#

Before you get too far into your tele-seminar planning, you must secure a tele-seminar conference telephone number and PIN#. In fact, get it early so you can send to your lists of invitees.

5.1 ❑ Conference Call Line & PIN#

Order the tele-seminar bridge line and PIN#s for both the moderator such as you and your guest speaker (if you have one) and your listening audience. Depending on the size of the listening audience that calls in, if it's less than 1000, you can take advantage of FREE tele-seminar conference service provided by my favorite tele-seminar company www.FreeConferenceCalling.com.

If you anticipate an audience greater than 1,000, you should be prepared to pay a, ranging from $50 to $500 per call. Every tele-seminar conference company is different.

5.2 ❑ TEST Your Tele-Seminar Conference Call Line & PIN#'s [CALL THEM!]

TEST your own tele-seminar conference call line number and (moderator + guest) plus PIN#s to ensure they work. With this information secured, you can move to the next step in your planning. If you experience any issues with the numbers, contact your conference call provider ASAP.

6.0 EMAIL MESSAGE

Now that you have your tele-seminar outline completed, tele-seminar call-in telephone number and PIN#s, time/date/day and duration of your tele-seminar, you can now write the script for your eMail announcement so your listeners can register for your event.

6.1 ❑ Create The eMail Message

When constructing the eMail message, you might follow this format and modify the sample to meet your specifications.

6.2 ❑ Add An eMail Message To Autoresponder

Add the eMail message you just drafted to an autoresponder. The autoresponder will be the auto-sending robot that automatically sends your crafted eMail to registrants. You can sign-up for an autoresponder service with Aweber.com, GetResponse.com or MailChimp.com, just to name a few services.

7.0 AUTORESPONDER EMAIL MESSAGE

7.1 ❑ Create Autoresponder In eMail

Using a system like Aweber, GetResponse or MailChimp to create the actual autoresponder that will deliver the eMail message and tele-seminar call-in details to those who register for your tele-seminar. You will need to create different autoresponders for different tele-seminars. The reason to keep these eMail

Dear _____,

Thank you for registering for my tele-seminar called:

[ENTER TELE-SEMINAR TITLE]

To join me on this teleconference, simply call the telephone number below on the day of the tele-seminar and then enter the PIN#, and you're on the call!

Day/Date of Call: __ __ / __ __ / __ __
Call Time: 00:00 P.M. (Eastern Time)
Call Number: 000-000-0000
PIN# = 00000

There is a handout for the tele-seminar. Please click on the link below and download the PDF file.

http://YourSite.com/handout.pdf

If you have any questions, please let me know.

I look forward to your call,

Coach's Name
YourSite.com

separate is because you want to always be using a current mailing list.

7.2 ❑ Test The Autoresponder Message

Test-send the eMail message you just added to the

autoresponder to yourself only as a so you can see what your eMail letter notification looks like in your eMail program. Check for any obvious formatting errors to ensure that there are no mistakes. Check that the call-in number, PIN#, day/date and time are accurate. If anything needs correcting, correct it in the autoresponder eMail message and resend it to yourself to again test it prior to sending it. Satisfied, you can move on to the next step in this sequence.

7.3 ❏ Create Opt-In (Registration) Form Tied To Autoresponder

Using a system like Aweber, GetResponse or MailChimp, create the opt-in form (associated with this autoresponder) to be used on your registration "web page." For example, I use Aweber.com because they offer a special tool that creates the exact HTML form-code you need for a registration form that you can place on your website. This is the "opt-in"/"registration" form you need so callers can enter their names and eMail addresses to register for your tele-seminar. This step will give you a head count of how many callers you can expect to call in.

8.0 TELE-SEMINAR REGISTRATION & THANK YOU WEB PAGES

Create the registration web page on your website so viewers can register for your tele-seminar online. Don't forget to create a thank you page. Once you have the names and eMail addresses from registrants, you can direct them to your thank you page, which will provide your tele-seminar callers with the telephone number and PIN# to access your tele-seminar.

8.1 ❏ Opt-In/Registration Web Page

This will direct potential callers to the place where they can register for your tele-seminar. Now, there are two ways to do this:

1. Simply add a new web page to your existing website that includes the opt-in/registration form you just created with your autoresponder program.

2. Or, you can register a completely new and separate domain name, build a web page on that domain name and place the opt-in/registration form on that page. What's the benefit? You can give out a website address that describes your event. For example: www.MyHealthSecretsTeleSeminar.com.

Note, if this is a pay-to-attend tele-seminar, you might ask people to simply register and pay for the tele-seminar via your shopping cart. For example, if you have to sell, buyers can click to buy that product, pay for it, and link an autoresponder to that product so that after payment is received, they'll get a receipt in their eMail inbox along with tele-seminar instructions.

8.2 ❏ Thank You Web Page

As soon as people register for the tele-seminar, it's important that you redirect them to a thank you web page that has the same tele-seminar call-in information posted on it in addition to them getting it in their eMail. This thank you page instructs the newly registered tele-seminar attendees to, "Check eMail for details about the upcoming tele-seminar." They can then print the details for ready access and/or add the event to their calendars.

8.3 ❏ Test BOTH!

After you build your opt-in/registration form web page and the thank you page, test both! Fill in the form with your own contact information. Does the form work? Are you redirected to the thank you page? Now, check your eMail. Did you receive the tele-seminar eMail message you wrote containing the call-in information? There's no room for error when communicating vital information.

9.0 PROMOTE YOUR TELE-SEMINAR

Depending on the kind of tele-seminar you're conducting, it's a good idea to promote your tele-seminar long before the date when you plan to have your event whether it's a free-to-attend or a fee-to-attend tele-seminar.

9.1 ❏ Online Marketing Tactics

You can promote your tele-seminars in several ways:

❏ On Your Website — Post your tele-seminar on your website and make it visible from the home page.

❏ On Affiliates' Website — Post your tele-seminar on your affiliates' websites and ask them to promote it.

❏ Social Networking Websites — Post it on your social media pages like Facebook, Twitter, LinkedIn, etc.

❏ eMail Your Database — Yes, eMail your clients, prospects and associates using a broadcasting software.

❏ eMail Other Databases — eMail the databases that belong to your associates, clients and affiliates.

❏ eZine Announcements — Make announcements via eZine, newsletters, reports and articles.

❏ Person-To-Person — Announce your tele-seminar by phone and one-on-one to everyone.

❏ Free Publicity — Make an announcement on the radio, TV or in print wherever the opportunity is.

❏ Video-Sharing Websites — Video/audio record all of your tele-seminars and share them online.

❏ Postcard Mailing — Use postcards to connect with other people's lists of clients, prospects and affiliates.

10.0 WHEN SHOULD YOU SEND OUT EMAIL REMINDERS?

Remind people of your tele-seminar several days in advance, one day and then the same day even hours prior to going live with your call. Reminders ensure better attendance.

10.1 ❏ Week Before The Tele-Seminar

Notify your list that paid to join your tele-seminar at least a week in advance. If your tele-seminar event isn't scheduled for several months, it's up to you to send regular reminders without overwhelming your list with constant contacts. Keep the message fresh and varied so they look forward to the tele-event. You don't want anyone asking for a refund, because they forgot the date or you sent too many reminders.

10.2 ❏ Week Of The Tele-Seminar

If your tele-event takes place this Thursday, for example, send a simple reminder on Monday, Tuesday, and Wednesday to gently let your list know that the deadline is fast approaching and you're excited about your event. Each day, you could send out a tip on topic you'll be presenting to stimulate positive caller enthusiasm.

10.3 ❏ 24 Hours Before The Tele-Seminar

There's value in reminding someone about an

event due to take place in the next 24 hours. People get busy and even when something is on the calendar, they get distracted and forget. Your friendly reminder will be appreciated.

10.4 ❑ Day Of The Tele-Seminar

Let's face it. People are busy and easily distracted and even when an important event is on their calendars, they forget. Reminders alert people visually and when they're short and to the point, they get the message such as, "The tele-seminar that you registered for today. We're eager for you to join us at 7:00 p.m."

10.5 ❑ eMail 1-3 Hours Before The Tele-Seminar

You can also eMail a quick note that says, "It happens in 1 hour! Be sure to call in 5-10 minutes early. It's going to be a great call."

11.0 CONDUCT YOUR TELE-SEMINAR

The day of your tele-seminar, you might be a little nervous. That's normal. Transform that anxiety into enthusiasm in whatever way turns your jitters off. For me, it's putting on my headphones for some heart-pumping music and for you or use imagery see yourself having a winning tele-seminar and launching your star. Keep a bottle of water handy while presenting in case you get dry mouth while chatting for the duration of your tele-seminar.

11.1 ❑ The Day Of The Tele-Seminar

On the day of your tele-seminar, review your outline, practice it again (at least the points you really want to drive home), make sure that technical equipment is working, and relax. Even though this is a tele-seminar, people will read volumes by your tone and demeanor.

11.2 ❑ An Hour Before The Tele-Seminar

Take a moment to collect yourself, take a deep breath, and get jazzed up, and ready to rock your tele-seminar. It's almost show time and you want to give your best performance.

Double check that you have all of the materials you'll need such as books/ magazine articles, website links, etc., so you aren't caught unorganized or unprepared.

11.3 ❑ 10 Minutes Before The Tele-Seminar

If other people are in the room such as a video/ audio recorder, guest speaker, support, be sure that everyone is ready for the call and follows the protocol you created for your tele-seminar. Clear your station of unnecessary items and turn your cell phone off so it doesn't distract you.

The key to any successful tele-seminar call is FOCUS, organization, high energy, fluidity, and passion for what you're about to talk about. Try to speak to your listeners as if they were in front of you, not on your computer or in your notes. When using a microphone, hold you head up while speaking versus moving it around and risking the callers not hearing everything that you have to say.

12.0 RECORD YOUR TELE-SEMINAR

Record every tele-seminar you conduct. Whether you're going to sell it or give it away to your audience, the trick to tele-seminars is establishing a level of trust and making if a more tangible experience. If people like what they hear, they'll want a recorded copy of your presentation. Follow these great tips:

12.1 ❑ Record Your Tele-Seminar

When speaking to your listeners, slow down your speech, use your best grown-up voice and articulate every word so that everyone understands you.

Depending on the tele-seminar service you use, they typically offer a FREE service/feature that allows you to record your tele-seminar calls. When you're connected to your own call, click the RECORD button within the online dashboard provided by your tele-seminar service (or other dial pad instructions on your phone). Let it record 2-5 minutes before your call starts, and 2-5 minutes after the call ends to ensure you record every word. Throughout your tele-seminar, monitor the recording process if you can to ensure it's working. Problems are rare, but don't take any chances. When you're recording is finished, give the system a few minutes to generate a downloadable MP3 file. You can then download it, open it and edit as needed.

12.2 ❏ Edit Your Tele-Seminar Recording

After you record your tele-seminar, it's important and highly advisable that you edit your audio recording. Why? If you plan to distribute copies to paying customers or prospects, you want it to sound professional. In other words, delete the "uums, aahs," any slang, etc.

If it takes a listener time to labor through 6-10 minutes of "Hi, how is it going?" or "Who is on the call tonight? " It's a sign of a poor speaker. Editing also gives you every opportunity to add some intro/outro appropriate music to your tele-seminar by creating a quality, professional sound.

12.3 ❏ Make Your Tele-Seminar Available For Sale or Giveaway

Now, that you've edited the audio recording of your tele-seminar, what's your plan for it?

12.4 ❏ GIVE IT AWAY?

If the tele-seminar was free to callers, you might want to make your recording available to others that were unable to join you on the call. You can also post it on your website for a broader reach of viewers to listen to. Even when offering a FREE product, ask viewers to sign in and then direct them to a page on your site that has the recorded version of your tele-seminar. Some tele-call service companies provide links that connect directly to a tele-seminar. So, inquire about that.

12.5 ❏ SELL IT?

Why not? If your call has value that people are willing to pay for, create a recorded product for your shopping cart and sell it from your website. As a digital product, the customer can download the MP3 audio file. Or, you could sell access to your call through a membership portal where you store all your tele-seminars on your website. All you need is membership software.

13.0 DISTRIBUTE YOUR TELE-SEMINAR [FOR SALE OR GIVEAWAY]

With your tele-seminar recorded (and edited) and ready to distribute, you have a several options:

13.1 ❏ Sell Your Tele-Seminar Recording

As I mentioned earlier, you can sell your tele-seminar recording to callers that participated on the call, others who missed the tele-seminar or prospects express an interest in the topic/training/ information you presented.

13.2 ❏ Transcribe Your Tele-Seminar Recording

You could also transcribe the audio recording of your tele-seminar and include the transcript with the tele-seminar product you're selling, or sell the transcription as a stand-alone product. You could also use the transcription for blogging material. When blogging, keep it short and highlight the more valuable components of your presentation.

In the event people express interest in the full recording, direct them to your website in your blog.

13.3 ❑ Bundle Your Tele-Seminar Recording(s)

Product bundling is just smart. Why not bundle your tele-seminar (recording and/or transcript) with other products you sell to add value to the package and price it accordingly. This is called mixed bundling, which many consumers favor. Sales have been known to soar when you bundle products into a package deal making it cheaper than buying individual products. However, I encourage you to use both options when selling because many buyers won't buy something when they only have one option and that is to buy a bundle.

13.4 ❑ Give Away Your Tele-Seminar Recording As A Bonus

Consider giving away your tele-seminar as a bonus with a compatible product you're selling or simply record it to a CD-RPM and offer it FREE to prospects to give them an overview of your skills and expertise and products/services and much more.

14.0 ❑ Follow-up With People After Your Tele-Seminar

Follow up after every tele-seminar with a reminder to "take action" regarding the special offer you might announced on the call.

14.1 ❑ Survey Them

What was the outcome of your tele-seminar? Ask your listeners! Send out a 5-10 question survey or invite listeners to comment on the call? For example, "What did you like most about the call? What did you come away with? What did we miss?

What would you like to learn more about?"

14.2 ❑ Product Offers

Since you spoke to your listeners after the call, you send an eMail with a special (product) offer only valid for a certain period of time and only for those who joined you on the call. Let them know when the offer ends and give buyers only 2-3 days to respond otherwise they'll lose interest or forget.

14.3 ❑ Offer Your Services

Do you offer services that might be of interest to the people who connected to your tele-seminar? You might send them a follow up eMail with a special offer to take advantage of certain prices related to the services you can provide.

14.4 ❑ Announce The Next Tele-Seminar

"If you liked that tele-seminar, we're having another one next week due to the great response we got from hundreds of people! If you have an idea for another tele-seminar related to our topic, let me know so we can be sure that we're meeting your needs. Encourage your family/friends/coworkers to join us on the next call."

THANK YOU PAGE
CHECKLIST
AFTER PURCHASING A PRODUCT

1. ❑ Post a message at the top of the page in a large font that reads, "THANK YOU FOR YOUR PURCHASE!"

2. ❑ A small, sub header should read, "INFORMATION ABOUT YOUR ORDER" or" WHAT TO DO NEXT!"

3. ❑ Create the message, "Check your eMail for an eMail receipt for your purchase. Use it for questions about the order we will be shipping you." You can tweak this for your needs.

4. ❑ Link to support pages, FAQ pages, video tutorials, infographics, guides, tutorials and instruction pages for customers with questions.

5. ❑ State when customers can expect their order to be shipped. typically, 2-4 weeks, but you may be able to provide a delivery date.

6. ❑ Provide easy instructions to download a product if it's a digital one.

7. ❑ Give instructions on how to access their new membership, if it's a membership website purchase.

W hen a customer buys a product from you, be sure you send that person to a thank you page. A typical thank you page should have a few essential components. Check my checklist for items that you can add to your thank you page so they're inspired to buy more or take another action while they're still at your site.

8. ❑ Provide opportunities to sign-up for your newsletter and disclose discounts for products or special announcements.

9. ❑ Giveaways make it easy for viewers to contact you for questions or concerns.

Many of **MY CHECKLISTS** have video tutorials that teach you more at www.MyTrainingCenter.com.

10. ❑ Post comments and testimonials from satisfied customers on the thank you page in written, audio or video form. Include photographs with testimonials. This inspires new customers to buy from you.

11. ❑ Post an audio recording of you personally thanking customers showing appreciation for sales and support. Add audio from happy customers.

12. ❑ Post other products on your thank you page. These products should be your top sellers. Use upgrades and add-ons to enhance their buying experience. Remind them of other products they could buy next time?

13. ❑ Post discount coupons on your thank you page to encourage more sales.

14. ❑ Offer a promotion for a product you want to move quickly like a fire sale. "Act now and take advantage of this steep discount for 24 hours only! CLICK HERE to buy yours."

15. ❑ Post a video of you thanking them personally, and/or anything else related to their order. Why not! Show a video of you making the product or packing their order. Make it personal, fun and creative. Be creative!!

16. ❑ Mention your affiliate program to encourage prospects to join. While they can't use discounts off of purchases, they might know others they can recommend to buy from you. Make it simple for new affiliates to sign up and ensure your program is worth their time and effort.

17. ❑ Ask customers/prospects to follow you on social media. Ask them to like your Facebook page, and post either on your Facebook page or a tweet on Twitter that a customer just bought from you, etc. Ask them to take a "selfie" picture when they post their comment.

18. ❑ Ask them to share your site via social media sharing icons. You can also offer a discount to them if they share your site.

20. ❑ Ask them to leave a comment about their shopping experience. Here's your chance to learn how to improve your customers' shopping experiences on your website.

21. ❑ Survey your customers and/or ask them to take a poll. Ask why they bought your product/service. You might be able to weave their comments into your sales copy for those products (with their permission).

22. ❑ Ask customers to tell you more about themselves. How will they use the product they bought? If it's a repeat customer, why do they keep coming back? What's their experience with the product?

23. ❑ Link to other parts of your site that might keep them there longer, such as your blog, video tutorial pages, and others of interest.

24. ❑ Ask them to participate on your site via podcasts, forums, blog article postings, etc.

25. ❑ Encourage customers to create an account with you AFTER they make a purchase. Asking them to create an account BEFORE they make a purchase can sometimes cause cart abandonment.

26. ❑ Include forms and other items in the sidebar on the thank you page so customers don't necessarily have to navigate elsewhere ... unless you want them to.

These items can also be added to your 404 (not found) error message pages.

TWITTER MARKETING
CHECKLIST

Twitter.com, a short (140 character) micro-blogging service is used by more than 304 million users at a rate of about 500 million tweets daily. Twitter can offer any business the opportunity to reach an enormous market as 80% of Twitter users are accessing it on their mobile phones and other portable devices as well. Your tweets can include a link to any web content (blog post, website page, PDF document, etc.) or a photograph or video. Here are a few tips for using Twitter:

❑ First, update/customize your Twitter profile with a rich biography, updated photo, custom background, and short description of your business story.

❑ Choose a Twitter ID that is robust and expresses your "brand." Use your professional name or your business name. This is done under *Settings* and then mention your Twitter ID in everything you do. Include it in your eMail signature, at the end of blog articles, etc. Notify literally everyone that you are on Twitter so they can follow you.

❑ To learn the ropes of Twitter and its many uses, set up a dummy account separate from your personal and/or business account so you can experience all the tools, features, functions, handles, hashtags, and more.

❑ What is a #hashtag? Hashtags categorize your tweets, which make it easier for others interested to find them. Turn keywords into hashtags. Create a hashtag by placing the # symbol in front of your desired keyword. For example, #productname, #keyword, and #whatyoudo.

❑ Thoroughly complete your Twitter profile to ensure that you take advantage of each feature that gives more details about your business so you can start building a following! A Twitter Tip: " Your Twitter experience is defined by whom you follow, not by who follows you." Choose wisely.

❑ Plan to tweet daily about your videos, articles, products, etc. Give useful information and answer questions.

❑ Ask your followers to retweet and mention your favorite tweets. Twitter has a follow button next to the handle of the person who just followed you to encourage users to follow more people. Their message reads: "This user followed you; why don't you return the favor?"

❑ Integrate Twitter with your other online marketing

social media marketing efforts (Facebook, LinkedIn and your blog). Share your Twitter content with other audiences on other networks by manually re-posting your tweets.

❑ Embed your tweets into your blog or website. This is as easy as copying the embed code and adding it to your blog or website, specifically in the sidebar or footer. WordPress has plugins that do this for you. Just supply your Twitter ID and how many tweets you want displayed.

❑ Write Tweets that spark conversations about product/service/business to earn followers and keep them engaged. Direct them to your website, videos and more.

❑ Your followers can help your business extend its reach, generate word of mouth awareness, and potentially make sales.

❑ Spy! Find out what's going on in your industry and what your clients are navigating to. You can use a tool like Topsy.com, a Twitter search engine, to help you with your search for related topics posted by your clients or competition.

❑ Start discussions with influencers to raise the profile of your business and build valuable connections, referrals and more.

❑ Track mentions when they occur and track brand mentions and keywords to follow what others are saying about you.

❑ Retweet (repost or forward a message posted by another user) to link you to experts in your coaching niche/industry.

❑ Take note of trending topics and hashtags to

connect others to your company. Tagging your tweets to relevant and trending hashtags can help you reach new users.

❑ Offer coupons, discounts or special deals to your Twitter followers. Run a Twitter contest such as, "The next 25 people who retweet me will receive 50% off coupon!" Invite past/current clients to post pictures of them using your product/service.

❑ Use images and videos to generate more views, clicks and shares versus plain text tweets.

❑ Track and analyze your tweets! Use Twitter's analytics tools to see what your followers favor most about your tweets. Learn what days are best to tweet for your business, what type of content is followed more, demographics, and more. Repeat what works, and tweak/dump posts that don't.

❑ Use Twitter Cards to attach rich photos, videos and media experience to tweets that drive traffic to your website. Simply add a few lines of HTML to your web page, and users who tweet links to your content will have a "Card" added to the tweet that's visible to all followers. With eight different card types to choose from, you can use Twitter cards to ask your audience to opt-in to your eMail list, register at your website, view/use a coupon, go to a landing page, download an eBook/app, and more without leaving Twitter's website. For more information, on Twitter cards, go to: https://dev.twitter.com/cards/

❑ Other Twitter software tools to help you tweet better include:

- InsightPool.com
- Tinytorch.com
- Tweepi.com
- Twitonomy.com
- TwtrLand.com
- YFrog.com

VIDEO MARKETING
CHECKLIST

VIDEO

THE BIGGEST OPPORTUNITY IN $$ MARKETING $$ EVER

When I think about video marketing, there's so much to consider. Let's start statistics and then we'll launch into a few different checklists for marketing your videos online for both fun and profit. This is what you should know about videos:

- ○ The average number of videos watched per day by Americans is roughly eight. (I usually view between four and 12.) This includes videos about news, marketing, product promotion, training, music, TV reruns, etc.

- ○ Videos help consumers digest more information in less time. That's a fact.

- ○ One minute of video is worth 1.8 million words or 3,600 average web pages so stop writing and start filming!

- ○ Videos are more cost effective and have a greater impact than any text you will ever write. You don't need a sales copy writer; you need a videographer and a video editor.

- ○ Video generates over 50% of all mobile phone traffic. With video, you can reach thousands, potentially millions!

- ○ More than 60% of users watch a video before engaging in any other behavior such as reading or listening to content.

- ○ At least 20% of people share videos on their phones. Are your videos worth sharing?

- ○ Upwards of 60% of people watch videos on social sharing websites. Are your social media channels set up for video?

- ○ Upwards of 70% of people watch video on YouTube and Vimeo. Do you have accounts on those sites? You need them.

- ○ Upwards of 90% of all information passed through our brains is visual. We process visuals a thousand times faster than reading!

- ○ Website visitors stay on your website longer when they're watching video opposed to reading content that you might have labored over. That's our reality.

- ○ Video inspire greater numbers of sign-ups, opt-ins, registrations, and purchases and in

---

less time versus reading ad copy.

○ Video does a much better job at educating, enlightening, informing, and convincing potential buyers. Videos keep them from checking out othr products/deals on other sites.

○ Video eMails generate higher click through rates than any text or images in HTML eMails.

WAYS TO INCORPORATE VIDEO IN WEBSITES, MARKETING & MAKING MONEY ONLINE

- ❑ Call-to-actions inside your videos ...
- ❑ Music (intro/outro) in your videos ...
- ❑ Screen capture videos showing how-to ...
- ❑ Sound effects in your videos ...
- ❑ Video answering frequently asked questions ...
- ❑ Video background(s) on your website ...
- ❑ Video message(s) about you ...
- ❑ Video messages about your products ...
- ❑ Video messages about your services ...
- ❑ Video messages from your staff/team ...
- ❑ Video tutorials on how to use your products ...
- ❑ Video testimonials for products / services ...
- ❑ Videos for your clients (new/current) ...
- ❑ Videos for your members (new/current) ...
- ❑ Videos for your prospects ...
- ❑ Videos used to educate and entertain ...

VIDEO SHARING WEBSITES

You can easily upload your videos to these websites for unlimited exposure. The larger your video footprint is online, the more leads and potential sales you can generate.

- ❑ YouTube.com
- ❑ Veoh.com
- ❑ Myspace.com
- ❑ DailyMotion.com
- ❑ Vimeo.com
- ❑ MetaCafe.com

- ❑ Break.com
- ❑ Esnips.com
- ❑ Ebaumsworld.com
- ❑ Atom.com
- ❑ Dropshots.com
- ❑ Share.ovi.com
- ❑ Sutree.com
- ❑ Tinypic.com
- ❑ Liveleak.com
- ❑ Vidmax.com
- ❑ Flixya.com
- ❑ Vidivodo.com
- ❑ Clipshack.com
- ❑ Vidipedia.org

PREMIMUM VIDEO HOSTING SITES

Users can upload, share and view videos on video sharing websites such as the list below. They offer premium video hosting and player services, greater control and flexibility when embedding video players on your website, high picture quality, analytics, optional storage for 100+ videos, full SEO visibility and so much more! Save on bandwidth and local hosting storage fees by hosting your videos with one of these websites. My preference is Vimeo.com.

- ❑ Vimeo.com
- ❑ SproutVideo.com
- ❑ Vzaar.com
- ❑ Vidyard.com
- ❑ Wistia.com
- ❑ Viddler.com
- ❑ BrightCove.com
- ❑ Oculu.com

MY FINAL THOUGHTS ON VIDEO MARKETING

Video is here to stay. Are you ready to play? Many startups and independent companies are leveraging the power of video marketing to communicate more effectively with strategic markets and key influencers. If you're not using video to promote your product/service/business, you're missing out on a key source of revenue.

Take time to learn how to make videos or pick up some tips if you're already producing videos. Review the video recording checklist for an overview how-to get started or tips on how to improve on your existing videos.

VIDEO RECORDING
CHECKLIST

To produce quality videos, follow my simple checklist for acquiring the right video equipment and accessories, video recording and editing software for promoting videos online! In this tutorial checklist, you will learn:

1.0 ❑ Know the PURPOSE for making videos! Before you purchase any equipment or software, determine, what is your purpose for creating videos? To sell product, share your knowledge, create awareness, etc. In fact, knowing your purpose will enable you to develop a solid plan, help justify your costs, ensure you message is clear, and know how you inspire and motivate your audience.

2.0 ❑ Make a LIST of video titles using keywords that will resonate. Depending on which product, service, series of video messages, etc. you anticipate creating, make a list of videos so you have something tangible to work from.

3.0 ❑ What type of video EQUIPMENT will you need? Now that you've formulated your ideas for videos that you'll record for your website, blog, social media connections, etc., thoroughly research video camera equipment, lighting and accessories. Your list should help you determine what you'll need. Lenses, for example, define the quality and sharpness of your video. Ask lots of questions and talk to experts for advice.

4.0 ❑ What SOFTWARE will you need to record, edit and play your videos? Recording video is essentially the easy part of make a video. The real challenge is getting your video clips imported to your computer for editing. Windows and Mac computers come with FREE editing programs otherwise you may need to purchase a video editing software program. Editing is a powerful skill, but know that it is an acquired skill that anyone can learn.

5.0 ❑ Are ready to launch your video? Is the market ready for your video? Is it unique, easily understood, checked for bugs, the call to action is clear, etc. Use a **.video domain extension** to point viewers to critical websites. Are you confident that your name defines what you are about, i.e., **massages.video**.

6.0 ❑ REHEARSE your video scripts. You only get one chance to make a good impression so don't think you can "wing it" because you're already a good speaker. Create an outline of what you'll say and than practice it. If you want to gain greater visibility, more traffic and more customers, make it memorable.

Many of **MY CHECKLISTS** have video tutorials that teach you more at www.MyTrainingCenter.com.

7.0 ☐ Who can PRODUCE your videos of YOU? Unless you're skilled at working the remote control and multi-tasking, I recommend you turn to an experienced videographer to film your shoot.

8.0 ☐ How will you record GREAT AUDIO for your videos? Whenever you shoot video, the big question always is, "How will your sound play on video?" If it's not crystal clear, you'll lose big time. Since recording sound can be a tricky, I recommend that you shoot several takes and then test them.

9.0 ☐ How about LIGHTS, BACKGROUND NOISE, SETTING, PROPS? It goes without saying that you need quality equipment to produce any kind of video. Some sound is easily spliced and replaced, but make an effort to avoid distortions altogether. The art of lighting is just that. Experiment until you get it right.

10.0 ☐ How Will You Upload & Post Your Videos To Your Website? Uploading your videos to your website is easy if you have the right software tools or web-based video sharing service.

11.0 ☐ Know how to UPLOAD videos to video-sharing websites. Plan to upload your videos to many video-sharing sites for maximum exposure. Most sites don't even limit video length or the number of videos you can upload. It's fast, fun, and easy to do with the right tools.

12.0 ☐ How do you convert videos to DVD format? Transferring video from VHS tapes to DVD is one way. Each way will involve hooking up your VCR to a DVD burning device. If you plan to sell DVDs, there are companies that will duplicate/package/fulfill your orders. Check out these resources.

RECOMMENDED VIDEO RESOURCES

Here is a list for video resource links at MyTrainingCenter.com and some of the topics covered:

- Clips & Footage (Free & Fee)
- DVD Duplication Services & Equipment
- Green Screen Software
- Green Screen Suits
- Green Screen Virtual Sets
- Green Screens & Equipment
- Lights & Lighting
- Making Money From Your Videos
- Online Video Storage
- Play Video On Your Website
- Studio Kits, Sets & Backdrops
- Teleprompter Software
- Teleprompters
- Tripods
- Upload Videos To Multiple Sites
- Video Adapters (All Kinds)
- Video Cameras/Camcorders
- Video Conversion Software
- Video Editing Software & Services
- Video Filming Services
- Video Players
- Video Sharing Websites
- Video Uploading Software
- Webcams

WEBINAR
CHECKLIST

Webinars are web-based seminars in a variety of formats such as lectures, meetings, teaching. training, workshops, etc. Webinars allow you to plan, implement and deliver information related to your topic. When it comes to conducting the perfect webinar, here's a quick checklist to ensure that you webinar is a success:

1. ❑ Get the webinar software such as WebinarJam, EasyWebinar.com, etc. You can choose to pay monthly or make a single payment for the use the FREE webinar software. For webinar software recommendations, go here:

MyTrainingCenter.com/tutorials/webinar-services

2. ❑ Test and practice using the webinar software until you're comfortable with it. Practice with a friend, associate or colleague BEFORE you go live. Learn all of the technical aspects to become a professional.

3. ❑ Create a topic and a title for your webinar.

4. ❑ Will it be a FREE or pay-to-attend webinar?

5. ❑ Create an outline for your topic, based on a 45-minute presentation.

6. ❑ Use either a PowerPoint slide or other visual presentation equipment. Your goal is to teach, train, entertain, or provide information to your attendees so your presentation should be spectacular.

7. ❑ Create an autoresponder (list) for each and every webinar you conduct. Keep your registrations separate from other webinars you conduct.

8. ❑ Create an opt-in form linked to the autoresponder assigned to your webinar so people can register for it. This form should include a field for: Name, eMail Address and possibly, ask a question for registrants to reply to: "What's your biggest question regarding this topic or field that I will be presenting?"

9. ❑ The most important component of your webinar will be the registration page where you'll want to drive as many sign-ups as possible for your event. There are many downloadable registration page templates. I suggest you

choose one that requires a first name, a last name and an e-mail address (three fields) only. The more fields you ask for the fewer people will register.

10. ❑ Promote the registration page and your webinar to your list and to other people's list to increase the potential number of sign-ups for your webinar.

11. ❑ Remind people about your upcoming webinar via eMail, text and/or voice messages the day before, the day of and even within an hour's notice of you conducting your webinar.

12. ❑ Conduct and record your webinar. Teach, train, entertain, interview guests, engage and interact with your webinar attendees.

13. ❑ Following the webinar, send a replay of the webinar via eMail to your guest(s) and attendees. Be sure that you mention products that you have for sale that are available to purchase, possibly at a discount for attending your webinar.

14. ❑ Remember to promote future online webinars at the end of current webinars. If you're planning a series of webinars, you can use one registration link to save time, however it restricts the ability to customize each individual webinar.

WEBMASTER/V.A.
CHECKLIST

I f you want to make money building websites or providing other business services for a fee, here's my checklist for becoming a master webmaster or virtual assistant. When you know the software to learn and skills to acquire, you're literally a walking money-making machine. The more resourceful and skillful you become, the more your services are in demand and the more money you can earn.

1.0 ❑ SKILL SETS TO HAVE

1.1 ❑ Website design skills (building new websites, revamping websites, WordPress websites, one-page websites, theme installation/customized, plugin installation/customized, eCommerce

websites, Blogs, websites for events, authors, speakers, coaching, etc.)

1.2 ❑ Graphic design skills (posters, postcards, business cards, flyers, bookmarks, book covers, eBook covers, 3D covers and product images, working with printers)

1.3 ❑ Affiliate marketing, affiliate program setup, customized, banner creation, paying affiliates

1.4 ❑ List management (adding contacts, exporting/importing, cleaning eMail lists)

1.5 ❑ eMail broadcasting, eZine Design/Broadcasting, Opt-in Form Creation

1.6 ❑ Autoresponders (create them, link to opt-in forms, eMail specific autoresponder lists, posting opt-in forms on website and sidebar, landing pages with opt-in form + autoresponder)

1.7 ❑ eCommerce / shopping carts (cart customized, payment gateway, adding regular/recurring products, membership products, coaching/consulting/service products, event registration products, product pages, links to shopping carts, create discounts/coupons, check regular/recurring orders)

1.8 ❑ Installing and tracking website statistics (Google Analytics, StatCounter.com, etc.)

1.9 ❑ Search engine optimization (meta tags, page

MY CHECKLISTS

optimization, XML sitemaps, SEO plugins)

1.10 ❑ Website Security (WordPress security plugins, malware scanning, threat removal, hosting company support calls, etc.)

1.11 ❑ Audio recording/editing/mixing skills (add audio to websites, create audio libraries, protect audio behind memberships, record seminars and tele-seminars, record podcast shows and interviews, help clients organize audio on their computer)

1.12 ❑ Video recording/editing/mixing skills (video record client messages, workshops, classes; create video products; edit video)

1.13 ❑ Book publishing design skills (layout, cover designs, formatting, submission, getting books printed, adding client's book(s) to their website, affiliate program for book sales)

1.14 ❑ eBook publishing design skills (layout, cover designs, formatting, submission to Kindle, SmashWords.com and/or BookBaby.com)

1.15 ❑ Social media skills (Facebook, Twitter, Pinterest, Google+, Instagram, LinkedIn)

1.16 ❑ Product creation support (books, eBook, home-study courses, audio/video products, downloadable file products, workbooks, duplication/replication, fulfillment options)

1.17 ❑ Tele-seminar support setup, get tele-seminar call-in number+guest+host PIN codes, setup registration page, opt-in form and autoresponder, recording calls, live chats, edit the MP3 recording of the call, post the call online, add the call to the shopping cart if selling)

1.18 ❑ Webinar support (webinar software setup, webinar registration page, autoresponder and opt-in form for the registration page, record/edit webinar, post on website), answer questions)

1.19 ❑ Podcasting skills (help clients setup and produce/edit/publish podcast)

1.20 ❑ Accounting/bookkeeping (FreshBooks.com, QuickBooks, Quicken, Excel, Online Banking)

2.0 ❑ SOFTWARE NEEDED

2.1 ❑ WordPress plugins and themes

2.2 ❑ Graphic design software (Adobe® Photoshop, Adobe® Fireworks, Adobe® Illustrator, Artweaver, Inkscape)

2.3 ❑ Publishing software (Adobe® InDesign

2.4 ❑ Audio recording software (Sony's Sound Forge "Audio Studio", Audacity)

2.5 ❑ Video recording/editing/mixing software (Camtasia, Premier, After Effects)

2.6 ❑ FTP Software (Filezilla, FTP Voyager, etc.)

2.7 ❑ Website hosting software (order hosting, cPanel, WHM, setting up eMail accounts)

2.8 ❑ List management software (Aweber.com, GetResponse.com, MailChimp.com)

2.9 ❑ Accounting/bookkeeping software (FreshBooks.com, QuickBooks, Quicken)

2.10 ❑ Password Protection & Form-Filling software (Roboform.com)

2.11 ❏ Desktop sharing software (Teamviewer.com)

2.12 ❏ Fax to eMail software (OneSuite.com)

2.13 ❏ Shopping cart companies (WooCommerce, Kartra.com, InfusionSoft.com, Cart66.com)

2.14 ❏ Affiliate software (iDevAffiliate.com, AffiliateWP.com, AffiliateRoyale.com)

2.15 ❏ Membership software (S2Member.com, MemberMouse.com, MagicMembers.com, MemberPress.com)

3.0 ❏ EQUIPMENT NEEDS

3.1 ❏ Computer (PC preferably, Mac)

3.2 ❏ Computer speakers (recommended)

3.3 ❏ Large monitor (24" ++) to display client work. Do NOT work on small monitors.

3.4 ❏ Audio recording/podcasting equipment (microphone, headset microphone)

3.5 ❏ Video recording equipment (tripod, lights, camera ... action!)

3.6 ❏ Scanner, laser printer and copier

3.7 ❏ Laptop computer

3.8 ❏ Headphones/headset for cell phone so you can work hands-free

3.9 ❏ Digital camera or cell phone camera

3.10 ❏ Digital video cameras) with tripods and green/black/white screens

3.11 ❏ USB headset

4.0 ❏ Resources

4.1 ❏ Domain name registration companies (ReallyCheapNames.com, GoDaddy.com, DirectNic.com, NameCheap.com, Enom.com, Dotster.com, 000Domains.com

4.2 ❏ Website hosting companies (FatCow.com, HostGator.com, BlueHost.com, JVZoo.com)

4.3 ❏ Stock photography websites (YayImages.com, Pond.com, 123RF.com)

4.4 ❏ Icon websites (FindIcons.com, IconFinder.com, IconArchive.com)

4.5 ❏ Social media websites (Facebook, Twitter, Pinterest, LinkedIn, Digg, Google+, Instagram)

4.6 ❏ Website stat counters (Google Analytics, StatCounter.com)

4.7 ❏ Webmaster tools (Google, IsItDownRightNow.com, WhoIsHostingThis.com,)

4.8 ❏ Google tools and services (Gmail, Forms, Drive, Calendar)

4.9 ❏ Podcasting services (Libsyn.com, iTunes.com, HipCast.com, PodBean.com)

4.10 ❏ Online radio show services (LATalkRadio.com, BlogTalkRadio.com)

4.11 ❏ Video sharing websites (YouTube.com, Vimeo.com, DailyMotion.com, ...)

4.12 ❏ Affiliate Nnetworks (JVZoo.com, ClickBank.com, Warrior Forum, E-Junkie.com)

5.0 ❏ Marketing Your Skills & Finding Clients

Many of **MY CHECKLISTS** have video tutorials that teach you more at www.**MyTrainingCenter.com**.

5.1 ❑ Your website (showcase skills; give work samples; share client testimonials; have forms on site to collect data from new / current customers; provide payment links for clients to go to, click on and pay you while you sleep!)

5.2 ❑ Advertising tactics (advertise on Facebook and places your target market hangs out)

5.3 ❑ Networking tactics (attend networking events/ seminars, distribute flyers with your services and how to reach you)

5.4 ❑ Ask for referrals (from clients (past/present), associates, colleagues, friends, and family)

5.5 ❑ Speak to potential clients, discuss services, be prepared to negotiate fees (no two clients are the same)

5.6 ❑ Closing the deal with confidence

6.0 ❑ WORKING WITH CLIENTS

6.1 ❑ Procedures for clients to send you materials for you to work on

6.2 ❑ Availability and accessibility to clients such as no calls after 8pm or on weekends

6.3 ❑ Your work hours (communicate when/where/ how you work best; find your groove)

6.4 ❑ Timelines for work completion (agree on deadlines)

6.5 ❑ Procedures for your showcasing work

6.6 ❑ Procedures for delivering finished work

6.7 ❑ Firing clients

7.0 ❑ GETTING PAID

7.1 ❑ Invoice methods, terms and strategies (how to submit your bill)

7.2 ❑ Setting fees (hourly; by the project size/ duration)

7.3 ❑ Deposit terms and guidelines

7.4 ❑ Payment terms and guidelines (pay as you go, weekly payments for on-going projects)

7.5 ❑ Final payment terms and guidelines (all work/ files turned over after final payment)

7.6 ❑ Payment methods (cash, check, credit card, PayPal)

7.7 ❑ Overdue payment terms and guidelines

8.0 ❑ REFUND POLICY

8.1 ❑ Raising your rates (demand for services could indicate a pay raise and working fewer hours because you can charge more; teach what you learn and know; reach out to groups or companies to reduce number of single payers)

8.2 ❑ Accounting, bookkeeping, tax deductions, calculating/paying business and personal taxes

Having read the above tips and suggestions, what do you know or what have you experienced that's not on this list? Create your own list of skill sets, resources, software and equipment you have mastered to become your own highly sought-after webmaster or virtual assistant that many businesses need.

WEBSITE BUILDING

CHECKLIST

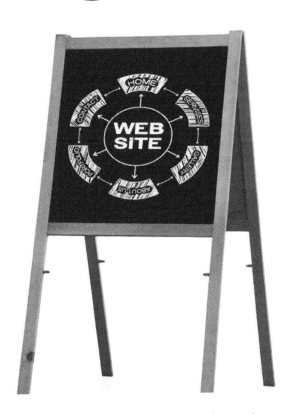

When setting up a website for the first time, there are many components to manage. With a workable checklist, you should be able to handle every activity with ease. If you already have a website, compare your site with the checklist below. Are you missing anything? Does the list give you any new ideas for enhancing your website?

1.0 ❑ DOMAIN NAME (WEB ADDRESS)

If you're going to have a website designed for you, you'll need to provide a "website address" (or domain name) where people can come visit you online! Don't settle for anything less than your own domain name. For example, http://Yahoo.com/your website won't cut it! For just a minimal fee of $9.97 per year, you can secure your own "website address" (or domain name).

1.1 ❑ Create a clever domain name (website address) where you can easily direct traffic.

1.2 ❑ Remember where you registered your domain name, so you can keep track of the annual expiration date. Many people neglect to renew their domain names and can lose them overnight. If you are notified that your domain name will expire, pay the annual fee immediately.

2.0 ❑ HOSTING SERVICE COMPANY

You will need to host your domain name (website address) with a website hosting company. While hosting a website can be costly, it is a must-have is service. Be sure that the company you select has 24/7 customer service and phone support.

The company I use to host MyTrainingCenter.com is FatCow.com. With a 24 hour telephone support system and fast servers, they earned my confidence of me and they never disappoint.

2.1 ❑ Order web hosting services at a company like HostGator.com to host your website on the Internet. Host Gator also has "reseller" packages that allow you to have one account with them or create an unlimited number of hosting accounts. This is a great idea for those who have (or intend to have) more than one website.

2.2 ❏ Write down your FTP login and password and keep it in a safe place. Remember where you host it, so you can make any necessary changes in the event your revolving door webmaster runs for the hills with all of your information!

3.0 ❏ CPANEL (WEB HOSTING SETUP, ADMIN & CONFIGURATION)

Once your hosting account is set up, verify that you have a cPanel administrative area sponsored by your hosting account. Every domain name / website hosting account should have a cPanel. cPanel, by the way, is short for "control panel."

The control panel is where you'll create eMail accounts using your domain name. You can also perform the following functions within your cPanel. You'll want to know how to do these things:

3.1 ❏ eMail Accounts — cPanel is where you'll create any number of eMail accounts, which you can use Outlook to check your eMail.

3.2 ❏ eMail Forwards (or Alias Accounts) — An eMail "alias" or "forward" is simply an eMail you create for the sole purpose of redirecting other eMails sent to you from another person.

For example, you might create any number of eMail aliases and forward the accounts possibly to your personal account versus creating separate eMail accounts via other eMail software programs such as Outlook, Outlook Express, Mozilla's Thunderbird, etc. This can become cumbersome to manage.

eMail alias accounts (a.k.a., forwarded eMail accounts) such as support@yoursite.com or feedback@ yoursite.com that redirect eMail sent to those eMail addresses to your primary eMail account for easy review/management. This is simple to check because you're dealing with one primary eMail account.

3.3 ❏ eMail Filters — If choose to block certain spam eMails from coming into your account, you can create any number of spam filters. The server will watch for certain emails you identify and delete them before they reach you. This is a real benefit. If some of your client(s) have Gmail as their eMail provider, Gmail does a superb job at sorting through valid eMail and bogus spam eMail. This step, however, is optional.

3.4 ❏ Checking eMail via "Web Mail" — Some clients like this option so they can check their eMail via a "web mail" platform. cPanel provides this option, too.

3.5 ❏ eMail Autoresponders — cPanel also provides for this option even though most eMail providers such as GMail provide what's called a "Vacation/Away" type of autoresponder. With cPanel, any email you can create you can also attach an autoreponder to it. If your client is going on vacation and they want to notify people when they'll return, set up this type of autoresponder. You can do that by creating an autroreponsder associated with any specific eMail which was created within cPanel. Remove the autoresponder when they return back to the office.

3.6 ❏ Create Subdomains — Subdomains look like www.AffiliateProgram.MyTrainingCenter.com. See the "AffiliateProgram." in the domain name? That's the "subdomain" part of the website. These subdomains are specifically designed to forward (or redirect) traffic to any website or web page you like! They're very easy to create and very convenient to have.

3.7 ❏ AddOn Domains — If you are on a basic/ shared hosting account, and you see this feature within your cPanel, you can save money by adding your additional domain names or create more websites for them using the same hosting account. This is beneficial because you don't have to purchase extra hosting or pay extra fees to host more websites. Just point the nameservers for each domain to the hosting company, add the domain, and start building. You'll find a folder for each additional domain within the root directory of your main website.

4.0 ❑ EMAIL ACCOUNTS

Whenever you set up your website, it's always a good idea to setup the following eMails to help support your site and provide a number of ways visitors, clients and affiliates can communicate with you. Now, many of these are just suggested eMails for you to create. Create what you like and/or create ones might not be selected.

4.1 ❑ Personal eMail Accounts [For Example — Bob@YourSite.com or BobSmith@YourSite.com]: The first eMail you should create should be yours! You definitely want to start showing off your domain name and what you do. So? Create an eMail address with your name in it and start using it! For example: Bob@YourSite.com or BobSmith@YourSite.com.

4.2 ❑ Help/Support eMail [For Example: Help@YourSite.com or Support@YourSite.com] — You might create an eMail where customers and clients can send you help and support questions. This eMail account can either forward to your personal account, if you handle the support issues yourself, or you could have it forward to someone else in your office if that's their role.

4.3 ❑ Affiliate eMail [For Example — Affiliate@YourSite.com or Affiliates@YourSite.com]: You might create an eMail where affiliates can send you questions about the affiliate program, commissions, marketing advice, etc.

Many affiliate tracking systems will ask you for an eMail address, enter this one: affiliate@yoursite.com. Also, you can either have this email forward to your personal account if you're personally managing this area of your business, or have it forwarded to another person in your office.

4.4 ❑ Billing eMail [For Example — Help@YourSite.com or Billing@YourSite.com] ... You might create a specific eMail just to handle billing issues. When you sign up for ANYTHING (i.e., web hosting, domain names, etc.) and a credit card is used, why not have all those issues be separated from all your other eMails by using a specific eMail just created for "billing issues." Create an eMail account called: Billing@YourSite.com. Unless you have an office manager or an accountant that works with you, you're better off forwarding these eMails to you.

4.5 ❑ Feedback eMail [For Example — Comments@YourSite.com or Feedback@YourSite.com] You might create an eMail where people can send you feedback and suggestions about your site, what you do, about the products you sell, etc. This can either be a separate eMail account you check individually, or an eMail alias (or forward) which redirects eMail to you or someone in your office assigned to handle these eMails.

4.6 ❑ Contact eMail [For Example — Contact@YourSite.com or Contact-Inquiry@YourSite.com] ... You might create an eMail where people can contact you, either via eMail or through an online contact form on your website's Contact Us page. When you get these eMails, you know they're simple a casual inquiry from your website, for the most part.

5.0 ❑ WEBSITE

MY CHECKLISTS

Assuming you've built your website using WordPress, which I recommend, or you are about to design it, here are a number of items (and specific pages) to keep consider when building the perfect website.

5.1 ❑ Link Navigation — Decide how you will line up the navigation links on your site, horizontally or vertically (along the side). It's best to align them along the top (under or over) the header in a horizontal fashion. Look at some of your favorites sites for good examples.

5.2 ❑ Home Page — Typically, the home page "writes itself." How? The home page serves should have a "table of contents" for your site and include links to several "hot topics" that are available within your website, but can be linked from the home page.

5.3 ❑ About Us Page — Visitors to your website might be interested in who designed the site or who owns it. The About Us page should identify this information. Always include a photograph of yourself (and/or your team), which makes the site more relatable, a description of what you do, how the site works, your business plan and how people can reach you. This link can often be placed at the bottom of the page, leaving room at the top for more "action-oriented" or "money-related" links such as "Products", "Services", etc.

5.4 ❑ Press Room Page — Every website should have a press room, especially if you are selling product/service, interacting with the public as a speaker, etc. The press room keeps visitors (and people who work in the media) up to date on your activities and any announcements. Did you release a new product, form a new alliance, or start using a new service to enhance your product/service? Press rooms also provide ready information about you that can be copied, photos of you/your team (web

size, 72 dpi and print size 300 dpi), plus press releases, quick links to social networking sites, and more.

5.5 ❑ Calendar Page — Are you a speaker? Do you conduct seminars, workshops and speak regularly? List your events on a calendar on your website so people can follow you.

5.6 ❑ Services Page — This is where you'll list all the services you provide to your clients/customers/ prospects.

5.7 ❑ eStore / Product Catalog Page — Here's where you'll list all the products you have for sale on your website. If you don't have a shopping cart yet (to sell products from your website) or you're not satisfied with the one you currently have, consider using MyMarketingCart.com. That's my shopping cart system.

5.8 ❑ Product Catalog "Thank You" Page — Once customers buy from you/your website, it's important to redirect them to a thank you page while checking out. This page might offer helpful information such as when they can expect delivery of an order, who to contact with billing questions, etc. Customers need to be reassured they made a wise purchase and your thank you page helps to confirm that.

5.9 ❑ Opt-In Box (Capture Names & eMails of Visitors) — One of your goals for your website should be to grow your contact list of prospects, clients and affiliates. To do this, you'll want to offer a FREE product/service in exchange for getting names and eMail addresses. With an opt-in box on your home page (in the top right corner), this will help to build your lists.

5.10 ❑ Opt-In "Thank You" Page — After your visitors or prospects opt-in and enter their names and eMail addresses, you should direct them to your thank you page. On this page, you might suggest they check their eMail a gift you're sending to them and offer some quick links to other relevant sections on your website.

5.11 ❏ Shopping Cart: Do you have a shopping cart to sell products (even services) from your website? If not, look into the power of MyMarketingCart.com.

5.12 ❏ Recommended Links/Resources (Page) — You definitely want to have a resource page on your website for several reasons. (a) You could list all the recommended resources that you have an affiliate relationship with. (b) When you speak to people on the phone or communicate via eMail them, refer them to a list of services that might benefit them. (c) If they sign up for services you recommend, you'll earn a commission because you are an affiliate for that program. Now, your site's almost paying for itself.

5.13 ❏ Affiliate Program — Do you sell products? Seminars? Services? Then, consider having an affiliate program on your site so others can help you make more money online. You'll need affiliate tracking software, which you can find at MyMarketingCart.com. Make sure you have pages that describe (a) your affiliate program details and how to sign up, (b) affiliate marketing and training materials and (c) your affiliate terms and conditions.

5.14 ❏ Legal Pages (Privacy Policy, Terms of Service, etc.) — Your website should include a set of legal statement pages disclosing a Terms Of Service page, Privacy Policy page, Income Disclaimer page and a Copyright Notice page. These pages can be drafted automatically with software found at AutoWebLaw.com. You can also review them and tailor the

wording to your specific business/website needs.

5.15 ❏ Contact Us (Page) — Every site should include a contact page that lists your company name, business/mailing address, telephone numbers, fax number, eMail address (optional) and a web-based contact form, which people can complete in order to contact you online. Make sure your address and telephone numbers are located at the top of the contact page and easy to find. Don't make them struggle to find that information.

5.16 ❏ Contact Us "Thank You" Page — After people contact you online, through a web-based contact form, you might want to provide an automatic thank you for contacting you. A specially designed thank you page will confirm receipt of their message and reassurance that a representative will contact them within 24 hours (or some reasonable time). These assurances communicate customer care, expressed interest in the customer's question/concern, timeliness and prompt action for resolution.

5.17 ❏ Site Map — Search engines love site maps and so do visitors to your site that can't find what they're looking for. A site page simply lists every possible link within your website. It's efficient and highly effective for viewers.

5.18 ❏ Blog — If you blog, attach the link to your blog on your website so customers/ prospects are kept current with your activities such as the new book you authored or the speaking engagement scheduled for next month and more. You can quickly install a blog if you have the

---

kind of hosting account that provides access to a cPanel administrative area.

5.19 ❑ Social Media — Don't forget to add your social media links and share icons to your website so visitors can share your website content with their peers, fans and followers.

5.20 ❑ What else? — What else would you like to see on your website? I strongly encourage you to look at other websites for ideas and test how easy they are to navigate!

INSTALL WORDPRESS
CHECKLIST

When it comes to installing WordPress on a new domain name and hosting account, while you could do it with the quick software installation wizards, I like to install WordPress by hand so I am in control of everything. Here's the checklist I follow every time I want to install WordPress to ensure it's successfully just the way I want it every time.

1.0 ❑ WITHIN CPANEL

1.1 ❑ If you have cPanel on your hosting account, which you should always try to get when you order a new website hosting account, log into it, and click on MySQL® Databases. Here you'll create a new database, username and password and then assign that user name and password to that newly created database and assign all the functions allowed to that newly created database. This should take no more than 5 minutes to complete. Make note of the database name, username and password in your computer. You'll need it later as you are about to read in this checklist.

1.2 ❑ Download the latest version of WordPress to your computer by going to:

WordPress.org/download

1.3 ❑ Inside the cPanel, click on the File Manger icon and a new tab will open showing you the contents of the server where you'll host your WordPress website. Click on "public_html". In the right-hand window, upload the WordPress zip file you just downloaded and uncompress it in the root directory.

1.4 ❑ Install WordPress on the new hosting account by going to your domain name in a new tab window. Follow the steps to install WordPress. This should take 1-2 minutes. Have a database title, username and password ready to complete the installation.

1.5 ❑ When WordPress installation is complete, you will be redirected to a login screen to log into the dashboard of your newly installed WordPress website. Congratu-

---

lations! This part is done. WordPress is ready for you to set up the WordPress dashboard.

2.0 ❑ WORDPRESS WEBSITE SETUP

Once logged into the dashboard, there are a few things you'll want to do right away. They are:

2.1 ❑ Install my recommended list of admin-related plugins. The list is all inclusive and thorough. Install all of these plugins before you start adding pages and posts and uploading images to your website.

2.2 ❑ Select a theme for your site. Check out my checklist for choosing the right theme for your WordPress site prior to making your decision.

2.3 ❑ Confirm and customize the WordPress admin dashboard before getting started. Look for Permalinks and General, which are both found under SETTINGS.

2.4 ❑ Turn on a COMING SOON message so you can work on your website without visitors seeing what you're doing, before you're ready to showcase it to the world.

THAT'S IT! YOU'RE PRETTY MUCH DONE INSTALLING AND SETTING UP WORDPRESS THE WAY I DO IT!

WORDPRESS PLUGINS

CHECKLIST

While there are dozens of WordPress plugins you could install in your WordPress website to enhance the performance. The following plugin checklist focuses only on those plugins I consider essential to running, managing and maintaining your WordPress website from an administrative perspective.

In all of my WordPress websites, I always install these plugins to manage both small and large websites. I highly recommend you print this checklist and check off the steps as you accomplish them.

The next time you install WordPress and/or have a WordPress website built for you that you will ultimately manage, be sure these plugins are installed to maximize the site's greatest potential.

1.0 ❑ ADMIN PLUGINS

1.1 ❑ **Ozh' Admin Drop Down Menu** — Ozh' Admin Drop Down Menu moves all the dashboard admin links from the left side of your screen to a neat horizontal row of drop down menu items at the top of your screen.

1.2 ❑ **Admin Menu Editor** — Admin Menu Editor is a WordPress plugin that will let you manually edit the Dashboard menu. You can reorder the menus, show/hide specific items, change access rights, and more.

1.3 ❑ **Coming Soon Page & Maintenance Mode** — Sticky Widget Area is a WordPress plugin that helps you to engage your visitors in checking out your sidebar content while scrolling through your web pages.

1.4 ❑ **Admin Management Xtended** — Admin Management Xtended lets you make quick edits and other modifications to pages and posts without having to click on the title for a full page edit. This is a real time-saver.

1.5 ❑ **Reveal IDs** — This plugin (Reveal IDs) shows the IDs on admin pages and posts.

1.6 ❑ **Single Category Permalink** — Reduce permalinks (category or post) that include an entire hierarchy of categories to just having the lowest level category.

1.7 ❏ **Duplicate Post** — This plugin allows to clone a post or page, or edit it as a new draft. This is very helpful when you want to create a new Page or Post and there are certain elements, features or settings associated with the page or post that you want to maintain.

1.8 ❏ **Admin Slug Column** — This plugin allows you to make a WordPress page or post link to the URL of your choosing, instead of a WordPress page or post URL. It also will redirect people who might go to an old URL versus the new one you've chosen.

1.9 ❏ **Bulk Move** — If you need to move or remove posts in bulk from one category to another, or by tagging them, this is the WordPress plugin for you.

1.10 ❏ **Change Your Admin Username** —This is a small WordPress plugin that will let you easily edit your username from within WordPress. It's useful if you want to change it to something other than "admin."

1.11 ❏ **Better Delete Revision** — Better Delete Revision not only deletes redundant revisions of posts from your WordPress Database, it also deletes other database content related to each revision such meta information, tags, relationships, and more.

1.12 ❏ **Upload Larger Plugins (Large File Sizes)** — This plugin replaces the built-in WordPress plugin uploaded with one that allows you to upload a plugin of any size.

1.13 ❏ **WP User Avatar** — WP User Avatar is a WordPress plugin that lets you choose any image from your WordPress Media Library as a custom user avatar.

2.0 ❏ PAGE MANAGEMENT & PAGE BUILDER PLUGINS

2.1 ❏ **Visual Composer: Page Builder for WordPress** — Visual Composer for WordPress is a drag and drop front-end and back-end page builder plugin that will save you loads of time working on site content. You will be able to take full control of your WordPress site, build any layout you can imagine with no programming knowledge required.

2.2 ❏ **TinyMCE Advanced** — This plugin will let you add, remove and arrange specific buttons on your WYSIWYG ("what you see is what you get") Visual Editor toolbar.

2.3 ❏ **Shortcodes Ultimate** — Shortcodes Ultimate is a WordPress plugin that provides mega packs of shortcodes. With this plugin you can easily create tabs, buttons, boxes, different sliders, responsive videos and even more.

2.3 ❏ **pageMash > Page Management** — With pageMash, you can quickly and easily manage a multitude of pages with the slick drag-and-drop style interface. pageMash lets you sort, hide, edit, rename, and organize several pages at a time.

2.4 ❏ **CMS Tree Page View** — This plugin adds a CMS-like tree overview of all your pages and custom posts so you can view them all at a quick glance. Within this tree, you can edit pages, view pages, add pages, search pages, and drag and drop pages to rearrange the order.

2.5 ❏ **Page Links To** — This plugin allows you to make a WordPress page or post link to a URL of your choosing instead of a WordPress page or URL post. It also will redirect viewers that go to your old (or "normal") URL to the new one you've chosen.

WORDPRESS PLUGINS

3.0 ❑ POST CATEGORY MANAGEMENT PLUGINS

3.1 ❑ Category & Taxonomy Terms Order — Order categories and all custom taxonomies terms (hierarchically) use a drag and drop, sortable javascript capability. No theme update is required.

4.0 ❑ MEDIA LIBRARY / IMAGE PLUGINS

4.1 ❑ Enhanced Media Library — Enhanced Media Library is a WordPress plugin that's great when you need to upload and manage a lot of varying types of media files.

4.2 ❑ Lightbox Plus Colorbox — Lightbox Plus Colorbox implements Colorbox as a lightbox image overlay tool for WordPress.

5.0 ❑ EXPORT/IMPORT PLUGINS

5.1 ❑ WordPress Menu Exporter — This plugin only exports WordPress Menus (like Posts, Pages, etc).

5.2 ❑ Widget Importer & Exporter — Widget Importer & Exporter is a WordPress plugin that helps you move your widgets from one WordPress website to another.

5.3 ❑ Export Categories — Export Categories is a WordPress plugin that will only export your WordPress categories. It won't export your posts or pages. For that you will need to use another type of plugin.

5.4 ❑ WP Export Categories & Taxonomies — WP Export Categories & Taxonomies is a simple WordPress plugin that lets you export your Post Categories, Tags and Taxonomies into a WordPress .xml file. You can also import them into other WordPress websites, which is a tremendous time saver versus recreating them from scratch manually.

6.0 ❑ SECURITY PLUGINS

6.1 ❑ All In One WP Security & Firewall — The All In One WordPress Security plugin will take your website security to a whole new level. It reduces security risk by checking for vulnerabilities by implementing and enforcing the latest recommended WordPress security practices and techniques.

6.2 ❑ Hide My WP Website — Hide My WP helps boost your WordPress website security and it also allows you to have more attractive URLs and permalinks!

6.3 ❑ iThemes Security Plugin — iThemes Security (formerly Better WP Security) gives you over 30+ ways to secure and protect your WordPress site.

6.4 ❑ BulletProof Security — BulletProof Security provides the additional website security protection that every WordPress website should have.

7.0 ❑ SEO PLUGINS

7.1 ❑ WordPress SEO by Yoast — Improve your WordPress SEO by writing more effective content giving you a fully optimized WordPress site with one WordPress SEO plugin -- Yoast.

7.2 ❑ Google Analytics for WordPress — The Google Analytics for WordPress plugin allows you to track your blog easily and with lots of metadata such as views per author and category, automatic tracking of outbound clicks and page views.

7.3 ❏ **SEO Ultimate** — This all-in-one SEO plugin gives you control over your page and posts title tags, meta descriptions, keywords, no index, meta tags, slugs, canonical, auto links, 404 errors, rich snippets, and much more!

7.4 ❏ **Google XML Sitemaps** — This plugin generates a special XML sitemap that aids search engines such as Google, Bing, Yahoo and Ask.com to better index your blog.

8.0 ❏ VARIOUS PLUGINS WORTH MENTIONING

8.1 ❏ **Global Content Blocks** — These create short codes that you can add to HTML, PHP, forms, opt-ins, iframes, Adsense, code snippets, reusable objects, etc. to posts/pages and preserves formatting.

8.2 ❏ **Ninja Forms** — Ninja Forms is a drag and drop WordPress plugin that lets you build custom contact forms, eMail collection forms, surveys, and other forms you might need for your WordPress website.

8.3 ❏ **Drop Shadow Boxes** — Drop Shadow Boxes is a WordPress plugin that provides an easy way to add a shadow effect to your images on posts, pages and within widget areas.

8.4 ❏ **Opt-In Panda & Social Locker** — Developed by the same company, these two plugins help you grow your eMail list and presence on social media.

WANT MORE? I'VE GOT MORE!
OVER 400+ RECOMMENDED PLUGINS
www.MyTrainingCenter.com/resources

- WP Admin Plugins
- WP Advertising Plugins
- WP Affiliate Plugins
- WP Amazon Plugins
- WP Amazon S3 Plugins
- WP Anti-Spam Plugins
- WP Audio Plugins
- WP Author Box Plugins
- WP Background Plugins
- WP Backup Plugins
- WP Banner Plugins
- WP Book Plugins
- WP Calendar Booking Plugins
- WP Calendar Plugins
- WP Category Plugins
- WP Comment Plugins
- WP Content Block Plugins
- WP Dating Site Plugins
- WP Directory Plugins
- WP eCommerce Plugins
- WP eLearning Plugins
- WP eMail Plugins
- WP Event/Registration Plugins
- WP Export / Import Plugins
- WP Feedback Plugins
- WP File Management Plugins
- WP Flip Book/Page Plugins
- WP Form Plugins
- WP Forum Plugins
- WP Gravitars & Avitars
- WP Holiday Plugins
- WP Image Plugins
- WP Image Slider Plugins
- WP Landing Page Plugins
- WP Legal Plugins
- WP Links Plugins
- WP List Building / Opt-In Forms
- WP Login Plugins
- WP Maintenance Page Plugins
- WP Media Library Plugins
- WP Mega Menu Plugins
- WP Membership Plugins
- WP Menu Plugins
- WP Mobile Menu Plugins
- WP Mobile Plugins
- WP Notification Bars
- WP Page Builder Plugins
- WP Page Peel Plugins
- WP Page Plugins
- WP Podcasting Plugins
- WP Polls & Survey Plugins
- WP PopUp Plugins
- WP Post Plugins
- WP Pricing Table Plugins
- WP Rating Plugins
- WP Scrolling Plugins
- WP Search Plugins
- WP Security Plugins
- WP SEO Plugins
- WP Shopping Cart Plugins
- WP Shortcodes
- WP Sidebar Plugins
- WP Social Community Plugins
- WP Social Media Lock Plugins
- WP Social Media Plugins
- WP Social Reputation Plugins
- WP Speed / Cache Plugins
- WP Stats & Hits Plugins
- WP Support Ticket Plugins
- WP Time Countdown Plugins
- WP Title (Show/Hide) Plugins
- WP Tooltip Popup Plugins
- WP Traffic Building Plugins
- WP User Plugins
- WP Video Player Plugins
- WP Video Playlist Plugins
- WP Views Plugins
- WP White Label Plugins
- WP Widget Plugins
- WP WYSIWYG Editors

WORDPRESS SECURITY

CHECKLIST

W ebsite security is a serious issue with every website, particularly, if yours generates revenue and has a lot of traffic. You cannot afford to have your site compromised or shut down by your web hosting company due to malicious malware installed on your site unaware or without your knowledge.

Website hacks, malware, and other forms of vicious cyber attacks on websites should not be feasible on any site. Loss of data, down sites, suspended hosting accounts serious problems when one is trying to earn a living online.

Protect your website, hosting reputation, and online income by becoming familiar with the benefits for installing a robust WordPress security plugin. Here's a checklist for several types of security measures.

KNOW HOW TO PROTECT YOUR WORDPRESS WEBSITE

1. ❏ Ability to add a simple math CAPTCHA to the WordPress login form to fight against brute force login attacks.

2. ❏ Ability to automatically lockout IP address ranges which attempt to login with an invalid username.

3. ❏ Ability to block fictitious Googlebots from crawling your website.

4. ❏ Ability to disable the right-click function, highlight/text selection, and copy option to protect your content.

5. ❏ Ability to hide your admin login page (http://yoursite.com/wp-admin/). You should rename it so your WordPress login page to only a name you know, such as, http://yoursite.com/imwonderful. This prevents bots and hackers from accessing your real WordPress login URL.

6. ❏ Ability to log all 404 events on your website. This can help clean up dead-end pages on your website. You should also be able to choose to automatic block IP addresses that are hitting too many 404s.

7. ❏ Ability to prevent image hot-linking, which is when other websites place your images

on their website by linking to yours. This can kill your bandwidth if you had hundreds of websites linking to hundreds of images on your website. Turn it off. Keep in mind, if you allow affiliates to link to banners on your website, don't turn off the banners your affiliates need.

8. ❑ Ability to see a list of all users who are currently logged into your site. If you don't recognize someone, you can check them out and decide to terminate their account if needed. I've seen it happen where people register and start blogging on your site with absurd, meaningless articles that have nothing to do with your website's theme or purpose so they can promote the garbage they sell.

9. ❑ Ability to use "honeypot login" that helps reduce brute force login attempts by robots.

10. ❑ Add a CAPTCHA to your WordPress comment form to add more security against spam comments.

11. ❑ Add CAPTCHA to WordPress Login form and forgot password form.

12. ❑ Add fire wall protection to your site with .htaccess file to stop malicious script(s) before it even reaches the WordPress code on your site.

13. ❑ Add script to your .htaccess file so you can block unacceptable countries from visiting your website such as China, Iran, Russia, Nigeria, etc.

14. ❑ Allows you to specify one or more IP addresses in a special white list (a list of people/ products viewed with approval).

15. ❑ As the admin, you can view a list of all locked out users.

16. ❑ Ban users by specifying IP addresses or use a wild card to specify IP ranges.

17. ❑ Block "bots" from constantly accessing your xmlrpc.php file and wasting server resources.

18. ❑ Brute force login attack prevention.

19. ❑ Database scanner feature can be used to scan your database tables. It will look for suspicious-looking strings, javascript and HTML code in some of the WordPress core tables.

20. ❑ Deny malicious query strings that show up in your WordPress database.

21. ❑ Detect if there is a user account that has the default "admin" username and change the username to a value of your choice.

22. ❑ Easily backup your original .htaccess and wp-config.php files in case you need to use them to restore broken functionality.

23. ❑ Easily change the default WP prefix in the database to a value of your choice with the click of a button.

24. ❑ Easily view and monitor all host system logs from a single menu page and stay informed of issues or problems occurring on your server so you can remedy them quickly.

25. ❑ Enable the famous "5G Blacklist" Fire wall rules courtesy of Perishable Press.

26. ❑ Forbid proxy comment posting.

27. ❏ Force logout of all users after a configurable time period of trying to login.

28. ❏ These back up files .htaccess and wp-config.php files have restore features.

29. ❏ Identify files or folders that have permission settings and if not secure, set the permissions to the recommend secure values with click of a button.

30. ❏ Instantly block Brute Force login attacks via our special cookie-based brute force login prevention feature. This fire wall functionality will block all login attempts from others including bots.

31. ❏ Modify the contents of the currently active .htaccess or wp-config.php files from the admin dashboard with only a few simple clicks.

32. ❏ Monitor the most active IP addresses that persistently produce the most SPAM comments and instantly block them with the click of a button.

33. ❏ Monitor/View login attempts that show the user's IP address, User ID/Username and Date/Time that show as failed logins.

34. ❏ Password strength tool to allow you to create very strong passwords.

35. ❏ Prevent comments from being submitted that don't originate from your domain to reduce the posting of SPAM bot comments.

36. ❏ Prevent people from accessing the readme.html, license.txt and wp-config-sample.php files of your WordPress site.

37. ❏ Protect your PHP code by disabling file editing from the WordPress administration area.

38. ❏ Schedule automatic backups and email notifications or make an instant DB backup whenever you need it with one click.

39. ❏ The file change detection scanner can alert you if any files have changed in your WordPress system. You can then investigate to verify a legitimate change or whether a bad code was inserted.

WordPress security evolves over time. Plugins evolve as hackers and spambot creators evolve. The best thing you can do to protect your website is to install any one of the recommended WordPress security plugins found on MyTrainingCenter.com. You can check them out, read more about them, and install one (or more) simply by clicking on the link provided: http://mytrainingcenter.com/learn/security-plugins-for-wordpress/

While there are several very robust WordPress security plugins, you cannot install all of them and hope they will doubly guarantee security. You normally would install one only. If you don't like the one you installed, uninstall it, and test another one. Many can be customized to meet your specific needs. By using more than one, multiple plugins working together are very often incompatible. So, research them, and try a couple of them. Most plugins working independently do a good job of preventing a fair number of attacks.

Check out these WordPress SECURITY PLUGINS over at: MyTrainingCenter.com

HOME > WORDPRESS PLUGINS > WP SECURITY PLUGINS

WP Security Plugins

WP SECURITY PLUGINS

All In One WP Security & Firewall

The All In One WordPress Security plugin will take your website security to a whole new level. It reduces security risk by checking for vulnerabilities, and by implementing and enforcing the latest recommended WordPress security practices and techniques.

LEARN MORE

WP SECURITY PLUGINS

Hide My WP Website

Hide My WP helps boost your WordPress website security and it also allows you to have more beautiful URLs and permalinks!

LEARN MORE

WP SECURITY PLUGINS

Wordfence Security

Wordfence Security is a free enterprise class security and performance plugin that makes your site up to 50 times faster and more secure.

WORDPRESS THEMES
CHECKLIST

Do you have a WordPress website? Are you looking for just the right theme to build your WordPress website? Here's my checklist for picking out the perfect theme and what to look for:

1.0 ❏ FREE VS. PAYING FOR A WORDPRESS THEME

1.1 ❏ **FREE THEMES** — FREE is good if you only need to build a very simple WordPress website. This includes membership websites because all you need is a lock on the front door with your protected pages secured behind it, and you're in business. You don't need anything elaborate (theme-wise) to build a membership website. However, if you choose to build a website with special functions, features, look

and design, the FREE themes are limiting. They don't have some of the bells and whistles or built-in premium plugins that paid premium themes can offer.

1.2 ❏ **PREMIUM THEMES** — When building a new website, I prefer Premium WordPress themes that come with a bundle of built-in features that will enhance any website. If you plan on build an elaborate WordPress website and need specialized features to function on your website that only a premium theme can provide, premium is the only way to go.

1.3 ❏ **PAYING FOR INDIVIDUAL OR GROUP THEMES** — WordPRess themes can be purchased individually or in groups. For example, an individual theme might cost $20-60 whereas for $80, you get full access to all of their themes. The benefit for buying in groups makes sense if you have a number of WordPress websites and you want to show variety. Another benefit to buying the group plan would be to try out different themes for the one website you want to build.

By buying a group of themes, you have flexibility to experiment and test what works best for you. On the other hand, if you're just building one website only with no future plans to build more, stick with the individual plan. Read all the fine print because many of these design companies do not offer refunds if you aren't satisfied with the one theme you selected. How can you tell if it's the right one for you?

MY CHECKLISTS

2.0 ☐ WHAT "FEATURES" SHOULD YOU LOOK FOR WHEN PURCHASING A PREMIUM WORDPRESS THEME?

When it comes to choosing the right premium theme for your WordPress website, here's what I look for:

☐ 100% Responsive

☐ Animated CSS3 Transitions Effects

☐ Blog Layouts (Small, Medium, Large)

☐ Blog Post Formats (Standard, Video, Link, Audio, Quote, Gallery, and Image)

☐ Blog Layouts (Standard, Full Width, Masonry Sidebar, Masonry Full Width)

☐ Boxed/Wide Layouts

☐ Built-In Page Builder (Visual Composer)

☐ Built-In Short codes

☐ Built-In Sliders

☐ Built-In Audio/Video Players

☐ Child Theme Ready

☐ Content Boxes

☐ Counter

☐ Demo Files Included

☐ Font Awesome Icons Included

☐ Full Width Page & Post Options

☐ Google Analytics Integrated

☐ Google Maps Integrated

☐ Header/Logo Area Customization

☐ Icon Progress Bar

☐ Infinite Scroll Option for Blog & Portfolio

☐ Looks Good On Cell Phones & Tablets

☐ Lots of Transitions

☐ Mega Menu (Optional)

☐ Multiple Widget Areas

☐ One Page & Multiple Pages

☐ Templates (Full/Right/Left Side Bar/Landing Page)

☐ Parallax Page Design Options

☐ Portfolio Formats (Image/Video/Audio/Gallery)

☐ Portfolio Layouts (Small, Medium, Large)

☐ Pricing Tables

☐ Ready Demo Data Included

☐ Responsive Menu Looks Good

☐ Search Function

☐ Show/Hide Features

☐ Sidebar Control Per Page

☐ Social Media Integration

☐ Sortable Portfolio

☐ Tabs & Accordion Design Features

☐ Unlimited Colors and Fonts

☐ WooCommerce Compatible

Specifically, I look to see how these areas look on a theme page, before you make my purchase.

☐ What do header/logo/navigation areas look like?

☐ Does a mega menu come with this theme?

☐ What do the sidebars and widgets look like?

☐ What do the pages look like?

☐ Blog post page layouts look like?

❑ What does a blog layout look like?

❑ What do the portfolio pages look like?

❑ How do WooCommerce shop pages look?

❑ What does the footer area look like?

❑ What's my overall perception of the theme I'm considering? Modern? New? Clean?

3.0 ❑ TYPES OF THEMES

If you're looking to build a specific WordPress website, there are specific themes that can help you do that. For example, what kind of site do you want to build? Maybe one of these types of themes can help you:

❑ Appointment WordPress Theme

❑ Artist / Music WordPress Themes

❑ Auction / Classified WordPress Themes

❑ Automotive WordPress Themes

❑ Catalog WordPress Theme

❑ Coming Soon WordPress Theme

❑ Corporate / Business WordPress Themes

❑ Dating Website WordPress Theme

❑ Digital Download WordPress Themes

❑ Directory WordPress Themes

❑ eBook WordPress Theme

❑ eCommerce / Store WordPress Theme

❑ Education WordPress Theme

❑ eLearning WordPress Themes

❑ Food WordPress Theme

❑ Image / Photo Gallery WordPress Themes

❑ Job Board WordPress Themes

❑ Landing Page WordPress Theme

❑ News / Magazine WordPress Theme

❑ One Page Sales Letter WordPress Theme

❑ Personal / Creative WordPress Themes

❑ Portfolio WordPress Themes

❑ Price Comparison WordPress Themes

❑ Professional/Consultant WordPress Theme

❑ Real Estate WordPress Themes

❑ Restaurant WordPress Themes

❑ Reviews WordPress Theme

❑ Spa Salon WordPress Theme

❑ Travel WordPress Theme

❑ University WordPress Themes

❑ Video WordPress Themes

❑ Yellow Pages WordPress Theme

4. ❑ SAVING & INSTALLING WORDPRESS THEMES

4.1 ❑ Once you've selected a theme, SAVE IT to your computer. FREE or premium theme should be save in an obvious, retrievable location. I have a folder on my computer called WORDPRESS. Within that folder, I have two other folders called PLUGINS and THEMES. It's within the THEMES folder where I'll download and saved the themes I purchased. Whenever I need a theme, I know which folder to go to for that theme.

4.2 ❑ INSTALL IT inside the WordPress site that you're building such as inside the WordPress dashboard, under APPEARANCE / THEMES, so you can effortlessly upload your WordPress theme and then activate it.

4.3 ❑ CUSTOMIZE your theme once it's activated. Every theme needs customizing. In no special order, you'll need to:

❑ Upload a logo and a favicon. Determine the height and padding of the header/logo area.

❑ Customize header and footer background colors.

❑ Customize typography. (i.e., font size and font style for the body text, navigation text, sub-navigation text, text in the header and footer, ...)

❑ Determine the website background colors.

❑ Determine menu type.

❑ Determine site layout. (i.e., boxed or wide/full-width)

❑ Customize blog options and layout.

❑ Customize portfolio options.

❑ Customize WooCommerce options.

❑ Customize social media accounts and icons you want displayed on your site.

❑ Customize accent colors or color scheme.

❑ Insert Google Analytics code into your theme.

❑ Add any customized CSS code into your theme.

❑ Customize footer copyright text, number of columns and colors.

Check out some very cool themes at: www.MyTrainingCenter.com

CHECKLIST

Blog
/blog/

def: A website where a writer or group of writers chronologically express their opinion on a subject

Now that you have WordPress installed on your website, you can start blogging? Writing blogs is not only great for personal use, but if you are looking to attract a wider audience for your business, blogging can enhance your professional image and your products/services. Imagine reaching billions on the Internet!

1. ❏ **By default, WordPress uses web page URLs that have question marks and numbers in them to identify posts and pages.** WordPress also offers you the ability to create custom page and post URLs for your permalinks and archives.

This can improve the aesthetics, usability, search engine listings and the forward-compatibility of your page and post links. So, inside the dashboard, under SETTINGS > PERMALINKS, select "Post Name" so your pages will look like this:

http://yoursite.com/**name-of-article**

Instead of:

http://yoursite.com//**?page_id=8140**

2. ❏ **Under POST CATEGORIES**, rename the default **Uncategorized** category title to something like **My Blog** so you can assign all your posts to a main category, provided you don't create other categories later on. If you know of other categories your articles might fall under, create them now.

3. ❏ **Under APPEARANCE > MENUS, add a menu item to your main navigation called BLOG** and then link it to the **My Blog** category (or what you named it). Some WordPress themes let you add posts (articles) on a specific page in your blog by choosing a post category or all categories. Do this in the navigation menu instead of a post category.

4. ❏ **Create your first POST article by giving it a NAME and a SLUG (page name).** Click the **SAVE DRAFT** button, instead of the Update button, because you don't want to publish an empty article quite yet.

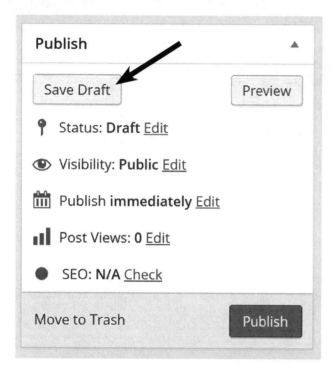

5. ❑ **Does your WordPress theme offer you different post (article) formats?** You'll find this option in the right hand column under a section called **Format.**

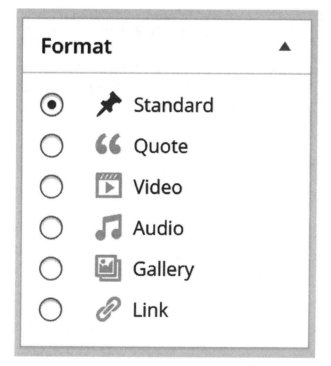

6. ❑ **Proceed to write your article.** You can choose to use the default WordPress window edit area or you could install a Page Builder plugin such

as Visual Composer to create professional looking article pages with columns, animation, custom sidebars, and more.

7. ❑ **Write a short 1-3 sentence EXCERPT** for your post. If you don't write one, some themes will pull the entire first paragraph of your post and post that on the article listing pages for certain categories. NOT GOOD. Some themes allow you to limit how many words or characters are pulled to generate that excerpt. GOOD. If you don't customize that part of your theme, write a short excerpt on the same page of your post.

8. ❑ **Assign a few TAGS** (keywords) to your post (article). About 3-10 tag words will suffice. Tags act like keywords in an article. If someone clicks on a tag word, other articles could show up for viewers if articles share similar tags.

9. ❑ **If a post (article) belongs to a DIFFERENT CATEGORY,** check the appropriate box to reassign it or create a new on the same page.

10. ❑ When you're ready to post an article, **OPTIMIZE the post for SEARCH ENGINES.** You can install any number of SEO plugins such as Yoast (WordPress SEO), All In One SEO, or SEO ULTIMATE to enhance your posts (articles) for search engines. Each one should have a TITLE, KEYWORDS and a DESCRIPTION.

11.0 ❑ When you're finished with the above steps, **PUBLISH your post (article)** by clicking on the PUBLISH button. Congratulations!

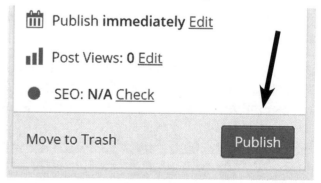

MOVING A WP SITE
CHECKLIST

I f you ever plan on moving your WordPress website from one hosting company to another, here's how I do it. Here's my personal checklist for moving whole WordPress websites.

1.0 ☐ WHERE WORDPRESS WEBSITE RESIDE ON CURRENT SERVER?

1.1 ☐ If you have cPanel, typically found at http://yoursite.com/cpanel, log into it, and click on the File Manager icon so you can view and manage all the files and folders on your website server.

1.2 ☐ When the File Manager window opens, click on the "public_html" link in the left column

to view everything on your server in the right-hand column.

1.3 ☐ Highlight every file and folder on the server, in the right-hand column, by clicking the Select All tool in the top right-hand column. When everything is highlighted in blue, you've done it correctly.

1.4 ☐ Click the "Compress" icon in the uppermost navigation row to "zip up" every file and folder (that you just highlighted) on your server. Note, if you have a large website with a thousands of files (including images) and folders, consider performing this task (highlight + compress) in stages. For example, highlight and zip up folders A-J into one zip file. You could name it "A-J-FILES-AND-FOLDERS.zip" and then continue with that method of zipping files with folders K-P, R-Z. With the final zipped group of folders, carefully select the root files as well. There are only about 15 of them. Use the CTRL key to select and include them all in the final R-Z zipped file.

1.5 ☐ After you have compressed (or zipped) your files/folders, you should look at these new zipped file sizes. The file size for one (or multiple) zipped file can range between 100MB up to 1GB. It's best to keep these file sizes down to 100MB-300MB and no more. The reason is, when you download them to your computer, you'' need to re-upload them to a new server. Well, if you have a .zip file

---

size that's 500MB or more, it's going to take a long time to download and re-upload. The lag time occurs in the uploading stage. If a huge 500+MB file is 80% uploaded and for some unknown connection problem, you'll be forced to restart the upload process. It's much better to keep these file sizes under 500MB if possible. If you happen to compress all the files and folders and the file size turns out to be 700MB, delete that .zip file and start over. Proceed to zip up small groups of folders such as FOLDERS-A-J.zip, K-P, R-Z, etc. Don't forget to include your root files in the last zipped procedure.

2.0 ❑ WHERE WILL YOU MOVE/HOST YOUR WORDPRESS WEBSITE ON THE NEW SERVER?)

2.1 ❑ If you have cPanel on the new hosting account, which you should always try to get when you order a new website hosting account, log into it and click on MySQL® Databases. Referencing the database by name, username and password from the current wp-config file mentioned earlier (found in the root folder of your current WordPress website), proceed to create a new database, with the same username and password and then assign that user name and password and functions to the new database you created. This takes a total of 1-3 minutes to complete.

2.2 ❑ Download the latest version of WordPress to your computer inside that sub-folder you created to store all your WordPress files/folders, by going to: https://wordpress.org/download

2.3 ❑ Upload and uncompress this WordPress zip file on your new web server in the root directory.

2.4 ❑ Install WordPress on the new hosting account

by going to your new hosting account within a browser. Installation should take 1-2 minutes.

2.5 ❑ Within cPanel on the new server, click on the phpMYadmin icon. Find the new WordPress database you just created. Select all the tables you see in that database and DROP them or delete them. This empties the database making room for you to import your old one with all your WordPress website data.

2.6 ❑ With this new database now emptied, IMPORT the saved .sql file of your current WordPress database into the newly emptied database. This will take just a few seconds to upload. When finished, you should see a green highlight bar with a success message in it. Completed!

2.7 ❑ Within the cPanel on the new server, click on the File Manager icon to open up the File Manger window of the new server account. Click on public_html to expose the recently installed WordPress files you just installed in Step 2.4 above. Upload your huge saved zipped file(s) that you downloaded from your old server, and which contain all the files and folders of your WordPress website. Move these into the root folder. Unzip them after they have been fully uploaded. YOUR entire WEBSITE HAS BEEN PROPERLY MOVED OVER … EVERY FOLDER … 100%.

3.0 ❑ WHAT'S LEFT TO DO?

3.1 ❑ Change the name servers so your old site now points to the new website server. Within 24 hours, your old site will be pointing to the new site that is now up and running.

3.2 ❑ Within File Manager, create a test directory/

folder called "test." Every few hours, while the name servers are propagating, type in any browser http://yoursite.com/ns and when you see "Index of /ns" pop up with a linkable phrase called "Parent Directory", you know your website has moved over 100% to the new server. Until you see that page, you will get a 404 or similar error message because you don't have that folder created on your new server.

3.3 ❑ When your WordPress website is fully moved over to the new server, you can confidently cancel hosting services at the previous website hosting company. I caution you to wait a couple days for peace of mind. Keep the old account active until you're fully satisfied that the new hosting server is hosting all of your files and everything is functioning as it should.

4.0 ❑ QUICK WAY TO MOVE A WORDPRESS WEBSITE

A fast way, but not always the ideal way to bring over content from one WordPress website to another is to simply export everything out of it and then import it into the new WordPress website installation. However, , if you want to move only parts of your site, here are few tips before making that move:

- ❑ Export (then import) pages.
- ❑ Export (then import) post categories.
- ❑ Export (then import) posts.
- ❑ Export (then import) menus.
- ❑ Export (then import) your widgets.
- ❑ Export (then import) theme settings.
- ❑ Export (then import) other settings.

The only problem with this method is that WordPress

websites are complex. There are customized details at every turn. Do you remember where everything is? Do you remember how you customized your SEO plugins or your security plugins? What about all those content blocks you created and more?

Don't forget about the images in your media library. Images must be moved too when migrating from one hosting company to another. Your images in your media library need to be brought over using the same the steps outlined in the checklists above that covered highlighting the /uploads folder, zipping it all up, download it, re-uploaded it, unzipping it and moving it over the newly installed WordPress uploads folder on the new server.

The same goes for plugins. Plugins must be brought over, unless you want to add them individually, which can be a real chore and many would require re-customizing as you did in the old WordPress website.

It's highly recommended that you move the entire image database, files and folders in a few single zip/export/download/upload/unzip procedures as outlined above in CHECKLIST STEPS 1-3. The steps above ensure your website is brought over 100% intact and not bit by bit, which could really ruin a website. Move the image files intact for peace of mind, complete assurance, and functionality. Master the checklists above prior to moving any WordPress website to a new hosting server. It's how I do it now with confidence, speed, and accuracy.

MY CHECKLISTS

HOW I LIKE TO MOVE WORDPRESS WEBSITES ...

In the screen shot below, and on MyTrainingCenter.com inside my video tutorials on moving a WordPress website, I go into rich detail how I like to compress (or zip up) all the files and folders on the server into a single ZIP file for a specific website. Then, I'll download that zip file to my computer and from there, the process begins for moving a WordPress website ...

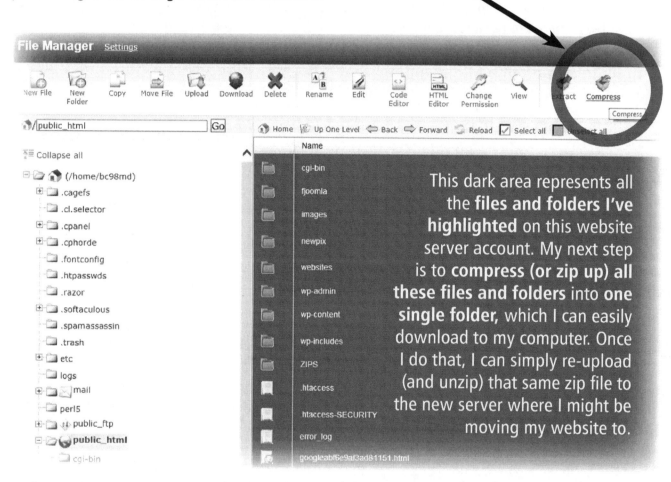

This dark area represents all the **files and folders I've highlighted** on this website server account. My next step is to **compress (or zip up) all these files and folders** into **one single folder,** which I can easily download to my computer. Once I do that, I can simply re-upload (and unzip) that same zip file to the new server where I might be moving my website to.

Do know, there are a few more steps to this entire process (of moving a WordPress website from one location to another) than what I have room to go into. So, be sure to check out my video tutorials on how I like to move WordPres files and much more at ... you know where:

Learn more about moving WordPress wesbsites at your favorite online training website ...

www.MyTrainingCenter.com

BART'S BOOKS, COACHING & TRAINING

Wow! This is some book of checklists, eh? Would you believe it if I said I have even more checklists for you? I tried not to write a phone book size collection of checklists for you, but can you believe that it takes this much strategy, planning, and know-how (step-by-step) to run a successful business? Who knew, right? Anyhow, you've come a long way since the first checklist, and I want to congratulate you. Check out even more checklists at my website below. See you there!

www.MyTrainingCenter.com/checklists

To your continued success,

Bart Smith

Bart Smith, TheMarketingMan.com
AND FOUNDER OF THESE WEBSITES

MyTrainingCenter.com
ReallyCheapNames.com
BreakThroughBS.com
BartsCookies.com ... and many more!

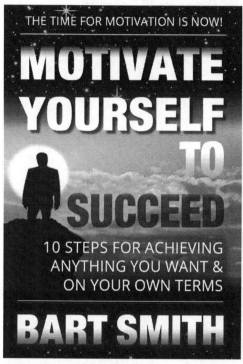
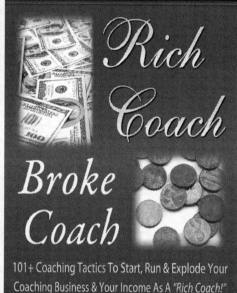

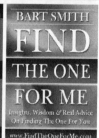

Check out some of my other websites below at your convenience. All sites are designed with the intention to help you cut through the B.S. in business and/or in your personal life.

www.MyTrainingCenter.com

Learn how to make money online, start a business, build websites, set up a shopping cart, write/self-publish books/eBooks, record and sell audio/video products, use social media, market online/offline, use computers, and more at Bart's training website.

www.ReallyCheapNames.com

Do you need a domain name for your business? Check to see if your business, product, service, book title or money-making idea is available in the .com, .net or .org domain name. Hurry!

www.BreakThroughBS.com

Break through all kinds of B.S. in your life (health, personal, politics, relationships and more) by visiting Bart's main *B.S.* site at www.BreakThroughBS.com.

www.AssessYourBS.com

Do you suffer from *B.S.*? Take my quick, online assessment questionnaire to find out. It's FREE and it will help you to identify areas (in business/life) you might want some help with.

www.DumpYourBS.com

Dumping *B.S.* (on the BMAN) can be healthy, even therapeutic. When you don't want to share what's troubling you with the world, but you want to get it out, contact me via phone, website or eMail to dump your *B.S.* on me. Maybe I can help!

www.BSReport.com

This is Bart's *B.S.* online newsletter (or eZine). Sign up here to get the latest B.S. updates, comical satire, and life tips from Bart!

www.CoachWithBart.com

We could all use a personal coach, mentor, or advisor at some point in our lives to help us diffuse the *B.S.* and out of a rut. Coach with Bart and see how FAST your life turns around and you start living life with intention.

www.FindTheOneForMe.com

Bart's dating website is designed for those looking for real relationships, love, and a potential soul mate. Let Bart's dating site help you find the one for you! The site is based on principles found in Bart's many books, namely, *Laws Of The Bedroom* and *Find The One For Me*.

www.BartsCookies.com

Have you tried Bart's *world famous chocolate chip cookies?* At least check out the photographs and videos of them at his website, www.BartsCookies.com. Bart bakes milk chocolate, dark chocolate, milk+dark chocolate, white chocolate, white+macadamia nut, and peanut butter+milk chocolate chip cookies.

ORDER YOUR COOKIES AT:

BARTSCOOKIES.COM

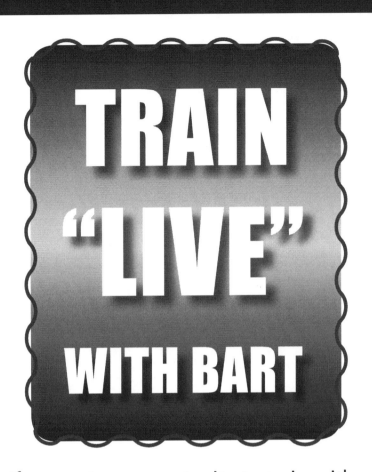

If you get an opportunity to train with me LIVE, I promise a fun, exciting, and highly motivational experience with NON-STOP marketing and money-making ideas and training on a variety of topics such as:

☑ **WORKSHOPS**
☑ **TELE-SEMINARS**
☑ **WEBINARS**

★ Writing / Marketing Books

★ Recording Audio Products

★ Interviewing / Publicity

★ Marketing / Promotion

★ Speaking / Presenting

★ Video Recording

CHECK MY CALENDAR FOR UPCOMING EVENTS:

http://MyTrainingCenter.com/calendar

Made in the USA
Charleston, SC
30 September 2016